Jump Up and Kiss Me

Jump Up and Kiss Me

Spicy Vegetarian Cooking

641.5

Jennifer Trainer Thompson

Ten Speed Press
Berkeley, California

Ten Speed Press
Box 7123
Berkeley, California 94707

Distributed in Australia by E. J. Dwyer Pty. Ltd., in Canada by Publishers Group West, in New Zealand by Tandem Press, in South Africa by Real Books, and in the United Kingdom and Europe by Airlift Books.

Cover design by Nancy Austin.

Library of Congress Cataloging-in-Publication Data

Thompson, Jennifer Trainer.
    Jump Up and Kiss Me: Spicy Vegetarian Cooking / Jennifer Trainer
Thompson
        p.   cm.
    Includes index.
    ISBN 0-89815-761-7
    1. Vegetarian cookery.   2. Spices.   3. Cookery, International.
I. Title
TX837.T468   1995
641.5'636—dc20

Printed in Canada

First printing, 1996

  2 3 4 5 6 7 8 9 10 — 99 98 97

This book is dedicated to my parents, Elinor and Potter
Trainer, who have always jumped up and kissed me.

Contents

Acknowledgments

Introduction

Starters & Light Fare

Appetizers

Salsas

Tortilla, Rice, & Bean Dishes

Baked & Grilled Entrées

Sandwiches

Salads & Side Dishes

Fruit & Vegetable Sides

Breads

Desserts & Drinks

Basics

Appendices

Index

ACKNOWLEDGMENTS

I am grateful to many people for their help in creating this book. Stuart Krichevsky, agent and friend, kept me super-strung on Scotch bonnets. Lorena Jones was all that one could ask for in an editor: thoughtful, helpful, and seemingly tireless. Many people shared their wonderful recipes, including Johanne Killeen and George Germon, Emeril Lagasse, Steve Cobble, Jim and Diana Starke, Tung Nguyen and Kathy Manning, Jose Marmolejo, Scott Avery, Chelsea Sleckman, Jody Fijal, and especially Carol Govan, Deborah Callan, Maureen Luchejko, Lisa Esposito, and Elizabeth Wheeler. I learned a lot about cooking from Liz while sequestered on small sailboats in the Atlantic for days at a time, and keep returning to her pasta gratin with mustard greens, buttercup squash pizza, and white bean soup. Hubey Plummer gave great beer suggestions and my recipe testers—Lori Garvie, Audrey Liese, and especially Jody Fijal—were invaluable. And Joe kept me humming. Thank you all.

INTRODUCTION

My passion for chiles and curries led me to spicy vegetarian cooking. My previous book was about cooking with hot sauces, and as I incorporated chiles and spices into various vegetable dishes (to make them interesting, not necessarily to enflame them) I came to realize just how much herbs, spices, and other seasonings can transform the simplest ingredients and create exciting vegetarian dishes with generous, spirited flavors.

The chipotle chile, for example, brings a deep, woody, smoky flavor to dishes, blending beautifully with tomatoes, grilled dishes, or sauces. Freshly grated ginger is sharp, almost effervescent, on the palate. Lightly chopped cilantro creates aromatic salsas and other dishes. Fresh-squeezed lime is zesty, tart, and tropical. The use of these simple ingredients can reinvent a dish.

Equally important in spicy vegetarian cooking is the cooking technique. In India, cooks dry-roast spices in a skillet, which brings out the natural oils and creates a heavenly perfumed aroma. Curry spices are added early in the cooking process to create layers of flavor and flickers of fire. In Tuscany, vegetables are browned in olive oil to create an earthy richness. In Mexico, vegetables such as chiles, tomatoes, onions, and corn are roasted over open fires, lending them a smoky, rustic complexity.

In some respects, this book wouldn't have been possible fifteen years ago, because so many ingredients were considered wildly exotic and weren't widely available. Thankfully, we are no longer limited by availability, because a quiet revolution occurred in the 1980s, when a few young entrepreneurs came up with the novel concept of flying freshly harvested foods from faraway locales to city markets within twenty-four hours. Calling themselves "Flying Foods," these folks (and soon others) made it possible for diners to enjoy fresh Dover sole and black-berries at New York restaurants in the dead of winter. While food still tastes best just picked from the vine, we are indeed fortunate that there is now a wide variety of produce available year-round. I live in a small New England town that sees snow from November through April, yet my local supermarket stocks enough cilantro, okra, habanero chiles, papayas, and starfruit to make a winter meal bright. If you can't find an ingredient, your local grocer can usually find it for you at the wholesale markets. Or you might try some of the mail-order sources listed on pages 342–344. I've also offered substitutions wherever possible.

While most dishes in this book have a zing and piquancy, spicy food isn't necessarily hot. You won't experience backdraft on these pages. Fire-eaters can customize the spice level by adding more of a particular ingredient. Or, where chiles are concerned, instead of incorporating just the flesh into a dish, also cook with the seeds and membranes, which is where the heat is contained. Taste the dishes as you cook, and create the level of spiciness you enjoy.

Several years ago, I bottled my own hot sauce. While the names of many hot sauces suggest the possible torture and hellfire associated with devilishly hot chiles—names like Last Rights, Hellfire & Damnation, and Armageddon— I wanted a name that reflected the passion and joy that spices bring to food. Calling the sauce Jump Up and Kiss Me, I went on to create other food products (not all of which are "hot") and the name stuck, in part because I believe that a passion for good food reflects a passion for life and its other pleasures.

And so, by all means, celebrate the bright flavors of these recipes and Jump Up and Kiss Me.

Starters

& Light Fare

Appetizers

Appetizers begin the evening with a flourish, and form a centerpiece that draws guests in and encourages lively conversation. Take a few minutes to make an easy hors d'oeuvre and greet people with a savory starter, rather than store-bought cheese and crackers. My husband is a big fan of "treats" before dinner, as he calls them. Even when we're not entertaining, we try to have something in the refrigerator or pantry that we can pop on a fiesta plate and enjoy while we relax before dinner and discuss the day's activities. Many of the appetizers in this chapter, such as the Bruschetta with White Bean–Roasted Garlic Spread and Roasted Peppers, will also make a tasty lunch or even a simple dinner with a salad.

Sundried Tomato Relish with Cayenne Toasts

Serves 6

Layers of flavor perform in this bite-sized appetizer with its crunchy cayenne-laced toast, smooth goat cheese, and lusty topping of sundried tomatoes and walnuts. I was first served a version of this canapé at NOLA, a Creole restaurant in Philadelphia, and keep returning to it when friends come for dinner, serving it with drinks and a bowl of kalamata olives. The toasts may be made early in the day and stored in an airtight container, then warmed in the oven just before serving. Use an excellent quality olive oil to brush on the toasts—there's a big difference in flavor. (If you're on a diet, you can omit the goat cheese.)

Sundried Tomato Relish

1 yellow onion, minced

1 tablespoon olive oil

1 clove garlic, minced

1 cup oil-packed sundried tomatoes, drained and chopped

1/4 cup chopped walnuts

4 large fresh basil leaves, chopped

1 teaspoon red wine vinegar

Freshly ground black pepper

Pinch of salt (optional)

Cayenne Toasts

1 loaf French bread, cut into 1/4-inch-thick ovals

Extra virgin olive oil

Ground cayenne pepper

4 ounces goat cheese

To make the relish, sauté the onion in the olive oil until softened, about 10 minutes. Add the garlic and sauté 1 minute more. Transfer to a small bowl and toss with the sundried tomatoes, walnuts, basil, red wine vinegar, black pepper, and salt. If dry, add a little extra oil or red wine vinegar.

To make the toasts, prepare the grill or preheat the broiler. Brush both sides of the bread with oil and dust one side with cayenne. Grill or broil the slices about 4 inches from the heat on both sides until golden brown and slightly crisp.

To assemble the canapés, arrange toasts cayenne side up on a serving plate, spread each toast with goat cheese, and top with a generous dab of the Sundried Tomato Relish. Or set out the toasts, goat cheese, and relish and let guests assemble their own.

OLIVES

When having friends over for dinner, I usually set out one appetizer and a bowl of olives. The saltiness goes well with drinks, and people love to nibble on the savory fruit. The flavor and texture of olives can vary enormously, depending on soil and climate as well as how they were grown, harvested, and cured. Green olives are picked unripe and pickled in brine; black olives are generally harvested ripe, then pickled in brine and sometimes oil. A good olive should be firm and not too salty. Some favorite varieties include:

Amfissa: A soft, fleshy, subtly sweet, dark purple olive from the Greek foothills of Mount Parnassus.

Atalanti: Large, greenish brown, round, and fleshy, with a bittersweet fruitiness.

Ionian: Mild, bright green, firm, and delicate.

Kalamata: Firm, pungent, meaty, and dark purple, cured in wine vinegar brine.

Nafplion: Small, dark green, and nutty.

Niçoise: Small and jewel-like, brownish-purple, tender and sweet.

Provençal: Cracked green olives from the Les Baux Valley in France, pickled in brine with herbs.

Thasos: Black, rich, and mellow, coated with olive oil; from Thasos, an island in the north Aegean Sea.

PASS THE PEPPER POD, PLEASE

What exactly did Peter Piper pick: Peppers? Chiles? Pods? Cayenne? The wording has been confusing ever since Christopher Columbus (in search of black pepper and other spices) landed in the West Indies, and — thinking he'd found the East Indies — mistook the chile plant for black pepper and called it a "pepper," thus setting the confusion in motion. A simple road map:

Peppers (aka chiles) are the fruit from shrubby plants of the genus *capsicum*. Some peppers are sweet (bell peppers), while others are fiery (chile peppers, or hot peppers). They range in color from green to red, yellow, orange — even purple, depending on the variety and how long the fruit stays on the vine. For varieties of chile peppers, see pages 36-38.

Pure chile powder: A rich, earthy powder made by grinding dried red chiles, usually New Mexican red chiles. Far superior to commercial chile powders, pure chile powder is easy to make; simply pulverize dried chile pods in a spice grinder or using a mortar and pestle. You may substitute different dried chiles and make your own habanero powder, ancho powder, and other spicy blends.

Chile powder: The chile powder found in supermarkets is usually a blend of ground dried chiles, oregano, thyme, and other spices. It can be used instead of pure chile powder in any of these recipes. Chile powder is also sometimes called "chili powder," because it's the main ingredient in flavoring the meat stew called "chili."

Ground cayenne pepper: Made by grinding cayenne pepper pods, this powder is orangy red and quite hot, and sometimes labeled "ground red pepper," "cayenne powder," or "cayenne pepper."

Crushed red pepper flakes: Popular in pizzerias, these are made by crushing a combination of several hot chile peppers, seeds included.

Paprika: A powder ground from the pod of a mild Hungarian red pepper (called *paprika* in Hungarian). A hotter paprika, made by grinding the seeds and placenta with the pod, is called hot paprika. Spanish paprika is milder than Hungarian paprika.

Black pepper: Made by grinding black peppercorns, black pepper (of the genus *piper nigrum*) is no relation to the chile pepper. For more information on peppercorns, see page 160.

If you're interested in learning more about chiles, there's an organization called the International Connoisseurs of Green and Red Chile. They have pods (chapters) throughout the United States, with each chapter headed by—what else?—a Pod Father. Pod-humous awards are coveted, and Utah even has a Latter-Day Pod. Pod-on me.

Caponata

Serves 6

Ancho chile peppers give this traditional Italian appetizer a Mexican twist. The ancho is one of my favorite peppers; it's actually a dried poblano pepper, with an earthy, slightly sweet, almost fruity flavor. This mildly spiced dish can be made hotter by adding more anchos or a jalapeño. Serve with slices of rustic bread that have been brushed with olive oil and grilled.

1 large eggplant, peeled and diced

2 ancho chiles, stemmed and seeded

1/4 cup olive oil

1 small yellow onion, finely diced

2 cloves garlic, minced

1 tablespoon capers

1/4 cup cracked Provençal green olives, pitted and chopped

1/2 cup tomato purée

3 small juicy tomatoes, finely diced

1 small bunch fresh cilantro (leaves only), chopped

1 teaspoon freshly ground black pepper

2 tablespoons red wine vinegar

Sprinkle the eggplant with salt and let it sit in a colander for 30 minutes to draw out the moisture.

Preheat the oven to 350°. Roast the anchos on a rack in the oven until you can smell them, 1 or 2 minutes, then soften by soaking them in hot water for about 15 minutes.

Heat oil in a large skillet. When the oil is hot, add the eggplant and stir to brown completely. Add the onion and cook until translucent. Remove the chiles from the water, dice them, and add them to the eggplant. Add the remaining ingredients and cook for 15 minutes, or until the flavors have married. Adjust the salt and heat level to your liking.

> Do not cease to drink beer, to eat, to intoxicate thyself, to make love, to celebrate the good days.
>
> —Ancient Egypt

Spinach and Potato Samosas

Serves 4

These curry-laced treats are a tasty accompaniment to soup and salad. They also make a savory appetizer with hot sauce, chutney, or a yogurt-based dressing. The red creamer variety of potato works well because of its tender skin and light, creamy texture, but other small potatoes may be substituted.

Filling

3/4 pound tiny, red creamer potatoes (about 10 to 12), scrubbed well and quartered (do not peel)

3 large cloves garlic, peeled and quartered

1 1/2 teaspoons salt

8 ounces fresh spinach leaves, trimmed of stems

1/4 cup thinly sliced scallions

2 jalapeños, seeded and minced

1 tablespoon chopped fresh dill

1/2 teaspoon ground coriander

1/2 teaspoon crushed red pepper flakes

1/4 teaspoon ground mace

Salt and pepper (optional)

Pastry

1 1/2 cups all-purpose flour

1/4 cup whole-wheat flour

1 teaspoon salt

1 teaspoon curry powder

1/2 teaspoon ground cayenne pepper

1/2 teaspoon ground cumin

2 teaspoons caraway seeds

1/3 cup tepid water (85° to 90°)

1/4 cup plus 1 tablespoon canola or safflower oil

1 large egg white, lightly beaten

To make the filling, place the potatoes, garlic, and 1/2 teaspoon of the salt in a medium saucepan with water to cover. Cover tightly, bring to a boil, reduce heat, and simmer until potatoes are tender when pierced with a fork, about 15 minutes. Drain, reserving 1 cup of cooking liquid. Place potatoes and garlic in a medium bowl, mash together, and set aside to cool.

Bring reserved potato water to a boil in a medium saucepan. Set a wire steaming basket in the pan. Add the spinach and cover. Steam until wilted, about 1 minute. Drain well and cool. Squeeze out excess moisture and chop the spinach (this should yield about 1/2 cup). Add the spinach and all the remaining filling ingredients to the mashed potato mixture and stir well. Taste and adjust with salt and pepper if desired. Cover and set aside while preparing the dough.

Preheat the oven to 375°. Line an 11 by 17 inch baking sheet with parchment. In a medium bowl, place the flours, salt, curry, cayenne, cumin, and caraway. Whisk to blend well. Make a well in the center of the flour and add the water and oil. With a fork, slowly work the flour into the liquid. Using your hands, continue to blend the dry and liquid ingredients until they hold together. Turn onto a clean work surface and knead until smooth and the dough holds together, about 3 to 5 minutes. Form into a ball, then flatten slightly. Set aside, covered with a towel, about 5 minutes. Divide into 18 pieces.

Roll each piece into a circle about 4 inches in diameter (keeping the remaining dough covered while working). Place 1 generous tablespoon of filling in the center of dough. Fold over to make a half-moon shape. Crimp edges with a fork to seal in the filling. Place on the parchment lined baking sheet in 3 rows about 1 inch apart. With the tip of a sharp knife, gently pierce the top of each pastry in two places. When you are ready to bake, lightly brush them with the beaten egg white.

Bake samosas until golden and the bottom of each pastry browns slightly, approximately 12 to 15 minutes. Serve warm.

Note: These samosas reheat well in a 350° oven for 10 minutes.

SHIITAKE MUSHROOMS

There are many interesting mushrooms on the market—matsutake, enoki, chanterelle, morel—with a lot more flavor and texture than small, white button mushrooms. Button mushrooms are flavorful only when allowed to "mushroom" into a larger size, which is now fashionably called a portobello. I'm partial to shiitakes, which are rich, hearty, and woody. Slice shiitakes into stir-fries, or grill the caps whole after marinating them in a spicy sauce for an hour or so.

Roasted Shiitake and Walnut Pâté

Makes 2 cups

This easy dish has the rich texture of a traditional pâté, but is much healthier. Serve it with toasted pita bread or grilled French bread.

1/2 cup walnuts

1/2 cup lentils

2 chipotle chiles, stemmed (and seeded if less heat is desired)

1 cup sliced shiitake mushroom caps

2 cloves garlic, minced

2 tablespoons chopped yellow onion

1 tablespoon olive oil

2 handfuls parsley (include tender stems)

3 tablespoons extra virgin olive oil

1 tablespoon balsamic vinegar

1/4 teaspoon salt

1/4 teaspoon freshly ground black pepper

1/4 teaspoon dried thyme

Preheat oven to 350°. Place walnuts on a baking sheet and roast in oven for 5 minutes.

In a covered saucepan, bring lentils to a boil with enough water to cover them generously, lower heat, and cook until soft, about 20 minutes. While the lentils are cooking, drop the chipotles into the same saucepan to soften, about 15 minutes.

Toss the shiitakes, garlic, onion, and 1 tablespoon olive oil in a small bowl. Spread in a shallow baking pan and roast for 15 minutes. Drain the lentils and chipotles, and purée in a food processor along with the shiitake mixture and the remaining ingredients. Taste and adjust seasonings.

West Indian Bean Fritters

Serves 4

Easy to make, fritters are a popular hors d'oeuvre in the
Caribbean. They can be prepared in advance and kept warm
in the oven, or made in the morning before the sun gets hot,
then reheated as the sun sets. Trinidadians favor split pea
fritters and serve the bite-sized morsels with a toothpick.
Variations include black-eyed peas, soybeans, or your
favorite small beans. (Just make sure beans have been
soaked overnight if you buy them dry.) Serve fritters topped
with a thin layer of sour cream, a thin layer of a fruity
Caribbean hot sauce, and a squeeze of fresh lime.

1 16-ounce can cooked small beans

1 small yellow onion, finely chopped

1 clove garlic, minced

1 tablespoon habanero hot sauce or curry powder

Freshly ground black pepper to taste

Vegetable oil, for frying

Sour cream, for garnish

Hot sauce, for garnish

Lime slices, for garnish

Combine the beans, onion, garlic, hot sauce, and black
pepper in a large bowl, and stir to mix well. Pour vegetable
oil 1/4 inch deep into a frying pan and heat until hot but not
smoking (about 325°). Drop heaping teaspoons of the fritter
mixture into the hot oil, about 6 at a time. Fry on both sides
until golden, 4 to 5 minutes per side. (If the fritters turn dark
immediately, the oil is too hot.) Remove fritters with a slotted spoon and drain on paper towels. Serve hot with a small
bowl of sour cream, hot sauce, and a plate of lime slices.

Squash Blossom Fritters Stuffed with Corn

Serves 6

This is a dish for high summer, when sweet corn is in season and squash plants are flush with bright yellow blossoms. These creamy-crunchy fritters make a great first course followed by a simple pasta with grilled vegetables. The garbanzo flour (found in health food stores) adds an Indian accent to this otherwise Southwestern-style dish. It's tasty served with Fresh Tomato Salsa (see page 59).

Filling

1 tablespoon peanut oil

1/2 cup finely chopped yellow onion

2 jalapeño chiles, seeded and finely chopped
  (about 2 tablespoons)

3 cups fresh corn kernels (about 3 large ears corn),
  coarsely puréed

2 tablespoons chopped fresh cilantro

1 tablespoon chopped fresh oregano

1 1/2 teaspoons finely chopped toasted cumin seed
  (see page 73)

2 teaspoons habanero hot sauce

1/4 teaspoon salt

1/4 cup sour cream

2 cups grated medium-sharp Cheddar cheese

Fritters

25 to 30 small (2-inch-long) squash blossoms

2 large eggs

1 tablespoon water

1 cup all-purpose flour

1 cup garbanzo flour

1/4 teaspoon ground cayenne or habanero pepper

1/2 teaspoon salt

Peanut oil, for frying

Fresh Tomato Salsa (see page 59)

Fresh cilantro, for garnish (optional)

Heat the peanut oil in a large, heavy saucepan over medium heat. Add the onion and jalapeños and cook, stirring until softened, about 5 minutes. Add the corn and cook, stirring frequently until the mixture is thickened, about 5 to 7 minutes. Stir in the herbs, cumin, hot sauce, salt, and sour cream. Simmer for 2 minutes, then remove from the heat to cool for a few minutes. Fold in the cheese. Spoon the stuffing into a pastry bag fitted with a large plain tip and refrigerate for 20 minutes, or until stiffened.

Trim the stems from the blossoms and remove their pistils gently from inside, taking care not to tear the petals. Pipe about 1 1/2 tablespoons of stuffing into each blossom, pinching together the points of the petals to enclose the filling. Refrigerate until ready to cook.

Whisk the eggs with the water in a large shallow bowl until well combined. Mix the remaining dry ingredients in a wide, shallow dish. Pour peanut oil 1/4 inch deep into a large, heavy sauté pan and heat over medium heat. Dip the stuffed blossoms in the egg and roll in the flour mixture until evenly coated. Fry the blossoms in the hot oil for about 5 minutes, turning once, until lightly browned and crisp. Drain on paper towels and keep warm in the oven on low heat while frying the remaining blossoms. Arrange several blossoms on a small plate for each serving, with a spoonful of Fresh Tomato Salsa on the side. Garnish with cilantro.

Tanzanian Potato Fritters with Tamarind Sauce

Serves 6

This African dish is thought to have derived from Indian cuisine, perhaps from shami kebab, which was improvised in many ways as it made its way to East Africa. There are many variations, with fillings ranging from eggs to peas. I first tasted this at the home of my neighbor Fahtma Kassamali, whose Iranian background and Tanzanian upbringing put a special spin on her culinary skills. It makes a tasty appetizer, but can also be served as a main course, accompanied by roasted bell peppers tossed with oregano and a hearty salad. To prepare this dish as an entrée, make 8 to 10 patties approximately 3 inches in diameter and 1/2 inch thick. The fritters can be made in the morning, then popped into a 350° oven for 10 minutes just before serving.

Filling

4 red potatoes

1 teaspoon minced garlic

1 teaspoon crushed fresh gingerroot

1/2 teaspoon ground cumin

1/2 teaspoon salt

1/4 cup chopped fresh cilantro (include tender stems)

1/4 cup freshly squeezed lemon juice

5 hard-boiled eggs, chopped

Batter

3 eggs

3 tablespoons milk

Pinch of salt

Freshly ground black pepper

1 1/2 cups bread crumbs

Vegetable oil, for frying

Tamarind Sauce (see page 293)

In a large stockpot, boil the potatoes until they are soft, then drain them in a colander. Pour cold water over the potatoes to cool them and discontinue cooking. Peel the cooled potatoes. In a large bowl, mash the potatoes, leaving some lumps. Add the remaining filling ingredients and mix well. Make 30 small fritters and set aside.

In a separate bowl, mix together all of the batter ingredients except the bread crumbs; place the crumbs on a separate plate. Pour vegetable oil 1/4 inch deep into a frying pan, heat the oil over high heat for 3 minutes, then reduce the heat to medium high for cooking. Coat each fritter with the batter and dredge it in the bread crumbs, covering all surfaces. Gently place the fritters in the hot oil. (You should be able to fry 4 at a time.) Cook until golden brown. Remove fritters and place on a paper towel to drain as you cook remaining fritters. Serve with Tamarind Sauce on the side.

Sweet Potato Fritters
with Jerk Sauce

Serves 4

I was first served this Jamaican appetizer by Cepha Gilbert, a Rastafarian who lives in Tampa and has a knack for combining simple ingredients in soulful ways. The crunchy fritters offer a perfect foil to the spicy sauce. Be sure to use white sweet potatoes.

2 white sweet potatoes
Vegetable oil, for frying
Jerk Sauce (see page 294)

Parboil the sweet potatoes until you can poke them with a fork (but don't let them get too soft). Cool the sweet potatoes under running water, then peel and slice them into 1/8-inch-thick pieces. Fill a large, heavy sauté pan with oil 1/4 inch deep, and heat over medium heat. Dust the sliced sweet potatoes in flour, then fry them for about 5 minutes, turning once, until lightly browned and crisp. Drain on paper towels, and serve with a dollop of Jerk Sauce.

Corn and Zucchini Fritters

Serves 4

Studded with potatoes, these dense tangy fritters are a hearty breakfast or brunch item. Serve with hot pepper jelly, sour cream and salsa, or fresh slices of papaya or cantaloupe.

1 cup all-purpose flour

1 1/2 teaspoons baking powder

1 teaspoon salt

1/2 teaspoon freshly ground black pepper

1 large egg

1 cup milk

1 baking potato, coarsely grated

1 small zucchini, coarsely grated

3 scallions, finely chopped

1 cup fresh corn kernels

3 green jalapeño or serrano chiles, roasted, peeled, seeded, and chopped (see page 40)

3 tablespoons vegetable oil

In a large bowl, mix together the flour, baking powder, salt, pepper, egg, and milk. Stir the potato, zucchini, scallions, corn, and chiles into the batter.

In a large skillet over high heat, add 1 tablespoon of the oil. Drop large spoonfuls of the mixture into the oil, flattening each mound slightly with a spatula. Cook the fritters until golden brown on one side, about 3 minutes, then turn and brown the other side. Transfer to a platter and keep warm. Repeat with remaining batter, adding oil to the skillet as needed. Serve immediately.

Good oil, like good wine, is a gift from the gods. The grape and the olive are among the priceless benefactions of the soil, and were destined, each in its way, to promote the welfare of man.

— George Ellwanger, *The Pleasures of the Table*, 1903

Bruschetta with Olive Tapenade and Herbed Ricotta Cheese

Serves 6

One of my favorite Italian foods is bruschetta, which is traditionally made by grilling dense, crusty bread over a fire, then rubbing it with garlic and brushing it with extra virgin olive oil. Many cooks have elaborated on this idea, and today bruschetta has come to mean grilled bread with a variety of toppings. This bruschetta can be served as a robust appetizer or with a salad and roasted red bell peppers dressed in extra virgin olive oil for a light supper.

Olive Tapenade

**1/2 cup assorted olives (cracked green, kalamata, and
    oil-cured are a great combination), pitted**

2 cloves garlic, minced

2 ripe tomatoes, finely diced

1/8 cup oil-packed sundried tomatoes, drained and chopped

1/8 cup pine nuts, lightly toasted and chopped (see page 73)

Herbed Ricotta Cheese

1 teaspoon finely chopped fresh rosemary needles

1/2 cup basil chiffonade

8 ounces ricotta cheese

1 tablespoon grated fresh Romano cheese

Freshly ground black pepper to taste

1 loaf Italian or other dense, crusty bread, sliced

Extra virgin olive oil

Pure chile powder

To make the tapenade, pulse the olives and garlic in a food processor until finely chopped. Transfer to a bowl, and gently stir in the tomatoes and pine nuts. In a separate bowl, combine the Herbed Cheese ingredients.

Brush the bread lightly on both sides with olive oil, then lightly toast both sides under the broiler or on the grill. Spread one side with a thin layer of Herbed Cheese, followed by a light layer of Olive Tapenade. Dust lightly with chile powder, and serve.

Bruschetta with White Bean-Roasted Garlic Spread and Roasted Peppers

Serves 6

This is the garlic lover's bruschetta! The white and black pepper combined with poblano chiles creates a unique heat.

2 red bell peppers, roasted, peeled, and seeded (see page 40)

4 poblano chiles, roasted, peeled, and seeded (see page 40)

1 cup extra virgin olive oil

1 teaspoon salt

2 cloves garlic, minced

1/4 cup roasted and peeled garlic cloves

2 cups cooked cannellini, baby lima, or navy beans (see page 333)

3 tablespoons freshly squeezed lemon juice

1 teaspoon freshly ground black pepper

1 teaspoon white pepper

1 teaspoon ground cayenne pepper

1 teaspoon dried oregano

1 loaf Italian or peasant bread

Slice the peppers and chiles into 1/2-inch-wide strips. Toss with 3 tablespoons of the oil, 1/2 teaspoon of the salt, and the minced garlic. Set aside.

In a food processor, purée the roasted garlic with the remaining salt. Add the beans and the remaining ingredients, except the oil. Purée well. With the machine running, drizzle in the remaining oil.

Brush the sliced bread on both sides with olive oil, and toast both sides lightly under the broiler. Spread white bean mixture on each piece and arrange a few strips of peppers on top. For extra zing, sprinkle each piece with a little more cayenne.

ROASTED GARLIC

Roasting gives garlic a luscious, buttery sweetness. To roast whole heads, preheat the oven to 350°. Remove the papery husk, leaving enough to keep the cloves intact, and slice off the top 1/4 inch of the head. Rub the head with olive oil, wrap in aluminum foil, and roast in the oven about 45 minutes. The garlic is done when it's soft and squeezable. When cool, squeeze out the individual cloves.

As ancient as corn and other South American ingredients, chiles are an extraordinary seasoning that enliven many dishes. Today markets, farmstands, and stores sell hundreds of fresh and dried chiles that offer vastly different taste profiles—some are fruity and herbal, others are tannic and smoky. Below are some varieties you're likely to find:

Anaheim: A long fresh chile (about 6 to 8 inches long and 1 inch wide) that turns from light green to red on the vine and is sometimes rather flattened in appearance. Red Anaheims are slightly sweeter, and both red and green Anaheims can be mild to medium hot. Almost identical to New Mexico chiles, they are good in chiles rellenos or stuffed. Substitute New Mexico chiles.

Ancho: About the size of a flattened plum, these auburn-colored dried chiles have the leathery wrinkled skin of a raisin and a sweet, earthy flavor and aroma. Made by drying poblano chiles, anchos are used in mole sauces, seasonings, and commercial chili powder. Substitute pasilla or New Mexico dried red chiles.

Banana: Also known as the Hungarian wax or Hungarian yellow wax chile, this crisp, pale yellow chile measures about 6 inches long. Medium hot and juicy, they are only available fresh. Substitute Santa Fe Grande.

Cascabel: A small (1- to 2-inch) round reddish brown dried chile with a thick glossy skin and seeds that rattle (hence the name, which means "jingle bell" in Spanish). With a mild to medium heat, cascabels have a pleasantly earthy flavor. Substitute cayenne or guajillo.

Cayenne: Approximately 4 to 6 inches long, these thin curved chiles have a pointy tip and are available fresh green or red, depending on how long they have been allowed to ripen on the vine. More often they are sold dried, when they are usually a bit smaller (2 to 4 inches long) and bright red. With a thin fiery heat, they are used in Louisiana sauces and Cajun and Creole seasonings. Substitute serrano, Thai, Korean, or Tabasco.

Chawa: This pale yellow fresh chile measures about 4 inches long, and has a mild, somewhat sweet flavor. Substitute banana or Hungarian wax.

Cherry: Also known as Hungarian cherry or hot cherry, this small round pepper (green to bright red in color) resembles a large cherry in shape. With mild to medium heat (depending on the crop), this pepper has a subtle sweetness and is available fresh or pickled. Substitute other pickled peppers.

CHIL

Chipotle: Made by smoking jalapeño peppers, these dried brown crinkled chiles measure from 1 inch to 3 inches long and have a woody, smoky, vaguely sweet heat. Substitute moritas or canned chipotle chiles in adobo sauce.

(Chile) de Arbol: Also known as the ginnie pepper or bravo (a hint of things to come), this skinny chile measures about 3 inches long and has a scorching short-lived heat. With more heat than flavor, they are sometimes available fresh (when they are green to red in color), but are more often sold dried, when they turn bright to dark red. Substitute cayenne, dried Thai, or tabasco.

Guajillo: Popular in Mexico, this long (6-inch) dried ebony-colored chile has a mild to medium heat and a sweet earthy resonance. When fresh, it is known as a mirasol. Very flavorful, it is used in stews, sauces, and seasonings. Substitute New Mexico chiles.

Habanero: Beware! This round crinkled chile, ranging in size from 1 inch to 2 inches, is the hottest in the world (habaneros can be 50 times hotter than jalapeños). Once you get past the heat, you'll notice a wonderfully fruity flavor, which makes habaneros the pepper of choice in Caribbean hot sauces and fruit salsas. They are a close cousin of the Scotch bonnet (same species, different cultivar), which is slightly smaller and rounder but has an equally powerful wallop. Also known as the Congo pepper, bonnie pepper, and Guinea pepper, fresh habaneros are picked green, yellow, orange, and red. They can also be found dried and, more recently, smoked. Substitute Scotch bonnet or datil.

Hungarian wax: See banana pepper.

Jalapeño: Perhaps the best known chile in North America, this fat fresh pepper is roughly 3 inches long, with a blunt apex. Green jalapeños are more readily available than red jalapeños, which are slightly sweeter. They both have a clean vegetable flavor and a decent heat that makes them a good all-around spice for many dishes. Too thick fleshed to be dried, jalapeños that are preserved by smoking are called chipotles. Substitute serrano.

Korean: Similar to the Thai chile, this thin (4-inch) long chile is hotter than the jalapeño, but not as hot as the habanero, and popular in the Korean dish kim chee. Substitute Thai or serrano.

Macho: The size of a bean, this fresh chile (red or green) lives up to its name and is almost as hot as the habanero. Substitute serrano or habanero.

Morita: Moritas are made from jalapeños that have been smoked, then dried. They are similar to chipotles, but not as intensely smoky and with a sweeter heat. Substitute chipotle.

E   S

New Mexico: The most harvested chile in New Mexico, these fresh green and red chiles measure about 6 to 8 inches long and about 1 inch wide. With a mild to medium heat, they can be slightly hotter than Anaheim chiles, which are derived from the New Mexico chile seeds that were brought by a New Mexico rancher to California in 1896. Also known as Hatch, chile Colorado, Anaheim, and California long green chiles (these border disputes never fade), they are available frozen, canned, fresh, and roasted. When fresh, they have a clean vegetable flavor and are good stuffed, roasted, or diced into soups and casseroles; dried they are earthy and warming and delicious in stews, sauces, and seasonings. The dried New Mexico red chile is often strung into a long braid of brick red chiles, called a ristra.

Pequin: Usually 1/2 inch long and shaped like a pine nut, this small dried red chile from Central America and Mexico has a torpedo heat. Substitute tepin.

Pimento: This mild heart-shaped chile measures about 4 inches long and ripens green to red. Thick fleshed and aromatic, it is good roasted or served as a garnish or in salads. When canned or bottled, it has a reddish orange color. (If the pepper is bright red, you've been sold a red bell pepper instead.)

Poblano: This dark green fresh chile is approximately 4 inches long and 3 inches wide, shaped like a small bell pepper with a pointed apex. Hailing from the city of Pueblo, Mexico (hence the Spanish name, "pepper from Pueblo"), the thick-fleshed poblano is delicious stuffed or roasted and generally has a mild heat, though some crops can be hot. Dried red poblanos are called ancho chiles.

Serrano: A small (1- to 2-inch-long) bullet-shaped fresh chile, with a clean fresh vegetable flavor and fiery heat that clocks in between a jalapeño and a habanero. Green serranos are more widely available than red serranos, which are slightly sweeter and add fiery color to a dish. Substitute jalapeño or half of a seeded habanero.

Tabasco: A small fresh chile that measures 1 to 2 inches long, with a pointy apex. Turning yellowish green to orange to red on the vine, tabasco chiles are used in the famous sauce of its name. (Indeed, Baton Rouge is named after the red stick that was brought into the fields for color likeness to judge a pepper's ripeness.) With a thin flesh and sharp heat, tabasco peppers hail originally from the city of Tabasco in Mexico. Substitute cayenne, tepin, or Thai.

Tepin: Also known as chiltepins, these small round chiles (about the size of pearls) are orange to red when ripe and reddish brown when dried. With a fiery quick-lived heat, they are named after the Nahuatl word for "flea." Substitute serrano or macho.

Thai: No longer than a pinkie finger and half as wide, this fresh red or green chile has a searing heat. Substitute fresh serranos or tepins.

Southwestern Bruschetta

Serves 6

Nothing beats the flavor of roasted corn combined with the smoky, woody heat of chipotle chiles, which are jalapeños that have been smoked for several days over an open fire. Serve with Toasted Corn Salsa on the side.

1 ancho chile

2 chipotle chiles

6 poblano chiles, roasted, peeled, stemmed, seeded, and finely chopped (see page 40)

1 yellow onion

1/2 teaspoon salt

Juice of 2 limes

1 tablespoon apple cider vinegar

1 teaspoon ground coriander

Rustic bread, such as a hearty corn-based or millet bread

2 cups Mexican cheese, such as Chihuahua cotija or anejo (see note)

Toasted Corn Salsa (see page 61)

Prepare a grill.

Preheat the oven to 350°. Roast the ancho chile by popping it in the oven just until you can smell it, about 2 minutes. Then, submerge the ancho and chipotles in hot water for 10 to 15 minutes to soften. Stem and chop the chipotle and ancho finely, and mix with the poblanos.

Peel the onion and place it on the hot grill, turning until it is blackened all over, about 7 minutes. Dice the charred onion and add to the chile mixture. Add salt, lime juice, vinegar, and coriander. Mix well and set aside.

Slice the bread and top with cheese. Melt the cheese under the broiler, then top each piece with a dab of the chile mixture. Serve with Toasted Corn Salsa on the side.

Note: If Mexican cheese is unavailable, substitute 1 cup Muenster and 1 cup Monterey jack cheese.

The quantity of chile disposed of was really prodigious: waggons laden with it, drawn each by six oxen, were arriving hourly from Aguas Calientes, yet their contents rapidly disappeared, piles of capsicum sufficient to excoriate the palates of half London vanishing in the course of a few minutes.

—*Ward's Mexico*, 1820s, describing the Zacatecas market in Mexico

COOKING WITH CHILES

Anyone who has bitten into a chile and felt the heat billowing through their mouth knows how powerful this fruit can be. The heat of the chile is contained in the inner ribs and the seeds; if you want a milder seasoning, remove the membranes and seeds with a sharp knife. You can also taste the flavor (but not the fire) of a particular chile by slicing off a bit of the outer skin and tasting it.

I'm often asked where to find fresh and dried chiles. If you don't live near an Asian or Mexican market, or can't find peppers in your local supermarket, ask the grocer to order them for you. I live in rural Massachusetts and have had great success obtaining a wide range of fresh chiles. I also order dried chiles through the mail from reputable sources (see Mail-Order Sources, pages 342-344).

Dried Chiles

- Look for chiles that have a good aroma and are supple, like raisins. Store in sealed containers in a dark, cool, dry place.

- Roasted dried chiles greatly enhance many dishes, which makes roasting well worth the small effort involved. Puncture chiles with a sharp knife, as you would a baking potato, and place them on a rack in a preheated 350° oven. Cook until you smell them, about 1 or 2 minutes. (Roasting too long will make them bitter.)

- To soften dried chiles, soak in hot (but not boiling) water for 15 minutes, or just until softened.

- Make your own chile powder by grinding dried chile pods in a spice or coffee grinder or with a mortar and pestle. You can mix and match chile pods to create unique spice blends.

Fresh Chiles

- Look for chiles that have smooth, taut skin—the same criteria you apply to bell peppers. Store chiles in the refrigerator.

- Roasting fresh chiles (and bell peppers) is an extremely easy process. Using a fork, hold the chiles over a grill or gas burner flame and rotate until they are blistered and blackened all over. Then place them in a paper or plastic bag and seal the bag for 15 to 20 minutes to steam them and loosen the skin. Peel away the thin outer skin, using your fingers. Keep a finger bowl of water handy for dipping your fingers to facilitate the skin removal. Don't rinse the chiles, or you'll lose the roasted quality. Stem and seed the peppers and use in your favorite recipe, or toss with olive oil and oregano for an intriguing side dish.

- When working with hotter chiles (such as habaneros), be sure to wash your hands with soap and water after touching them or wear latex gloves.

Texas Hill Country Guacamole

Makes 2 cups

I'm not a fan of bottled salsas, but the Stonewall Chili Pepper Company in Stonewall, Texas, makes a fantastic salsa that's hot as hell and laden with fresh habanero chiles, the hottest peppers on earth. Owner Jeff Campbell was the first farmer to grow habaneros commercially in the United States. If you can't find his salsa, substitute a little hot sauce or add some chopped fresh jalapeños or habaneros. If you use habaneros, be sure to add just a little at a time and taste as you go along — these babies are hot.

2 large ripe Haas avocados, peeled, pitted, and sliced

1/2 cup Stonewall Habanero Salsa (or 1 fresh habanero, seeded and chopped)

1 small red onion, chopped

Juice of 1/2 lime

2 cloves garlic, minced

Freshly ground black pepper

Salt to taste (optional)

In a large mixing bowl, mash the avocado coarsely with a fork. Gently stir in the remaining ingredients. Taste and adjust seasonings.

Babaghanoush

Makes 2 cups

Often called "eggplant caviar," this pungent, textured Middle Eastern spread can be served as a dip with crisp vegetables or crackers, or tucked into pita pockets with sprouts and roasted red peppers for a delicious sandwich. Be sure to choose a small firm eggplant with a green cap and stem and no blemishes. For this dish, I prefer Chinese eggplant, which are readily available and often sweeter in taste; they are slimmer than globular eggplant (their shape is roughly akin to a cucumber) and have a violet skin. Roasting the eggplant and garlic lends a beautiful mellow flavor to the dish.

4 small Chinese eggplant (about 2 pounds)

4 large cloves garlic, quartered

1 tablespoon olive oil

2 tablespoons freshly squeezed lemon juice

1/4 cup chopped fresh parsley

2 large firm but ripe plum tomatoes, seeded and chopped (about 2/3 cup)

1 teaspoon kosher salt

1 teaspoon freshly ground black pepper

2 teaspoons tahini

2 teaspoons dark sesame oil (sometimes called black sesame oil)

1/2 teaspoon ground cayenne pepper

1 tablespoon toasted sesame seeds, for garnish (see page 73)

1 teaspoon minced lemon zest, for garnish

1 small red onion, diced, for garnish

Preheat oven to 375°.

Make a slit about 3 inches long and 1 inch deep in each eggplant. Tuck the garlic pieces in the slit in each eggplant, pushing gently to mesh the garlic with the flesh of the eggplant. Drizzle the olive oil into the slits of each eggplant.

Place eggplant in a heat-proof baking dish and roast about 30 minutes. Cover dish with foil and bake an additional 30 minutes, or until tender.

Place lemon juice in a medium bowl. When eggplant is cool enough to handle, scrape flesh onto a cutting board and chop coarsely. Add immediately to the lemon juice. Add remaining ingredients and mix well. Garnish and serve. This dish will keep well several days refrigerated.

Artichokes with Rosemary-Curry Vinaigrette

Serves 4

I was introduced to artichokes in college by a Swiss friend. The experience is still etched in my mind—four of us sitting on floor pillows in her Cambridge apartment on a wintry afternoon, the sun streaming in the big bay window, listening to Billie Holliday. Dominique went into the kitchen to prepare a snack and emerged twenty minutes later with a bottle of wine and a bowl of steaming artichokes. They seemed breathtakingly exotic to me, and I ate very slowly, learning by observation how to eat such prickly things. The Rosemary-Curry Vinaigrette is also delicious drizzled over steamed broccoli.

4 whole artichokes

Juice of 1 lemon

Rosemary-Curry Vinaigrette

4 tablespoons Rosemary-Serrano Red Wine Vinegar (see page 321)

8 tablespoons Curry Butter (see page 312), melted

Rinse the artichokes, cut off their woody stalks and remove any tough outer leaves. Fill a large pot with water 1 inch deep and the lemon juice and bring to a boil. Place the artichokes in a wire basket steamer and steam, covered, until the artichokes are tender (about 20 to 40 minutes, depending on size). The artichokes are done when you can easily pull a leaf from the flower. Combine the vinaigrette ingredients in a small mixing bowl and transfer to 4 individual ramekins. Dip the artichoke leaves in the vinaigrette.

ALL CHOKED UP

The artichoke, a native of Sicily and North Africa, has a prickly past: Pliny even questioned why people paid good money for thistles. In sixteenth-century France, Catherine de Medici encouraged their cultivation, and in seventeenth-century Europe, they were purported to have such aphrodisiacal qualities that women were forbidden to eat them. By the eighteenth century, artichokes were back in vogue and considered a natural remedy for various ailments, including depression.

Today, artichokes are available year-round, although those grown in California are the freshest (and cheapest) from March to May. Baby artichokes are actually mature; they have just grown in the shade and aren't as big. In selecting artichokes, look for firm globes with leaves still tucked together tightly like any flower bud. Buy artichokes of similar sizes so they take the same amount of time to steam. If you plan to leave them in the refrigerator for a few days before steaming, put the stems in water to keep them fresh. Avoid buying artichokes with blackened tips, which indicate that they weren't picked recently. The most delicious part is the heart, which is won by removing all the leaves and cutting away the hairy yoke (choke) that protects it.

Avocados with Chipotle and Lime

Serves 4

The essence of nouvelle cuisine is to present the finest, freshest ingredients in a simple way. This dish does just that, counting heavily on a delicious avocado, which should be ripe, creamy, and of the Haas variety (the nubbly black avocados, not smooth the green-skinned ones, which can be watery). A delicate, deep red line of hot sauce painted across the avocado is visually dramatic, and the spiciness accentuates the avocado's cool smoothness. This dish makes an elegant and very easy first course for a dinner party.

1 medium-large Haas avocado

3 tablespoons Chipotle Hot Sauce (see page 291), at room temperature, or canned chipotle chiles in adobo sauce

1 tablespoon warm water

1 tablespoon drained and chopped oil-packed sundried tomatoes

1 lime

Skin the avocado, cut it in half lengthwise, and remove the pit. Slice the halves lengthwise into 6 to 10 thin slices, and fan them out on small plates (3 to 5 slices per serving).

Combine the chipotle sauce, water, and sundried tomatoes in a blender, and purée. Spoon a fine, decorative line across the fanned avocado slices. Cut the lime in half. Squeeze a bit of juice from one half of the lime over the top of each fan; cut the other half into 4 thin slices. Garnish the plates with lime slices and serve.

Chipotle Antipasto

Makes 1 cup

When my friends Jim and Diana Starke bought a smoker, they started smoking all sorts of foods, including jalapeños, which turn into chipotle chiles when smoked. One night on the island of Vieques, they served this torrid antipasto, which will tickle the fancy of fire lovers. Serve it with crackers.

10 chipotle chiles, softened in water, drained, and finely chopped

2 tablespoons minced garlic

2 yellow onions, minced

1/2 cup loosely packed chopped fresh cilantro

1 2-ounce can anchovy filets (optional)

1/4 cup olive oil

Blend all ingredients in a food processor until texture is smooth.

Spicy Mediterranean Tart

Serves 10 to 12

This tart borrows its tangy flavors from Greek cuisine, but takes on a peppery twist in both the crust and the filling. It's quite bold, and best enjoyed in small wedges—a perfect appetizer or side dish.

Crust

3/4 cup all-purpose flour

Pinch of kosher salt

1 tablespoon coarsely ground black pepper

1/4 cup finely ground walnuts

4 tablespoons softened cream cheese

2 tablespoons softened unsalted butter

2 1/2 to 3 tablespoons buttermilk

Filling

2 shallots, chopped

2 tablespoons butter

1 tablespoon chile oil

1/2 cup chopped plum tomatoes

1/2 cup oil-packed sundried tomatoes, drained

1/4 cup pitted and chopped kalamata olives

3 eggs

1/4 teaspoon salt

1/2 teaspoon or more crushed red pepper flakes, to taste

3 ounces feta cheese

2/3 cup sour cream (or well-drained nonfat yogurt)

To make the crust, combine the flour, salt, and pepper in a large mixing bowl. Add the walnuts and toss. Blend the cream cheese and butter in the food processor. Add the dry ingredients and the buttermilk, alternating, to the cream cheese-butter mixture, blending just until a dough is formed. Adjust the amount of buttermilk as needed to keep the dough from becoming sticky. Turn the dough out onto a floured board; shape into a ball, cover, and refrigerate for at least 1 hour.

When the dough is thoroughly chilled, preheat the oven to 425°. Remove the dough from the refrigerator and dust the top with additional flour to keep it from sticking to the rolling pin. On a floured sheet of waxed paper, roll out a 12-inch circle. Lift the dough with the waxed paper, place it face down in a 10-inch pie plate, and carefully pull back the waxed paper. Patch any tears with dough pinched from the edges. Trim the edges, but keep them high because the crust will shrink during baking. Prick the bottom and sides of the crust with a fork to keep it from buckling. Cover with aluminum foil and fill with dried beans. Bake until the crust is lightly browned, about 10 to 15 minutes. Remove the foil and the beans.

To make the filling, lower oven temperature to 375°. In a large frying pan, sauté the shallots in butter and chile oil until translucent. Remove from heat. In a large bowl, combine the shallots, the fresh and dried tomatoes, and the olives. In a separate bowl, beat the eggs with the salt and red pepper, and fold in the cheese and sour cream. Fold the egg mixture into the other filling ingredients and pour into the crust. Place the tart in the oven immediately and bake until the mixture sets and the top is lightly browned, about 20 to 25 minutes.

Sweet Corn Tamales with
Spicy Ancho Tomato Sauce

Makes 20 tamales

In Mexico, tamales are made for special occasions, ranging from fiestas to graveside suppers on All Saints' Day. This festive food is light and flavorful and can be served any time of day—for brunch, Sunday supper, or as a filling snack. Gather some friends on a Sunday afternoon and experiment with fillings: try spicy black beans, roasted hot and sweet peppers with a few dashes of a Caribbean hot sauce, or roasted squash and blue cheese.

24 medium to large dried corn husks

1/2 cup butter, cool but not chilled

1 cup lightly packed coarsely grated Cheddar cheese

1 1/4 cups masa harina

1/2 teaspoon baking powder

1 1/2 teaspoon salt

3/4 cup warm water

3 cups fresh corn kernels (3 to 4 ears)

Freshly ground black pepper

2 (8-ounce) sweet potatoes, roasted until just tender, peeled, and cut in 1/4-inch-thick slices

4 tablespoons chopped chives or scallions

Crushed red pepper flakes or habanero hot sauce

Spicy Ancho Tomato Sauce (recipe follows)

Except the vine, there is no plant which bears a fruit as great in importance as the olive.

—Pliny, Roman scholar, AD 79

Soak the corn husks in warm water until they are flexible, about 2 to 3 hours, then drain and set aside. Make ties from several of the longer corn husks by tearing off 40 1/8-inch-wide strips. Cover the leaves and ties with a damp towel to keep them from drying out.

Using an electric mixer, beat the butter in a bowl until it is light and fluffy. Add the cheese gradually, beating again until fluffy. In a separate bowl, mix the masa harina, baking powder, and salt by hand. Add the water slowly while working the mixture, until a stiff dough forms. (You may not need all the water.)

Put the corn and pepper in a food processor fitted with the chopping blade and purée coarsely. With the processor running, add the masa dough by the spoonful, and blend until the mixture is smooth. Add the butter mixture to the masa mixture by the spoonful, beating continuously until the mixture is light and fluffy (it will resemble pound cake batter).

To make each tamale, open the corn husk. Spread about 2 tablespoons of the tamale dough evenly over the husk. Stud the dough with about 1 tablespoon of sweet potato slices, then sprinkle with chives and red pepper flakes. Wrap the husk around the filling and tie the ends with the corn husk strips. (If husks are small, you may need to use two, overlapping the sides to make a rough rectangle.) Repeat until all husks are filled.

Steam the tamales in a bamboo steamer or a metal basket steamer over simmering water for about 1 hour, or until firm. For each serving, place 1 or 2 tamales on a plate and serve warm with the Spicy Ancho Tomato Sauce or your favorite hot sauce.

At dusk the people
came to the temple
and filled the court-
yards with lights and
bonfires. At midnight,
the conch shells, flutes,
and trumpets sounded.
Garlands were brought
forth, finely decorated
with strings of chiles,
corn, and all types of
grain. It was set down
at the door of the
chamber which held
the image of the god-
dess. The chamber had
been decorated and
made green with
numerous strings of
corn, chili, squash,
flowers, and all kinds
of seeds. It was a most
remarkable, most
ornate thing to see.

—Diego Duran,
sixteenth-century
Franciscan

Spicy Ancho Tomato Sauce
Makes about 4 cups

Accented with sweet cinnamon and orange rind, this smooth, spicy sauce goes well with corn dishes such as polenta, corncakes, or cornmeal pancakes. It would also taste good with a rice or bulgur pilaf made with raisins or other dried fruit, or inside a rice and bean burrito. The cream enrichment can be omitted.

1 small ancho chile
1 tablespoon vegetable oil
1 yellow onion, finely chopped
3 cloves garlic
1 teaspoon toasted and ground cumin seed (see page 73)
1/2 teaspoon dried oregano
3-inch strip orange zest
1 (2- to 3-inch) stick cinnamon
4 cups fresh or canned tomatoes, chopped, peeled, and seeded
4 tablespoons heavy cream (optional)
1/4 teaspoon salt

Toast the ancho in a 350° oven until aromatic, just 2 to 3 minutes. Place in a bowl, cover with hot but not boiling water, and set aside to soften for 15 to 20 minutes. Remove the stem and seeds, and set the pepper aside.

Heat the oil in a heavy saucepan over medium-low heat. Add the onion and cook, covered, until softened, about 5 minutes. Add the garlic, cumin, oregano, orange zest, and cinnamon and cook, stirring occasionally, for another 5 minutes, or until aromatic. Increase the heat to high and add the tomatoes and the ancho. Reduce the heat to low and simmer for about 25 minutes, until slightly thickened. Remove the cinnamon stick and orange rind.

Transfer the contents of the pan to a food processor fitted with a metal chopping blade. Process until puréed. Strain the mixture through a wire sieve into the saucepan. Return the mixture to the heat and add the cream and salt. Simmer over low heat for about 10 minutes.

Fried Cauliflower with Yogurt Aïoli

Serves 6

Aïoli is a Provençal mayonnaise sauce traditionally made with garlic (ail) and oil (oli). This version replaces the oil with yogurt, making a healthier sauce. This appetizer can also be served as a light entrée with a salad of sliced English hothouse cucumbers tossed with red apples, walnuts, golden raisins, and extra virgin olive oil.

Yogurt Aïoli

1 head roasted garlic (see page 35)
1 small red potato, peeled and boiled until soft
Juice of 1 lemon
2 cups plain yogurt

Batter

1 cup all-purpose flour
2 cups water
3 eggs, beaten
1/2 teaspoon salt
1 teaspoon ground coriander
1/2 teaspoon ground cayenne pepper
1 clove garlic, minced
1 tablespoon chopped fresh parsley

Vegetable or olive oil, for frying
1 head cauliflower, cut into florets

 To prepare the aïoli, squeeze the garlic out of the skin and purée in a food processor. Add the potato and purée. Add the remaining ingredients and blend thoroughly. Set aside.
 Combine the water and flour until mixed thoroughly. Add more water if necessary to achieve the consistency of thick pancake batter. Add the eggs, salt, and spices and mix well. If the batter is too thick, add more water. Pour oil 1/8 inch deep in a heavy skillet, and heat until hot but not smoking. Keeping the oil at medium heat, dip the cauliflower florets into the batter, one piece at a time to coat thoroughly, and fry until golden brown all over. Drain on paper towels. Serve with the aïoli.

Training is everything. The peach was once a bitter almond; cauliflower is nothing but cabbage with a college education.

—Mark Twain,
Pudd'nhead Wilson

Orzo-Stuffed Mushrooms with Lime and Pumpkin Seed Sauce

Makes 12 mushrooms

This light-tasting but hearty dish has a smooth, complex sauce that is rich with the flavors of tomatillos, lime, and serrano chiles and walks the line of heat with the orzo stuffing.

Stuffed Mushrooms

2 ancho chiles

1 1/2 cups uncooked orzo

12 portobello mushrooms

2 tablespoons olive oil

1 eggplant, diced and sprinkled with 1 tablespoon salt

1 yellow onion, finely diced

1 head roasted garlic (see page 35), skins removed

10 plum tomatoes, diced

1/4 teaspoon thyme

1/2 teaspoon oregano

1 teaspoon ground cayenne pepper

1/4 cup packed fresh basil leaves, chopped

1/2 cup grated Pecorino, Romano, or Parmesan cheese
   plus a little reserved for garnish

Salt to taste

Lime and Pumpkin Seed Sauce

1/2 cup shelled pumpkin seeds

4 small fresh tomatillos, husked, rinsed, and coarsely chopped

1/3 cup packed fresh basil leaves plus extra for garnish

1 bunch fresh cilantro, chopped, plus extra for garnish

1 large fresh poblano chile, seeded and coarsely chopped

3 serrano chiles

1/4 cup freshly squeezed lime juice

1 teaspoon salt

1/2 cup olive oil

Preheat the oven to 375°. Roast the anchos until you can smell them, about 2 minutes, then submerge in hot water for 15 minutes. Finely chop the anchos and set aside.

Bring 6 cups of water to a boil in a medium saucepan. Add the orzo, reduce the heat, and cook, uncovered, until the orzo is al dente, about 10 minutes. Drain and set aside.

Remove the stems from the mushroom caps and coarsely chop. Pour the olive oil into a large frying pan and sauté the mushroom stems with the eggplant and onion until eggplant begins to brown. Add the garlic, tomatoes, thyme, oregano, cayenne, and anchos, and sauté for 10 minutes. Combine in a bowl with the remaining mushroom ingredients. Stuff each mushroom with this mixture. Spritz a baking sheet with a little water or white wine. Place the stuffed mushrooms on the baking sheet. Bake for 20 to 30 minutes.

Prepare the sauce while the mushrooms bake. In a food processor, combine all sauce ingredients, except for the olive oil, one item at a time. Transfer to a blender, drizzle in the oil, and blend until smooth. Don't heat the sauce; instead, transfer it directly to a plate and top with the mushrooms. Sprinkle the reserved cheese on top of each mushroom and garnish with the reserved basil and cilantro.

Jalapeño Ice with Tomatoes

Serves 6

Served in tall stemmed glassware, such as martini glasses, this makes an elegant, refreshing first course for summer. Despite its name, this dish is not particularly fiery—the ice is slightly fruity, a bit spicy, and a terrific foil to the dog days of August, especially when served atop juicy vine-ripened tomatoes. You might also try a scoop of just the jalapeño ice on chilled melon soup or gazpacho—or serve it as a palate cleanser between courses. The ice can be made a few days ahead.

Jalapeño Ice

1 to 2 large jalapeños

2 teaspoons freshly squeezed lime juice

1 3/4 cups apple juice

1/4 cup crushed pineapple with juice

1/2 teaspoon ground white pepper

1/4 teaspoon kosher salt

4 small plum tomatoes, chopped

Minced red onion, for garnish

Chopped fresh cilantro, for garnish

To prepare the ice, stem, seed, and finely mince the jalapeños (you should have 1 heaping tablespoon). In a food processor, mix lime juice, apple juice, and pineapple and process about 30 seconds. (There will still be some texture from the pineapple.) Stir in the pepper and salt.

Pour juice mixture into a freezer-proof container. Cover and freeze approximately 2 hours, stirring once or twice. When ice is frosty but still soft, stir in the minced jalapeño. Freeze at least 2 more hours until set and frozen.

To serve, divide tomatoes equally among 6 stemmed glasses. Top tomatoes with a generous scoop of the Jalapeño Ice. Garnish with a sprinkling of red onion and cilantro.

Goat Cheese Poppers

Makes 24 poppers

I kept getting so many requests from friends for jalapeño poppers that I decided to experiment with different fillings. These "Goat Poppers" are milder than the Hot Jalapeño Poppers (see page 56) and are a bit fancier with the goat cheese and fresh rosemary filling.

24 jalapeño peppers

2 1/4 cups goat cheese

2 tablespoons minced garlic chives

3/4 teaspoon minced fresh rosemary needles

Salt to taste

Freshly ground black pepper to taste

5 eggs, lightly beaten

5 tablespoons milk

Flour, for dredging

Seasoned bread crumbs, for coating

Vegetable oil, for frying

Scoop out the stems, seeds, and membranes of the peppers (a grapefruit spoon is handy for this task), keeping the top of the pepper intact. Rinse and dry the peppers thoroughly.

With a fork, mash together the goat cheese, chives, rosemary, salt, and pepper in a small bowl. Fill each pepper with the cheese mixture. Chill for at least 1 hour in the refrigerator to harden the cheese.

Combine the eggs and milk in a bowl to make the batter. Dip the stuffed jalapeños into the batter, then roll them in the flour. Dip again in the batter, then roll in bread crumbs, repeating this step until they are coated thoroughly. Refrigerate until ready to fry.

Fill a large frying pan with oil 1/2 inch deep and heat until hot, but not smoking. Deep-fry jalapeños until golden brown, about 5 to 8 minutes. Drain on paper towels and serve.

HOMEMADE BREAD CRUMBS

Make your own bread crumbs by slicing a loaf of stale or toasted bread and processing in a food processor or blender until the desired crumb (fine, coarse, or chunky) forms. Mix crumbs with 4 tablespoons minced fresh parsley, 1 tablespoon dried oregano, 2 teaspoons dried thyme, 1 teaspoon dried basil, 1 tablespoon chopped fresh chives, and 2 teaspoons minced garlic. Homemade bread crumbs will keep in an airtight container for several weeks.

Hot Jalapeño Poppers

Makes 24 poppers

Poppers are fun to make for a party or with chile-loving friends. Serve with a mild tomato salsa and margaritas.

24 jalapeño peppers

3 cups grated Muenster cheese

3/4 teaspoon freshly ground black pepper

1 tablespoon Tabasco sauce

5 eggs, slightly beaten

5 tablespoons milk

Flour, for dredging

Seasoned bread crumbs, for coating (see page 55)

Vegetable oil, for frying

Scoop out the stems, seeds, and membranes of the peppers, reserving the jalapeño pepper seeds and membranes. (A grapefruit spoon is handy for this task.) Rinse and dry the peppers thoroughly. Mince enough seeds and membranes to yield 4 1/2 teaspoons.

With a fork, combine the seeds and membranes with the cheese, black pepper, and Tabasco sauce in a small bowl. Fill each pepper with the mixture and chill for at least 1 hour in the refrigerator.

Combine the eggs and milk in a bowl to make the batter. Dip jalapeños into the batter, then roll them in the flour. Dip again into the batter, then roll in bread crumbs, repeating this step until they are coated thoroughly. Refrigerate until ready to cook.

Fill a large frying pan with oil 1/2 inch deep and heat until hot, but not smoking. Deep-fry the jalapeños until golden brown, about 5 to 8 minutes. Drain on paper towels and serve.

Salsas

Salsa, which means "sauce" in Spanish, is a chunky, uncooked blend of fruits or vegetables. Traditionally, it's a medley of tomatoes, onions, and chiles, but there are many variations on the salsa theme: tropical fruit salsas, roasted corn salsas, even bean and nut salsas. Easy to make, several salsas set out in colorful bowls with tortilla chips can begin a cocktail hour, but salsas don't end there; they can be served on the side with grill menus, rice dishes, or chiles rellenos and even offer a healthy alternative to heavy cream sauces. Serve the Fire-Roasted Tomato Salsa with the Squash Blossom Fritters, for example, or surprise people with a platter of grilled mixed vegetables tossed with Pico de Gallo. Just make sure that you select the freshest ingredients for your salsa, as this simple dish emphasizes all their flavors and textures in living color.

CILANTRO

Cilantro (also known as Chinese parsley) is a pretty garden herb with pale pink and white flowers that appear in early summer. Resembling Italian parsley, the leaves are pungent, with a distinctive (some say "soapy") taste and aroma. Used in Mexican, Chinese, and Indian cooking, cilantro is an intense herb. It's also delicate and wilts easily, and should be stored wrapped in a paper towel in the refrigerator. Cilantro is a pungent garnish for many dishes and should be added at the last minute. I often mix the leaves into green salads for a surprising flourish.

The seeds are called coriander, an ancient and much-revered herb, which is mentioned in the Bible and was found in the tombs of the pharaohs. Aromatic, with a subtle sweet flavor and hint of citrus, coriander gives a lift to desserts and fruit dishes, and is an essential ingredient in curries. To enjoy a full flavor, buy the seeds whole and toast them lightly on medium-high heat in a toaster oven or dry skillet, then grind them in a coffee or spice grinder, or place them in a small bag and crush with a hammer or rolling pin. The extra effort is worth the delicious flavor—you'll never buy store-bought ground coriander again.

Fire-Roasted Tomato Salsa

Makes about 2 cups

For best results, be sure to use firm, garden-fresh, meaty, ripe tomatoes. Plum tomatoes may also be used to good effect. This salsa should be eaten as soon as it is made, as refrigeration will dull and flatten the fresh taste of the lightly charred tomatoes and peppers. Serve with crisp tortilla chips, or use as a sauce for grilled vegetables and rice.

4 medium tomatoes

1 small red bell pepper

2 to 4 jalapeño peppers

2 cloves garlic, finely chopped

1/4 cup finely chopped scallions

2 tablespoons chopped fresh cilantro

Juice of 1 lime

Salt to taste

Prepare a charcoal fire and allow it to burn down to glowing coals. Adjust the grill over the coals and allow it to heat for several minutes. Working quickly, char the tomatoes, bell pepper, and jalapeños on the grill until their skins are blackened and split. Set the vegetables aside to cool.

Skin and core the tomatoes, also removing most of the seeds. Coarsely chop tomatoes and transfer to a large bowl. Remove the skin, stems, and seeds from the peppers; chop finely and add to the tomatoes.

Add the garlic to the mixture and purée against the side of the bowl with a spoon. Stir in the scallions, cilantro, and lime juice, and season with salt.

Fresh Tomato Salsa

Makes 2 1/2 cups

Make this salsa in the peak of summer when tomatoes are hanging voluptuously from the vine. When refrigerated, the salsa will keep 3 to 4 days.

2 large ripe tomatoes, seeded and finely chopped
1/2 cup finely chopped sweet red or white onion
1 large jalapeño chile, seeded and finely chopped
2 heaping tablespoons chopped fresh cilantro
1/2 teaspoon salt
2 tablespoons freshly squeezed lime juice

Combine all of the ingredients in a nonmetallic bowl and refrigerate until ready to serve.

Chipotle-Tomatillo Salsa

Makes 3 cups

With a papery husk and bright green skin, tomatillos are a member of the Cape gooseberry family and have a tart, crisp flavor. They look like small green tomatoes (even though they aren't related) and are a good substitute for tomatoes in the wintertime. Serve this as a salsa, or tuck it into a warmed tortilla for a chipotle-tomatillo burrito.

2 pounds tomatillos, husked and diced
2 cloves garlic, minced
4 chipotles, softened and chopped
1 bunch fresh cilantro leaves, chopped
1 cup Vegetable Stock (see page 75)
Juice of 1 lime

Sauté the tomatillos, garlic, chipotles, and cilantro. Add the stock and lime juice and cook on low heat for 15 to 20 minutes.

Tomatillo-Almond Salsa

Makes 1 1/2 cups

Tomatillo salsas are popular in Mexico. In this one, the light crunchiness of the almonds complements the tart tomatillos beautifully and makes a perky winter salsa. Light and fresh, it's a good starter with chips and is also tasty with tortillas or as a condiment on a grill menu. This salsa is mild; chop in more jalapeños if you want to drive up the spice.

8 tomatillos, husked and chopped

1 small yellow onion, finely chopped

1/4 cup almond slivers, chopped

1/2 cup packed fresh cilantro and parsley leaves, finely chopped

4 tablespoons white wine vinegar

1 teaspoon dried oregano

1 jalapeño with seeds, chopped

1/4 teaspoon salt

1/4 teaspoon freshly ground black pepper

Combine all the ingredients in a large mixing bowl and serve.

Toasted Corn Salsa

Makes 3 cups

With the delectable taste of toasted corn, this is a welcome side dish on a grill menu or a good relish for the Southwestern Bruschetta (see page 39).

2 tablespoons olive oil

2 cups fresh or frozen corn (thawed if frozen)

3 tablespoons chopped fresh cilantro

1 small red bell pepper, finely diced

1 teaspoon granulated sugar

1/2 teaspoon ground cumin

3 tablespoons apple cider vinegar

2 tablespoons red wine vinegar

Juice of 1 lime

1 tablespoon orange zest

Juice of 1 orange

1/4 teaspoon ground cayenne pepper

Heat the olive oil in a cast-iron or other heavy skillet. Add corn and sauté on medium-low heat until lightly browned and caramel colored. Remove from the pan and let cool for 5 minutes. Add the remaining ingredients and stir to combine.

PITA POCKETS

Make an easy, healthful sandwich by stuffing pita bread with salsa fillings. Cut the pita in half, warm it for a few minutes in a toaster oven, then fill each half with:

◇ Borlotti Bean Salsa (see page 62), hummus, and fresh basil leaves

◇ Toasted Corn Salsa, fresh sliced tomatoes, and hot sauce

◇ Fire-Roasted Tomato Salsa (see page 58), romaine lettuce, alfalfa sprouts, and grated Cheddar cheese

Borlotti Bean Salsa

Makes 4 cups

Borlotti beans are preferred for their fresh taste, but if they aren't available, dried red kidney beans are a good substitute. For detailed information on beans, see pages 137-139.

1/2 cup dried black beans

1/2 cup dried borlotti beans

8 plum tomatoes (4 red and 4 yellow, if available), chopped into 1/2-inch pieces

1/2 large Bermuda onion, finely chopped

3/4 cup fresh cilantro, chopped

1/4 cup extra virgin olive oil

1/8 cup red wine vinegar

1/2 cup hot sauce

2 teaspoons pure chile powder

2 teaspoons ground cumin

3 jalapeño chiles, finely chopped

Juice of 1 fresh lime

Rinse and pick over the beans. Place beans in separate saucepans with cold water to cover and bring to a boil. Drain, add fresh water, and bring to a boil again. Reduce heat, cover and simmer until tender, about 1 hour for borlotti (or kidney) beans, 1 1/2 hours for black beans. (Do not add salt to the cooking water as it toughens beans.) Remove from heat and let cool in cooking water to keep skins intact. Drain, then combine the beans in a large bowl with the rest of the ingredients. Chill to bring out the flavors.

. . . but for the <u>frijoles</u> (beans) which followed, and which come in at the conclusion—like "God Save the Queen" at the end of a concert—we should have gone to bed famishing.

—English traveler in Mexico, 1864

Caribbean Sun-Splashed Salsa

Makes 3 cups

The combination of tropical fruit with habanero chiles produces a sweet heat that is soothing and explosive. This salsa is a good accompaniment to fried plantains or delicious served simply as an appetizer with slices of crisp chayote. Use papayas and mangoes that are barely ripe to hold the salsa together better. You might also try substituting other fruit, such as pineapple or kiwi.

1 ripe pineapple, peeled, cored, and diced

1 ripe mango, peeled and diced

1 ripe papaya, peeled, seeded, and diced

1 small red onion, finely diced

1/2 cup chopped fresh cilantro

Juice of 2 limes

1/4 cup freshly squeezed orange juice

1 tablespoon brown sugar

2 tablespoons dark rum

Pinch of salt

1 tablespoon apple cider vinegar

2 fresh habanero chiles or Scotch bonnet peppers, minced

Combine all of the ingredients in a large bowl. Allow the salsa to sit at room temperature for 30 minutes before serving.

TROPICAL PLEASURES

Tropical fruits are appearing on American restaurant menus everywhere. They are colorful, good for you, and as refreshing as a palm-fringed cove in the dead of winter. Add papayas, mangoes, and other fruit to drinks, yogurt, vinaigrettes, grilling marinades—even baby food.

PAPAYAS

Native to Malaysia, papaya (also known as paw paw) is rich in vitamins B and C, and can vary enormously in size—from the size of a big potato up to a 20-pound oval. The smooth skins range in color from yellowish green to dark green to greenish orange. Cut it in half and inside you'll find hundreds of small round edible black seeds, which can be scraped out with a spoon. Green unripe papaya is cooked like a vegetable in the Caribbean and tastes a bit like squash. When unripe, it's also used to make chutney and emits a white juice that is a natural meat tenderizer. Ripe papaya has a melonlike texture, with the floral perfume and flavors of melon and citrus. An islander once taught me to ripen a papaya quickly by scoring it and leaving it in a paper bag for two days, which did the trick. Fresh ripe papaya is delicious served cut open, seeded, and topped with a squirt of fresh lime.

Mango Tango Salsa

Makes about 2 cups

In this bright tropical dish, the jalapeños and basil counter the sweetness of the fruit, yielding a provocative salsa that is good with a grill menu.

1 ripe mango (or papaya), coarsely chopped into 1/2-inch cubes
1 1/2 cups coarsely chopped pineapple
1/4 cup paper-thin slivers of red onion
Juice of 1 lime
2 jalapeños, skinned, seeded, and minced
8 basil leaves, shredded
4 to 5 shakes of Melinda's Hot Sauce or other Caribbean hot sauce

Toss ingredients together gently in a bowl and serve immediately.

Pico de Gallo

Makes 3 cups

From Mexico, pico de gallo (which means "bite of the rooster" in Spanish) is a zesty combination of fresh fruit or vegetables and chiles. It can be served with tortilla chips as a snack, but it really shines as a garnish or condiment with quesadillas, enchiladas, or rice and beans. When cutting the fruit and vegetables, try different shapes to create an interesting visual effect—tiny cubes of watermelon and cantaloupe, small matchsticks of jicama, and paper-thin radish slivers.

3/4 cup seeded and finely chopped watermelon
1 cup finely chopped cantaloupe
1 cup finely chopped jicama
1 cup finely chopped radishes
2 jalapeños, seeded and minced
1 small red onion, minced
3 to 4 tablespoons finely chopped fresh cilantro
Juice of 1 lime
Pure chile powder

Combine all of the ingredients except the chile powder in a bowl and toss gently. Dust lightly with chile powder and serve.

Autumn Black Bean Salsa

Makes 5 cups

With the startling flavor pairings of ingredients like sweet potatoes and apples, this salsa from my friend Scott Avery is an easy-to-prepare appetizer that is delicious served with blue corn chips. It also makes a hearty pasta sauce (see note). The flavors taste best if the salsa is made the night before and allowed to sit at least 6 hours before serving.

1 large sweet potato, baked and peeled

2 cups cooked or canned black beans, drained (see page 333)

1 red onion, peeled and diced

1 clove garlic, minced

1 yellow or orange bell pepper, seeded and diced

1 jalapeño, seeded and diced

1 red apple, cored and diced

1/4 cup apple cider vinegar

Juice of 1 lime

1/4 cup fresh parsley, chopped

1/4 cup fresh sage, chopped

2 teaspoons ground coriander

1/8 teaspoon ground cayenne pepper

Kosher salt to taste

Grated sharp Cheddar cheese, for garnish (optional)

Toasted pumpkin seeds, for garnish (optional; see page 73)

Divide the sweet potato, placing half in a mixing bowl, and mash until smooth. Dice the remaining half and add to the bowl. Add the remaining ingredients and combine well. Allow the salsa to rest a minimum of 6 hours. Top with a sprinkling of cheese and pumpkin seeds just before serving.

Note: To serve with pasta, heat the salsa quickly in a sauté pan over high heat. Toss with freshly cooked pasta and serve immediately, topped with a sprinkling of cheese and pumpkin seeds. If you can't find fresh sage, add a bit more fresh parsley (to taste), adjusting the amount of jalapeño and cayenne to suit your palate.

MANGOES

Although mangoes are native to Asia, more than 500 varieties are now cultivated throughout the tropical world. They can be round or elongated and generally are the size of a large avocado. As they ripen, they turn from green to ruby red, orange, or yellow. The skin should be removed with a sharp knife. The juicy flesh is attached to a disc-shaped core, which is rather difficult to separate from the flesh, but can also be done with a sharp knife. Rich in iron and vitamin A, they have a distinctive sweet-sour flesh with a hint of varnish (oddly enough!) that is delicious. I generally prefer to eat mangoes at the beach, knee deep in water, where the juicy mess can truly be enjoyed.

Soups

Soups are welcome any time of the year. They refresh you off on a hot summer afternoon, they warm you on a winter night, they begin a meal with gusto. They are also highly portable in a thermos; indeed, there's nothing like wrapping your fingers around a steaming mug of soup at a fall football game or aboard a sailboat in Maine in late September.

A note about soup stock: an easy recipe for Vegetarian Stock is found on page 75. Make a big batch and store in several containers in the freezer so you needn't use packaged or canned stock. The difference in taste (and the amount of sodium) is noticeable.

Roasted Corn Soup with Chipotles

Serves 4

I first tasted this extraordinary soup by Lisa Esposito at Casa U-Betcha in Seattle. An actress and chef, she is one of a growing number of chefs nationwide who is serving authentic Mexican food. Lisa says that it's difficult to get people excited about this cuisine because it's so misrepresented in our country. Her culinary prowess at Casa U-Betcha is doing a lot to correct this. Rich and satiny smooth, this soup has the fullness of a traditional corn soup and the smokiness and lingering embers of chipotle chiles.

1 head roasted garlic (see page 35)

1 1/2 cups (10 ounces) corn kernels, fresh or frozen (thawed if frozen)

1 tablespoon olive or vegetable oil

1 yellow onion, finely diced

1 teaspoon salt

1/4 teaspoon ground cayenne pepper

1/4 teaspoon ground coriander

1/4 teaspoon ground cumin

2 cups milk

1 pint heavy cream

2 tablespoons puréed canned chipotle chiles in adobo sauce (see note)

Chopped scallions, for garnish (optional)

Squeeze out the cloves of roasted garlic, chop, and set aside.

Turn the oven to broil. Spread the corn in a single layer on a baking sheet and place under the broiler, shaking the sheet every few minutes until the kernels are caramel colored all over. Remove from broiler.

In a heavy stockpot, heat the oil and sauté the onion and garlic until the onion is transparent. Add the salt, spices, and corn, then add the milk. Carefully bring to a boil, reduce heat, and stir in the cream. Simmer for 15 minutes. With a slotted spoon, remove the corn and onion and transfer them to a blender or food processor. Purée with a little of the milk-cream mixture, then return to the stockpot. Add the chipotles, simmer another 10 minutes, and serve. Garnish the soup with scallions.

Note: If you can't find canned chipotles, soak dried chipotles in hot water for about 15 minutes (or until soft), remove the stems, and purée in a food processor. If you leave in the seeds, you'll have a scorcher of a soup.

It is the rare winter chill that persists in the face of a well-made soup. Obviously, warmth is a major factor. But the generous spirit that seems to guide the hand of the soup-making cook also presides over the dinner party where soup is the main attraction. Maybe it's the perfume that lingers after hours of simmering on the stove. Or the steam that covers the kitchen windows. Or the calm that enters the cook's soul when dinner has been assembled leisurely over days, not in a last-minute panic. But whatever it is, when soup is served, a mood of easy intimacy prevails.

—Molly O'Neill

Spicy White Bean Soup with Tomato

Serves 6

Puréeing half the beans will give you a smooth soup with a bit of texture. Remember to soak the beans overnight.

2 cups dry small white cannellini, lima, or navy beans
1 yellow onion, cut in half
1 bay leaf
1 celery stalk
2 tablespoons olive oil
1 cup chopped yellow onion
2 cloves garlic, chopped
1/2 teaspoon ground fennel
1/2 teaspoon ground cayenne pepper
1 1/4 cups canned peeled tomatoes, with juice
Freshly ground black pepper
1/2 cup chopped fresh parsley
3 cloves garlic, finely chopped
1 teaspoon dried thyme

Rinse the beans and soak overnight in cold water to cover generously.

Drain beans and cover with 2 quarts fresh water. Add the onion halves, bay leaf, and celery. Bring to a boil over high heat, then reduce the heat and simmer gently for 1 1/2 to 2 hours, or until the beans are very tender. Remove the onion, bay leaf, and celery with a slotted spoon. Salt to taste, purée half the beans in a blender, and crush the other half with their liquid. Set aside.

Heat the olive oil in a sauté pan over medium heat. Add the chopped onion and the garlic and cook, stirring for about 5 minutes, or until softened. Add the fennel and cayenne and cook a few minutes longer, until aromatic. Add the tomatoes and cook, breaking them up with a wooden spoon, until most of the liquid has evaporated. Stir the bean mixture into the tomatoes and simmer gently for 30 to 40 minutes. Season liberally with pepper. Combine the parsley, garlic, and thyme and stir into the soup just before serving.

Beautiful soup! Who cares for fish, game, or any other dish? Who would not give all else for two pennyworth only of beautiful soup?

—Lewis Carroll

Carrot Soup with Lemongrass

Serves 4

This pretty, Thai-inspired soup is thickened slightly with rice and laced with spices. The coconut milk and orange marry well with the carrot's sweet herbal flavor.

1 tablespoon vegetable oil
1 yellow onion, chopped into 1/4-inch dice
2 cloves garlic, finely chopped
1 teaspoon ground cumin
1 teaspoon ground coriander
1/4 teaspoon ground cayenne pepper
1/8 teaspoon ground cardamom
2 tablespoons white basmati rice
1 pound carrots, peeled and cut into 1/8-inch-thick slices
4 cups water
1/2 teaspoon salt
1/2 teaspoon brown sugar
4 quarter-sized slices peeled gingerroot
1 stalk lemongrass, tender part only, peeled and thinly
    sliced crosswise (about 3 tablespoons)
1/2 cup coconut milk
1 cup freshly squeezed orange juice
1 to 2 tablespoons freshly squeezed lemon or lime juice
4 tablespoons chopped fresh chives or cilantro, for garnish

Heat the oil in a heavy 3-quart stockpot over medium heat and add the onion. Cook, stirring for 2 to 3 minutes, until softened. Add the garlic and spices. Reduce the heat to low and cook for 5 minutes longer, then add the rice and continue cooking for 2 to 3 minutes.

Add the carrots to the pan and increase the heat to medium. Cook, while stirring, until the carrots are coated with the spices. Lower the heat and cover. Sweat the carrots, stirring occasionally, for about 15 minutes. Add the water, salt, brown sugar, ginger, and lemongrass and bring to a boil. Reduce the heat and simmer for 30 to 40 minutes, or until the carrots are soft. Remove and discard the ginger. Add the coconut milk and orange juice and simmer for 2 minutes. Set aside and allow the mixture to cool for a few minutes.

Purée the carrot mixture in batches in a food processor or blender. Strain back into the pan through a medium-fine sieve. Reheat, and adjust seasoning with the lemon juice. Serve hot, sprinkled with chives.

Do you have a kinder, more adaptable friend in the food world than soup? Who soothes you when you are ill? Who refuses to leave you when you are impoverished and stretches its resources to give you a hearty sustenance and cheer? Who warms you in the winter and cools you in the summer? Yet who is also capable of doing honor to your richest table and impressing your most demanding guests? . . . Soup does its loyal best, no matter what undignified conditions are imposed upon it. But soup knows the difference. Soup is sensitive. You don't catch steak hanging around when you're poor and sick, do you?

—Judith Martin
    ("Miss Manners")

Several years ago, I spent a month on an estate in Tuscany. My companions and I, all food lovers, made daily excursions to the markets and sampled the local cheeses, fruits, and vegetables. From the estate, we bought wine and olive oil, which came in wine bottles plugged with corks. The olive oil was fruity, fresh, and as pungent as the forest. Drizzled lightly on our food, it elevated the simplest dishes—late summer tomatoes, fresh breads, and homemade pasta.

There is a tremendous difference in quality between olive oils, and if you are featuring it uncooked in a vinaigrette or marinade, buy the best you can afford. Oils labeled "virgin" are made from the first pressing of olives and are untreated. "Extra" virgin is the finest, identified by its extraordinary aroma and fruity flavor. "Pure" olive oils (or those whose labels just say "olive oil") are a blend of refined and virgin oils and suitable only for general cooking. Olive oil pressed from unripe olives tends to be bright green in color and strong tasting, whereas ripened olives produce oil that is more subtle and softer tasting. The best olive oils on the market come from estates in Spain and Italy, where single varietal olives are grown and pressed in small batches.

Italian olive oil: Considering that 92 percent of the world's olive oil comes from the Mediterranean, where olive trees have been cultivated for more than six thousand years, it's not surprising that Italian olive oil is spectacular. Green, rich, fruity, and slightly peppery, good Italian oil is fresh and gutsy. I love the intense, robust oils from the Tuscany region, in particular from Fattoria Dell'Ugo. Laudemio Frescobaldi, which has a grassy aroma and hint of apples, and Tega Cardinale from Umbria, which smells and tastes of the forest, are also delicious.

Spanish olive oil: Yellow, buttery, and not as peppery as Italian oils, Spanish oils tend to be lightly fruity, with a subtle floral bouquet. Favored brands include Lerida (an estate-bottled oil from Catalonia), L'Estornell (pressed from Arbequina olives), and Baena (an unfiltered organic estate oil).

O L I V E

California olive oil: This oil is derived largely from mission olives, which Spanish Franciscan missionaries introduced to California in the late 1700s for lamp fuel. Many California oils on the market today are inferior blends, bought in large batches from the same few sources and then privately labeled. There are some notable exceptions, such as Lila Jaeger's Olive Oil from the Rutherford Hill winery in Napa Valley.

Greek olive oil: With Greece the world's third largest producer of olive oil, most of the olives are grown in Crete and Peloponnisos (where the town of Kalamata is located). Rustic and assertive, Greek oils are fruity, with the flavor of the olive shining through. Iliada is a good brand.

French olive oil: France is one of the world's smallest producers of olive oil, with much of the French oils from orchards in the Mediterranean provinces, particularly Provence. Pressed from ripe olives, French olive oil tends to be golden in color, with a subtle, sweet flavor. Recommended brands include A L'Olivier Extra Virgin Olive Oil as an everyday oil and Huile D'Olive from The Fresh Olive Company of Provence for a treat.

Judge an oil by its color, aroma, and flavor, swirling a bit around in your mouth before swallowing, as you would a fine wine. Olive oil needn't be refrigerated, but should be stored in a cool, dark place, because it can go rancid when exposed to light and air. If you want to preserve the flavor, resist the temptation to leave the pretty bottle on a sunny ledge in the kitchen!

O I L S

Curried Squash-Apple Soup

Serves 4

This is a takeoff on the curried pumpkin soup often served on the Barbados and other British-influenced Caribbean islands. The curry gives the soup a provocative lift, while the apple and port provide sweet comfort. With a distinctive bread, a green salad, and a terrific dessert, this makes a comforting winter meal.

4 tablespoons butter

2 yellow onions, chopped

2 cloves garlic, minced

1 to 2 tablespoons curry powder (depending on desired intensity of curry flavor)

1 tart green apple

2 pounds butternut squash, peeled and coarsely chopped

4 cups Vegetable Stock (see page 75)

1/4 cup pine nuts or squash seeds (see note), for garnish

1 tablespoon tawny port

Freshly ground black pepper

Heat the butter in a heavy stockpot over medium heat. Add the onions and cook, stirring often, until softened, about 10 minutes. Add the garlic and curry powder and cook, stirring, for 1 minute. Stir in the apple, squash, and stock, cover, and cook until the squash is soft, about 20 minutes.

While the squash is cooking, toast the pine nuts in a 350° oven until golden brown, 2 to 3 minutes. Remove the soup from heat and, when slightly cooled, transfer to a food processor and purée. Pour back into the pot, reheat, and stir in the port and black pepper to taste. Ladle into soup bowls, and garnish with pine nuts.

Note: You can substitute squash seeds for pine nuts, but they will give the soup a coarser taste and texture.

TOASTING NUTS, SPICES, SEEDS, AND BREAD CRUMBS

Briefly toasting nuts, spices, and bread crumbs is an easy process that will reward you with a roasted flavor and aroma. Toasted pine nuts, for example, can be sprinkled atop salads or soups, or tossed into stuffings and salsas. Toasting whole spices such as cumin or coriander before crushing them enhances their piquant flavors and adds zest to curried dishes, rice pilafs, or stews. Toasting bread crumbs makes their wholesome qualities even more evident. If you're as fond of that roasted taste as I am, you may want to toast batches of nuts and seeds just to keep on hand.

To toast nuts: Preheat an oven or a toaster oven to 350°. Spread nuts evenly on a baking sheet (or foil shell) and toast until they turn golden brown and aromatic, just a few minutes. Remove from oven and cool.

To toast sesame seeds and whole spices: Follow the instructions for toasting nuts. Or heat a dry heavy skillet over medium heat and dry-roast the seeds or spices in a single layer, shaking the pan or stirring frequently with a wooden spoon until aromatic, about 2 to 3 minutes.

To toast squash and pumpkin seeds: Preheat the oven to 350°. Remove the seeds and pulp from the squash or pumpkin. Comb the stringy pulp with a fork to dislodge the seeds. Place the seeds in a shallow pan (or a shallow shell made from aluminum foil) and coat lightly with 1 to 2 teaspoons of melted butter or with vegetable cooking spray. Spread the seeds in a single layer and toast in the oven, stirring occasionally, until the seeds are golden and crunchy, about 30 minutes.

To toast bread crumbs: Preheat the oven to 350°. Spread the bread crumbs evenly on a baking sheet (or foil shell) and toast in the oven until lightly browned and aromatic, just a few minutes. Remove from oven and cool.

Corn Gumbo

Serves 6

Gumbo (or gombo) is Creole patois for okra and refers to a soup made with a roux and thickened with okra. The secret of good gumbo is to slowly bring the roux to a toasty brown color, which gives this thick soup a rich, nutty flavor. Serve ladled over rice in soup bowls and set out a bottle of hot sauce.

3 tablespoons vegetable oil

3 tablespoons all-purpose flour

1 green bell pepper, chopped

1 stalk celery, chopped

1 yellow onion, chopped

1 16-ounce can stewed tomatoes, or 2 cups fresh
    chopped tomatoes

1 cup Vegetable Stock (see page 75)

2 cups okra, sliced into 1/4-inch-thick rounds

1 cup baby lima beans

1 cup fresh or frozen corn kernels

1 tablespoon Worcestershire sauce

2 tablespoons Tabasco or other Louisiana-style hot sauce
    (or more, to taste)

3/4 teaspoon salt

1/2 teaspoon dried thyme

1 cup water

3 cups long-grain white cooked rice (see page 334)

In a stockpot, heat the vegetable oil over medium heat and stir in the flour. Cook, stirring constantly, until the flour is browned, but not burned, about 10 minutes. Add the green bell pepper, celery, and onion and cook over medium heat until the vegetables are just tender. Stir in the tomatoes, stock, okra, lima beans, corn, Worcestershire sauce, hot sauce, salt, thyme, and water, and bring to a boil. Reduce heat and simmer 20 minutes to blend flavors.

Jadin loin, gombo gaté.

(When the garden is far, the gombo is spoiled.)

—Creole proverb
from Martinique

Vegetable Stock

Makes 12 cups

Vegetable stock is easy to make and tastes much better than what's available in cans or made from packages. Make a big batch and freeze in containers if not using promptly.

2 large yellow onions, chopped
2 tablespoons olive oil
4 cloves garlic, chopped
4 carrots, chopped
2 potatoes, quartered
4 celery stalks, chopped
One handful fresh parsley sprigs, chopped
2 sprigs fresh rosemary
1 teaspoon dried thyme
1 teaspoon dried oregano
1 teaspoon dried sage
2 bay leaves
20 whole black peppercorns
2 to 3 teaspoons salt
Pinch of ground cayenne pepper or pure red chile powder
20 cups cold water

Sauté the onions in olive oil in a large stockpot until soft. Add the garlic and sauté for 1 minute more. Add the remaining ingredients, bring to a boil, then reduce heat to simmer for 1 1/2 hours, partially covered. Strain liquid.

OKRA

This succulent vegetable, native to Africa, was introduced to the Americas by black slaves. Okra goes by many lyrical names: lady's finger in England (due to the tender green pods, no longer than a pinkie), *quiabo* in Brazil, *nkruma* in Ghana, and *gombo* in French. It's a popular vegetable throughout the South and Caribbean, as well as in India and the Balkans, and is rich in calcium, iron, and vitamin C. It will thicken sauces and stews and is delicious fried. You can find it fresh or frozen in many supermarkets throughout the year.

Main Courses

Stews

Stews are in a class by themselves, adding cheer to a winter kitchen and filling the house with fragrant smells. They're hearty one-dish meals that can be made on Sunday to tide the family over during a busy week. Stews can be served over a bed of couscous, rice, or polenta, or enjoyed by themselves in a deep bowl with buttered hot bread. If there are leftovers, a thick stew can also be folded into omelets for breakfast or spooned into pita pockets for lunch.

Portuguese Vegetable Stew

Serves 6

This thick, aromatic stew of fall vegetables brings together sweet winter squash, sweet potatoes, and carrots with cabbage and tomatoes. The cinnamon, marjoram, and cumin are often found combined in Mexican dishes.

1 1/2 pound butternut or buttercup squash, peeled, seeded, and cut into 3/4-inch dice (3 cups)

2 large sweet potatoes, peeled and cut into 3/4-inch dice (3 cups)

4 carrots, peeled and sliced crosswise into 1/4-inch-thick rounds (2 cups)

4 tablespoons vegetable oil

1 large yellow onion, finely chopped

1 large red bell pepper, seeded and cut into 1-inch-long slices

3 jalapeño peppers, roasted, peeled, seeded, and cut into 1/4-inch dice

4 cloves garlic, chopped

1 1/2 teaspoons marjoram

1 (2-inch) stick cinnamon

1 1/2 teaspoons ground cumin

1 tablespoon hot paprika

3 cups peeled, seeded, and chopped tomatoes, or 1 28-ounce can chopped tomatoes, with juice

1/4 pound cabbage, cut into 1-inch strips (about 2 cups)

1 1/2 cups cooked kidney or cannellini beans (see page 333)

Salt to taste

Preheat oven to 400°. Lightly oil (or spray with nonstick cooking spray) a heavy 12 by 18-inch shallow baking pan. Toss the squash, sweet potatoes, and carrots in 2 tablespoons of the vegetable oil and spread in a layer on the baking pan. Roast for 20 minutes, until barely tender. Set aside.

Meanwhile, cook the onion in the remaining 2 tablespoons of oil in a large, heavy stockpot over medium heat until softened, about 5 minutes. Add the bell pepper and jalapeños and cook, stirring for another 5 minutes until softened. Add the garlic, marjoram, and spices and cook until fragrant, about 2 minutes. Add the tomatoes and their juice and simmer 20 minutes, until slightly reduced. Add the cabbage and salt. Simmer for 10 minutes, then add the roasted vegetables and beans. Simmer gently for 20 to 30 minutes until the vegetables are tender. Remove the cinnamon stick and serve.

Green Street Ratatouille

Makes 12 cups

Steve Cobble is a chef who cooks with spices by the handful. At the Green Street Grill in Cambridge, Massachusetts, his food will make you sweat and tear up, then ask for more. "We're part of a circuit of restaurants in town that people visit for exciting food," he says. This terrific ratatouille with allspice is from his kitchen.

2 tablespoons olive oil

1 yellow onion, diced

1/4 cup minced garlic

2 tablespoons finely julienned fresh gingerroot

2 tablespoons finely sliced lemongrass

1 1/2 sticks cinnamon

1/2 tablespoon cracked allspice berries

1 1/2 hot cherry pepper, stemmed, seeded, and minced (seeds reserved)

1/2 Scotch bonnet chile pepper, stemmed, seeded, and minced (reserve the seeds)

2 cups white wine

2 cups freshly squeezed orange juice

1/2 cup pineapple juice

1 32-ounce can plum tomatoes, with juice

4 tablespoons tomato paste

1 1/2 chayote, diced

2 red bell peppers, stemmed, seeded, and diced

1 green bell pepper, stemmed, seeded, and diced

4 cups diced calabaza or butternut squash

1 medium eggplant, diced

Salt to taste

Freshly ground black pepper

Chopped fresh oregano leaves, for garnish

Chopped fresh thyme leaves, for garnish

Put 1 tablespoon of the olive oil in a large stockpot and over medium heat, sweat the onion, garlic, ginger, lemongrass, cinnamon, allspice, and chiles for about 8 minutes. Add the wine and cook 3 to 4 minutes. Add the orange juice, pineapple juice, juice from the tomatoes, tomato paste, and chayote and cook until soft, about 20 minutes. Add the bell peppers and tomatoes and cook until thickened, about 20 minutes.

Meanwhile, steam the calabaza until cooked, about 20 minutes, then set aside to cool. Pan-fry the eggplant in a skillet in the remaining tablespoon of olive oil until cooked, about 10 minutes, then set aside to cool. Add calabaza and eggplant and cook until the mixture comes together, about 10 to 15 minutes. Season with salt, black pepper, and a sprinkling of oregano and thyme.

Curried Winter Squash Stew with Red Lentils

Serves 6

This recipe, from my friend Liz Wheeler, evolved from one she found a few years ago in Julie Sahni's *Classic Indian Cooking*. This savory (and very spicy) stew is delicious served with plain boiled rice and is a wonderful way to take advantage of early fall squash and apples and the last fresh, ripe tomatoes. You can embellish the stew by adding finely shredded fresh basil during the final simmer or enriching it with up to 1 cup of heavy cream. To make a beautiful soup, purée the stew and swirl in a little heavy cream. It's a meal in itself with salad and bread.

1 (2-pound) butternut or buttercup squash, peeled, seeded, and cut into 1/2-inch dice

2 tablespoons vegetable oil

1/2 teaspoon salt

1 teaspoon ground cumin

1 teaspoon ground coriander

1/4 teaspoon ground cinnamon

1/4 teaspoon freshly ground black pepper

2 cloves garlic, finely chopped

1/2 cup red lentils

1/2 teaspoon turmeric

1/4 teaspoon ground cayenne pepper

1 bay leaf

3 cups water

2 tablespoons vegetable oil

1 cup finely chopped yellow onion

4 serrano chiles, seeded and finely chopped

1 1/2 tablespoons finely chopped gingerroot

1 large, tart apple (Granny Smith or Macoun), peeled, cored, and chopped (1 heaping cup)

2 cups fresh or canned, peeled, seeded, and chopped tomatoes, with juice

Salt to taste

Arugula

Cilantro

Dill

Lavender

Rosemary

Sage

ASSERTIVE HERBS

Preheat the oven to 400°. Toss the squash cubes with the oil, salt, spices, and garlic. Spread in a roasting pan, cover, and bake until barely tender, about 15 to 20 minutes. Uncover and set aside.

Pick over and wash the lentils. Place them in a saucepan with the turmeric, cayenne, bay leaf, and water. Bring to a boil, then reduce the heat and simmer gently, partially covered, until just tender, about 20 minutes.

Meanwhile, heat the oil in a heavy 3-quart saucepan over medium heat. Add the onion, chiles, and ginger, and sauté until the vegetables are softened, about 5 minutes. Add the apple and sauté 2 to 3 minutes, or until it begins to soften. Add the tomatoes and simmer until the mixture is slightly thickened, about 15 minutes. Season with salt. Add the squash and lentils to the tomato mixture and stir together gently. Simmer very gently over low heat for 20 to 30 minutes. Add more salt to taste and remove the bay leaf. (If you purée the stew, you may want to add up to 1 cup of water to thin it.)

It is a tree of the Sun, and under the Celestial sign Leo, and resisteth Witchcraft potently, as also all the evils old Saturn can do the body of man . . . neither witch nor devil, thunder nor lightning will hurt a man where a bay tree is.

—Nicholas Culpepper, *Complete Herbal*, 1653

Black Pepper

Cayenne

Cumin

Fenugreek

Ginger

Hot Paprika

Mustard

Hearty Green Chili with Black Beans

Serves 8 to 10

Making a robust green chili without meat has always been a challenge for cooks, as the flavor of pork or beef is an integral component of Mexican and New Mexican chili dishes. In this recipe, the corn tortillas are puréed along with generous amounts of cumin, coriander, and ground chile powder to give soul to this heartwarming stew. It's delicious garnished with chopped cilantro, finely diced red onions, diced tomatoes, and sour cream...or enjoyed by itself. Serve with warm flour tortillas.

8 tomatillos, husked and rinsed

1 large yellow onion, diced

1 chayote, cored and chopped

1 large baking potato, finely diced

1 green bell pepper, chopped

1 red bell pepper, chopped

4 fresh jalapeños, minced

1 head roasted garlic, minced (see page 35)

2 cups diced fresh or canned New Mexico green chiles

1 16-ounce can chopped tomatoes, with juice

1 1/2 cups Vegetable Stock (see page 75)

1/2 cup water

2 teaspoons salt

3 teaspoons ground cumin

1 tablespoon ground coriander

1 tablespoon dried oregano

2 teaspoons freshly ground black pepper

1 tablespoon pure chile powder

2 cups salted tortilla chips

2 cups cooked black beans (see page 333)

Chopped fresh cilantro, for garnish (optional)

Finely diced red onions, for garnish (optional)

Finely diced tomatoes, for garnish (optional)

Sour cream, for garnish (optional)

Heat a large sauté pan or skillet on high heat and char the tomatillos by shaking the pan occasionally, until they are blackened all over. Chop the tomatillos (including skins and seeds). In a large, heavy stockpot, heat the oil over medium-low heat. Sauté the onion, chayote, potato, and bell peppers until wilted. Add the jalapeños, roasted garlic, green chiles, tomatoes, stock, water, salt, and spices to the stockpot and stir. Cover, and simmer for 30 minutes.

In a blender, purée the corn chips with 1 cup of the stew, adding more stew if necessary. Add puréed chips to the stockpot, and add the black beans. Stir, and cook for 15 minutes. To serve, ladle into bowls and garnish with the cilantro, red onions, tomatoes, and sour cream.

Moroccan Vegetable Stew with Couscous

Serves 6 to 8

Moroccan food is startlingly aromatic. Perfumed with the fragrance of cardamom and accented with the sweetness of currants, one bite of this spicy stew will have you thinking you've just arrived in the city of Fez for a culinary adventure. It's delicious served with Fennel Salad (see page 189).

2 tablespoons olive oil

1 large yellow onion, chopped

6 cloves garlic, minced

2 red potatoes, diced

1 cup diced carrots

2 teaspoons ground cardamom pods or cardamom powder

1 zucchini, cut in half and sliced

1 yellow squash, cut in half-moons and sliced

1/2 cauliflower, cut into florets

2 teaspoons curry powder

1 teaspoon salt

1 teaspoon freshly ground black pepper

1 teaspoon ground cayenne pepper

1/2 cup raisins or currants, soaked 15 minutes in warm water to plump

1 16-ounce can diced tomatoes

1 15-ounce can tomato sauce

2 tablespoons honey

1 15-ounce can garbanzo beans

6 cups water

3 cups uncooked couscous

1/2 cup dried figs, coarsely chopped

1/3 cup sliced almonds

1 pint plain yogurt, for garnish

1 bunch fresh mint, chopped, for garnish

In a heavy stockpot, heat the olive oil and sauté the onion, garlic, potatoes, carrots, and cardamom. Stir until fragrant, then add the zucchini, yellow squash, and cauliflower. Add curry powder, salt, black pepper, and cayenne and stir. Drain the raisins and add to the pot along with the tomatoes, tomato sauce, honey, and garbanzo beans. Cover and simmer for 30 minutes, or until the vegetables are tender, adding up to 1 cup of water if the stew appears dry.

While the stew is cooking, bring the water to a boil in a saucepan and stir in the couscous. Cook for 1 minute, then cover and turn off the heat, letting the couscous sit for 10 minutes. After the couscous has sat for 5 minutes, stir the figs and almonds into the stew.

To serve, fluff up the couscous with a fork. Spoon a mound of couscous on each plate and form a well in the center. Ladle a portion of stew into the well. Garnish with several tablespoons of the yogurt and fresh mint. Serve the remaining yogurt on the side.

COMPLEMENTARY HERBS

Basil

Bay

Chives

Fennel

Lemongrass

Oregano

Parsley

Tarragon

Thyme

Shiitake Stew with Crisp Polenta

Serves 4 as an entrée or 6 as an appetizer

In the small town where I live, chef Scott Avery at Savories Restaurant serves this rich shiitake stew, which is satisfying on a winter night by the restaurant's roaring fire.

Polenta
1 cup cornmeal
1/2 cup cold water
2 cups boiling water
1 cup grated Parmesan or Romano cheese
Salt to taste
Freshly ground black pepper to taste
Crushed red pepper flakes to taste
Flour, for dusting
Olive oil, for frying

Mushroom Stew
2 tablespoons olive oil
1 shallot, minced
8 large shiitake mushrooms, stemmed and thinly sliced
4 oil-packed sundried tomatoes, drained and diced
1/4 cup brandy
1 teaspoon Worcestershire sauce
1 teaspoon thyme
Dash of nutmeg
Salt to taste
Freshly ground black pepper to taste
1 cup heavy cream
2 cups chopped raw spinach

In a large mixing bowl, stir together the cornmeal and cold water to make a smooth paste. Add to boiling water and stir vigorously with a wooden spoon. The polenta will thicken and form a ball. Add the cheese, salt, and black pepper and beat by hand for 1 minute until elastic and smooth. Place the polenta in a loaf pan lined with plastic wrap, cover, and chill for at least 4 hours, or overnight.

Remove the polenta from the loaf pan by inverting it onto a cutting board. Slice it into 1/4-inch-thick squares or triangles. Roll the top edge (and sides, if you like it hot!) of each polenta slice in hot pepper flakes, then dust the entire surface with flour. Heat the olive oil in a sauté pan over moderate heat, and brown and crisp the polenta slices on each side. Transfer to a serving platter or individual soup plates.

To make the stew, heat the oil in a saucepan over moderate heat and add the shallot, stirring while sautéing until lightly browned. Add the mushrooms and sundried tomatoes, sautéing until the mushrooms have absorbed the oil and the pan is dry. Remove pan from stovetop and add the brandy. Lower heat and return pan to the stovetop, being wary of flames. Cook on low for 1 minute, then add the Worcestershire sauce, thyme, nutmeg, salt, pepper, and cream. Bring to a simmer and reduce heat. Simmer for 20 minutes, or until the cream has reduced by half. Add the spinach just before serving and stir until just wilted. Serve stew over the polenta.

Curried Vegetable Stew with Tamarind and Coconut Milk

Serves 6

This vegetable stew is my friend Liz's interpretation of various Indian and Thai recipes that use curry. The coconut milk provides a smooth, rich background for the spicy curried vegetables. If you want to reduce the heat somewhat, remove the seeds from the chiles. Serve with plenty of plain basmati rice to soak up the sauce.

Tamarind Purée

3 ounces seedless tamarind pulp

1 cup boiling water

Curry

2 teaspoons ground coriander

2 teaspoons ground cumin

1 teaspoon ground fenugreek

1/2 teaspoon ground turmeric

1/2 teaspoon freshly ground black pepper

1/2 teaspoon ground cinnamon

2 whole star anise (or a dash of ground fennel seed)

3 tablespoons vegetable oil

1 large yellow onion, sliced lengthwise into 1/8-inch slices (about 1 1/4 cups)

2 teaspoons finely chopped gingerroot

3 cloves garlic, finely chopped

6 red Thai chiles, stemmed and thinly sliced crosswise

1 large red bell pepper, seeded, and cut into 1-inch-thick slices (about 1 1/4 cups)

3 cups bite-sized cauliflower florets

4 ounces portobellos, shiitakes, or other flavorful fresh mushrooms, sliced 1/4 inch thick

1/2 teaspoon salt, or more to taste

1 14-ounce can coconut milk

1 cup water

1 1/2 cups cooked garbanzo beans, yellow lentils, or channa dal (see page 333)

2 cups fresh or frozen snow peas or sugar snap peas

3 to 4 tablespoons chopped fresh cilantro

Place the tamarind in a bowl and cover with boiling water. Crush with a fork and set aside to soften for 1 to 2 hours, breaking up the pulp occasionally. Put through a sieve, using a spoon or spatula to push through the pulp. Discard the fibrous material in the sieve. Measure 1/3 cup of tamarind purée and set aside.

Combine the spices in a small bowl and set aside.

Heat the oil over medium heat in a heavy 4-quart pot with a tight-fitting lid. When it is hot, add the onion, ginger, garlic, and chiles, and cook, stirring, until the onion is softened, about 5 minutes. Add the spices and cook, stirring until fragrant, about 3 minutes. Add the red bell pepper, cauliflower, and mushrooms, and sprinkle with salt. Stir vegetables with a wooden spoon until they are coated with the spices, and continue to cook, stirring, for 5 minutes. Increase the heat to high, and add the tamarind purée, coconut milk, and water to the pan. Bring to a simmer, then reduce the heat and simmer gently for 20 minutes, stirring occasionally. Add the garbanzo beans and simmer for 10 minutes until the vegetables are just tender. Add the peas and simmer for 5 minutes until they are just tender. Remove the star anise. Add salt to taste and sprinkle with cilantro.

Allspice

Anise

Cardamom

Cinnamon

Cloves

Coriander

Mace

Nutmeg

Star Anise

WARMING

SPICES

North African Lentil Stew

Serves 6

Hearty and laced with the deep flavor of chiles, this is the perfect stew for a cold winter night. You can vary the ingredients according to taste and availability—instead of butternut squash, try acorn squash or pumpkin, and perhaps use Swiss chard or spinach instead of the kale. Serve with couscous or rice followed by a salad of greens with orange slices.

2 tablespoons olive oil
1 large yellow onion, chopped
3 jalapeño chiles, seeded and diced
3 garlic cloves, minced
1 tablespoon pure chile powder
1 teaspoon ground cumin
1 cup dried lentils
1 16-ounce can chopped tomatoes, with juice
3 cups Vegetable Stock (see page 75)
1 (2-pound) butternut squash, peeled and cut into 1/2-inch dice
1 large bunch (about 1 pound) kale, chopped
Salt to taste
Freshly ground black pepper to taste

In a large stockpot, heat the olive oil over medium heat. Add the onion, chiles, and garlic and cook until the onion is tender, about 5 minutes. Add the chile powder and cumin and cook 1 minute. Add the lentils, tomatoes, and stock and heat to boiling. Reduce heat to medium-low, cover, and simmer until the lentils are tender, about 30 minutes, adding a bit of water if necessary. Add the squash and simmer until tender, about 20 to 25 minutes. Add the kale and cook until just wilted, about 5 minutes. Season with salt and pepper.

He who plants a coconut tree plants food and drink, vessels and clothing, a habitation for himself and a heritage for his children.

—Anonymous

God bless the Italians, who not only gave us pasta and pizza, but also polenta, a creamy porridge made of cornmeal and water. You can serve polenta steaming hot with butter, shaved Parmesan cheese, and plenty of freshly ground black pepper. Or cool the polenta, cut it into shapes, and grill or pan-sear.

Pasta, Polenta, & Pizza

The beauty of pasta, polenta, and pizza is that they taste great year-round and are extremely versatile: serve them as an antipasto, for lunch, or as a light dinner with salad.

COOKING PASTA

When cooking pasta, always use a large pot of salted water, which will allow the water to swirl through the strands and prevent the released starch from clumping the strands together. Dropping a spoonful of olive oil into the pot will also prevent the pasta from sticking. Bring the water to a rolling boil before adding the noodles.

Pasta with Summer Tomato Sauce

Serves 4

This light sauce rings of the fresh flavors of summer. Toss with a black pepper linguine or your favorite pasta topped with freshly grated Parmesan cheese.

Summer Tomato Sauce

1 1/2 pound plum tomatoes, diced
1 bunch scallions, chopped
2 teaspoons granulated sugar
1 cup fresh basil, cut into 1/4-inch strips
1 teaspoon salt
Freshly ground black pepper
1/4 cup extra virgin olive oil
3 tablespoons balsamic vinegar
4 jalapeños, seeded and minced
Pinch of salt
1 pound black pepper linguine or other pasta
Freshly grated Parmesan cheese, for garnish

Combine all of the sauce ingredients in a bowl and set aside.

Bring water and salt to boil in a large stockpot. Add linguine. Cook until al dente, then drain. Toss pasta with sauce. Sprinkle with Parmesan cheese and serve.

Pasta with Cannellini Beans and Broccoli

Serves 4

Quick and colorful, this dish is a full meal with a green salad.

Pinch of salt

1 pound pasta (penne, ziti, or spaghetti)

3 tablespoons olive oil

4 garlic cloves, minced

2 cups cooked cannellini beans or other white beans, plus 2 tablespoons cooking water (see page 333 and note, below)

4 cups bite-size pieces of broccoli, steamed

Juice of 1/2 lemon

1/4 cup dry white wine

1 to 1 1/2 teaspoons crushed red pepper flakes

1/3 cup fresh flat-leaf parsley, chopped

Bring water and salt to boil in a large stockpot. Add pasta and cook until al dente. While the pasta is cooking, heat the oil in a medium saucepan. Add the garlic and lightly brown. Add the beans and their liquid, broccoli, lemon juice, wine, and pepper flakes. Stir and simmer until heated completely, 5 to 10 minutes.

Drain pasta and transfer to serving bowl. Add the parsley to the sauce and toss with the cooked pasta.

Note: If using canned cannellini beans, add all the liquid from the can (instead of the 2 tablespoons cooking water).

Buckwheat Pasta with Peanut-Coconut Sauce

Serves 4

With its layers of flavor, this robust pasta sauce is rich and filling, and light eaters may prefer it as a savory appetizer. For hearty eaters, it's good as an entrée served with a cucumber salad and the Green Papaya Salad (see page 190). This recipe serves 4 as an entree or 6 to 8 as a small pasta course.

3 tablespoons olive oil

1 small red bell pepper, diced

1 small green bell pepper, diced

1 small yellow onion, diced

1 tablespoon minced fresh gingerroot

1/2 cup diced plum tomatoes

1 tablespoon miso

1 tablespoon Jamaican jerk sauce

4 cups coconut milk

1/4 cup freshly squeezed lime juice

Pinch of salt

1 pound buckwheat pasta (see note)

2 tablespoons sesame oil

1 cup crunchy peanut butter

1/4 cup fresh basil, cut into 1/4-inch-wide strips

1/2 cup fresh cilantro

Chopped fresh cilantro, for garnish

Lime slices, for garnish

Finely chopped peanuts, for garnish

    Heat the olive oil in a large frying pan. Sauté the bell peppers, onion, and ginger until the onion is translucent. Add the tomatoes, miso, and jerk sauce and stir well. Add the coconut milk and lime juice and simmer for 30 minutes.

    Meanwhile, bring stockpot water and salt to boil. Add buckwheat pasta. Cook until tender, then drain. Transfer to a large bowl and toss with sesame oil.

    Stir the peanut butter into the sauce until well incorporated. Add the basil and whole cilantro leaves, stir, and remove from the heat. Pour over the cooked buckwheat noodles. Garnish with chopped cilantro, lime slices, and peanuts.

Note: Buckwheat pasta is available in health food and gourmet stores.

PASTA

We have Thomas Jefferson to thank for introducing pasta to America in the 1700s after an ambassadorial trip to Naples. (And it still took another hundred years for the first pasta factory to open in New York!) Today the abundance of pasta shapes and varieties available can be confusing. All pasta is made from a dough (pasta means "paste" in Italian) of grain or flour and water. Italian-style pasta is made from durum-wheat semolina. Flavored pastas are made by combining Italian-style pasta with vegetables such as tomatoes or spinach, or spices such as black pepper. Asian noodles are made with flour other than semolina, such as buckwheat or mung bean flour. Egg noodles are typically made from semolina combined with other wheats, such as farina. Below is a field guide:

Agnolotti: Half-moon-shaped stuffed pasta.

Anellini: Tiny pasta rings. Good in soups.

Bavettine: Thin linguine.

Bean thread noodles: Thin translucent noodles made with mung bean flour.

Buckwheat: Long grayish brown noodles that are fragrant, light, and rich in protein. Combines well with Asian-inspired sauces made with coconut milk, peanuts, and chiles.

Cannelloni: Large pasta tubes that are typically stuffed, sauced, and baked.

Conchiglie: Shell-shaped pasta. Delicious in soups.

Egg noodles: Made with wheat flour and semolina. Delicious in soups, stir-fries, or with sauces.

Farfalle: Little bow tie-shaped pasta. Good with vegetables and in salads.

Fettuccini: Long ribbons made of egg noodles.

Fusilli: Corkscrew pasta.

Lasagna: Fat pasta ribbons, featured in baked dishes.

Linguine: Long, thin ribbons. Delicious served with a simple sauce or combined with lentils or cheese.

Manicotti: Pasta tubes suitable for stuffing.

Orzo: Rice-shaped pasta.

Penne: Round, tubular pasta that holds sauce well.

Ramen: Slender, yellow, corkscrew wheat noodles, popular in Chinese dishes.

Ravioli: Pasta squares or rectangles that are delicious stuffed with legumes or nuts.

Rice noodles: When dried, rice noodles are sold as thin long white strands. In their fresh form, they are sold in sheets. Transparent rice noodles are lighter in color. Popular in stir-fries and soups.

Rigatoni: A grooved, tubular macaroni that holds sauce well.

Spaghetti: Long, thin ribbons that are available as spaghettoni (thick strands), spaghettini (more slender), and capellini (thinnest).

Soba: The Japanese word for buckwheat pasta (see above).

Somen: Thin, white wheat-flour noodles.

Tagliatelle: Flat egg noodles, similar to fettuccini. Good with simple sauces, cheeses, and nuts.

Tortellini: Stuffed pasta rings.

Udon: Tan-colored flat whole-wheat noodles.

Vermicelli: The thinnest cut ribbon pasta. Good with lentils, garlic, and olive oil, or in soups.

Ziti: Pasta tubes.

Chilled Soba Noodles in Spicy Peanut Sauce

Serves 4

Cold spicy noodles blend beautifully with the piquant flavors in this sauce, creating a well-rounded dish. This pasta is spicy, but not blazing, and creates a nice warm mouth-feel.

1/2 cup creamy peanut butter

2 tablespoons soy sauce

2 tablespoons rice wine vinegar

2 tablespoons red chile garlic paste or sauce

1 round tablespoon minced gingerroot

4 tablespoons sesame oil

1/2 cup coconut milk or water, or a combination of the two (see note)

8 ounces soba noodles (buckwheat pasta), or other Asian-style noodles, cooked and chilled

6 scallions, thinly sliced

1 tablespoon lightly toasted sesame seeds (see page 73)

Combine peanut butter, soy sauce, rice wine vinegar, red chile garlic paste, and ginger and mix thoroughly, either by hand, with a whisk, or in a blender. Add the oil and mix. Add the coconut milk and mix well. Pour sauce over noodles and toss. Garnish with scallions and sesame seeds.

Note: If you want to reduce the fat content of the dish, use water to thin the sauce rather than coconut milk; either way, the results are delicious.

Linguine with Spicy Lentil Sauce

Serves 6

Combining pasta and beans is an economical way to get a balanced meal in one bowl. This recipe comes from my friends Johanne Killeen and George Germon, the chefs and owners of Al Forno Restaurant in Providence, Rhode Island. Browning the vegetables in olive oil, a technique they learned in Tuscany, increases the depth of flavor—a useful tip for vegetarian cooking. This recipe serves 6 for dinner or 10 to 12 as a small pasta course.

7 to 8 tablespoons extra virgin olive oil

1 cup finely chopped celery

2 carrots, scraped and finely chopped

2 large yellow onions, chopped

2 cloves garlic, coarsely chopped

1 to 2 fresh jalapeños or other hot peppers, seeded and chopped

1 teaspoon kosher or sea salt

1/2 teaspoon crushed red pepper flakes

1 1/2 cups lentils

5 cups water

1 1/2 pounds imported spaghettini or linguine fini

Finely minced zest of 1 lemon

1/2 cup coarsely chopped fresh flat-leaf parsley

Heat 6 tablespoons of the olive oil in a heavy saucepan. Add the celery, carrots, onions, and garlic. Sauté over medium-high heat, stirring occasionally, until the vegetables are soft and beginning to brown, about 15 minutes. Add the chiles, salt, and pepper flakes. Continue to sauté, allowing the vegetables to brown, about 5 to 10 minutes, while watching carefully and stirring often so they don't burn. Add the lentils and water, and bring to a boil, then lower the heat, cover, and simmer until the lentils are soft but not falling apart, about 20 minutes for fresh lentils. (If the lentils are old, they can take as long as 40 minutes to cook, and you may need to add more water.)

Cook and drain the pasta, and add it to the lentil sauce with the 1 to 2 remaining tablespoons of olive oil. Fold in the lemon zest and parsley and serve immediately.

Linguine with Vegetables

Serves 6

This fragrant Vietnamese-inspired linguine dish comes from
Tung Nguyen and Kathy Manning, who for the past 15 years
have been cooking wonders at Hy-Vong, a tiny Vietnamese
restaurant in the Little Havana district of Miami.

Tomato Sauce

1/3 cup vegetable oil

1 large white onion, chopped

6 large cloves garlic, chopped

4 ripe tomatoes, ends trimmed, cut in half, and cut in
    1/4-inch-thick slices

3 tablespoons fish sauce (see note)

1 pound linguine

2 cups vegetable oil

1 pound firm or soft tofu

8 tablespoons butter

9 large cloves garlic, chopped

1 large white onion, cut in half, then cut into 1/4-inch-thick slices

5 tablespoons fish sauce (see note)

4 carrots, sliced crosswise diagonally into 1/4-inch-thick slices

2 small bunches broccoli, cut into florets and 2-inch-long sticks
    from peeled stem

1/2 head cauliflower, cut into florets

1 14-ounce can straw mushrooms, drained

1 cup snow peas, tips removed

4 cups bean sprouts

3/4 cup unsalted dry-roasted peanuts, finely chopped

3/4 cup toasted almonds, finely chopped (see page 73)

1 to 2 tablespoons Simple Vietnamese Hot Pepper Sauce
    (see page 105), or 3 minced serrano chiles

3 scallions, thinly sliced, for garnish

To make the Tomato Sauce, heat the vegetable oil in the skillet. Add the onion and garlic and cook over medium-high heat until onion is translucent and the garlic is lightly browned. Add the tomato, mix well, and cook over medium heat, stirring occasionally until the tomato is cooked and the mixture becomes a sauce, about 10 to 15 minutes. Add the fish sauce and set aside for later use.

Cook the linguine al dente and drain. Set aside.

Heat the vegetable oil in a large skillet. Cut the tofu lengthwise into 1/2-inch pieces, then stack the slices and cut them crosswise into 1/2-inch pieces. Fry the tofu in the vegetable oil until golden brown, then remove with a slotted spoon and set on paper towels to drain. Drain the skillet of oil.

Melt the butter in the large skillet or in a wok. Add the garlic and onion and cook until the garlic is browned and the onion is limp and translucent. Add the linguine and stir well to separate. Add the fish sauce, carrots, broccoli, cauliflower, mushrooms, snow peas, bean sprouts, tofu, and Tomato Sauce and stir well to combine. Cook over low heat, covered, for 10 minutes (or longer for softer vegetables). Just before serving, add the chopped nuts and hot pepper sauce and mix well. Serve topped with scallions.

Note: You may substitute a pinch of salt dissolved in the same amount of water for the fish sauce.

Rice Noodles with Coconut Milk and Vegetables

Serves 6

This unexpectedly light, Thai-inspired dish is brightly flavored with chiles, lemongrass, and aromatic herbs. The differing textures and flavors of the peas, water chestnuts, and spinach are heightened by the velvety but assertive coconut milk sauce.

8 ounces dry rice noodles (rice sticks)

1 tablespoon vegetable oil

Sauce

3 to 4 cloves garlic, finely chopped

4 to 6 Thai chiles, seeded and finely chopped

1/3 cup chopped shallots

1 stalk lemongrass, tender part only, sliced finely crosswise (about 3 tablespoons)

1 13-ounce can coconut milk

2 tablespoons freshly squeezed lime juice

Vegetables

1 tablespoon vegetable oil

1 yellow onion, thinly sliced lengthwise

1 tablespoon shredded gingerroot

1 heaping cup trimmed snow peas (about 4 ounces)

1/2 cup fresh or canned sliced water chestnuts

2 packed cups trimmed, washed, small spinach leaves

1/2 teaspoon granulated sugar

1 1/2 cups fresh mung bean sprouts

3 large scallions, shredded

2 tablespoons light soy sauce

2 teaspoons sesame oil

4 tablespoons shredded fresh basil

4 tablespoons chopped fresh cilantro

Soak the rice noodles in cold water for 30 minutes, or until they soften. Drain and cook the noodles in a large stockpot of boiling salted water for 30 seconds, or until cooked through but firm. Drain immediately and rinse under cold running water. Drain well and toss with the oil.

Combine the sauce ingredients in a pan and simmer over medium heat for 5 minutes. Set aside while preparing the vegetables. Heat the 1 tablespoon of oil in a large skillet over high heat. Add the onion and ginger and stir-fry for 1 minute, then add the peas and water chestnuts and stir-fry 30 seconds longer. Add the spinach leaves and toss until they begin to wilt.

Add the sugar, bean sprouts, and scallions and toss well. Add the coconut sauce and stir well. When it is bubbling, add the noodles, soy sauce, sesame oil, and herbs and toss just until heated through. Remove from the heat and serve immediately.

Vietnamese Fresh Rice Noodles with Chiles and Mint

Serves 6

Fresh rice noodles are available at Chinese markets, sold in white sheets that are folded and wrapped in plastic. They will keep in the refrigerator 2 to 3 days. This dish, from the Hy-Vong restaurant in Miami, makes a good main course served with steamed asparagus, preceded by a savory soup.

2 cups vegetable oil

5 large shallots, cut crosswise into 1/8-inch-thick slices

1 pound firm tofu

6 tablespoons butter

9 cloves garlic, minced

1 large white or sweet Vidalia onion

2 12-ounce packages fresh rice noodles

2 tablespoons fish sauce (see note)

2 tablespoons soy sauce

1 teaspoon freshly ground black pepper

4 cups fresh bean sprouts

Sauce

4 large cloves garlic, finely chopped

1 cup water

1/2 cup fish sauce (see note)

2 tablespoons granulated sugar

2 tablespoons plus 1 teaspoon freshly squeezed lime juice

2 fresh serrano peppers, minced

1 tablespoon Simple Vietnamese Hot Pepper Sauce
    (recipe follows), or 2 minced serrano chiles

2 scallions, thinly sliced, for garnish

Sprigs of fresh mint, chopped, for garnish

3 tablespoons finely chopped unsalted dry-roasted peanuts,
    for garnish

3 tablespoons finely chopped roasted almonds, for garnish

Heat the vegetable oil in a wok or saucepan. Add the shallots and fry, stirring frequently so they brown evenly. When they are dark brown, transfer them with a slotted spoon to a colander and drain well. Set aside.

Cut the tofu lengthwise into 1/2-inch slices, then stack the slices and cut them crosswise into 1/2-inch pieces. (This will give you 1/2 by 2-inch pieces.) Fry the tofu in the vegetable oil until golden brown. Drain well on paper towels.

In a large frying pan with a tight-fitting lid, melt the butter over medium heat. Add the garlic, stirring to brown. While the garlic is browning, cut the onion lengthwise, then cut each half crosswise into 1/4-inch-thick slices. Add the onion to the frying pan and cook until translucent.

Cut 1 package of fresh rice noodles in half and then in half again. Cut each quarter into 1/2-inch strips. Separate the noodles. Repeat with the second package.

Reduce the heat to low and add the rice noodles to the butter mixture. Add the fish sauce, soy sauce, and black pepper and mix noodles together well. Add the tofu and turn the heat to high, stirring gently for 1 to 2 minutes. Add the bean sprouts, cover, and turn off the heat. Set aside, covered.

Meanwhile, to make the sauce, place the garlic in a bowl and add water, fish sauce, and sugar. Stir to dissolve the sugar, then add the lime juice and mix well. Add the serrano peppers and mix well. Transfer to a small pitcher to serve as an accompanying sauce for the noodles.

Just before serving, remove the lid from noodle dish, add the hot pepper sauce, turn on the heat and stir the dish gently for 1 minute. Remove from heat and spoon onto individual plates. To garnish, sprinkle fried shallots over the noodles, then sprinkle each serving with scallions, mint, and top with a sprinkling of nuts. Serve with the sauce.

Note: You may substitute a pinch of salt dissolved in the same amount of water for the fish sauce.

Simple Vietnamese Hot Pepper Sauce
Makes 3/4 cup

6 serrano chiles
4 large cloves garlic
1/2 tablespoon granulated sugar

Blend all of the ingredients in a food processor until finely minced and well mixed.

Rice Noodles with Vegetables, Tofu, and Watercress

Serves 4

This savory dish cooks quickly once the ingredients are assembled. The crisp-tender, colorful vegetables and creamy eggs contrast with the soft noodles, which absorb the flavorful soy and sesame oil. Toasted sesame seeds or cashew nuts (see page 73) can be added for extra flavor and texture. Use crisp lettuce or finely shredded cabbage if you lack watercress.

6 ounces dry rice noodles (rice sticks)

6 tablespoons vegetable oil

4 cloves garlic, peeled and crushed

1/2 pound firm tofu, cut into 1/2-inch cubes

4 tablespoons thinly sliced seeded serrano chiles (about 8 chiles)

1 large red bell pepper, cored, seeded, and cut into 1/8-inch slices (about 1 cup)

2 cups broccoli florets (about 1/2 inch in diameter)

1/4 cup sliced fresh or canned water chestnuts

1 teaspoon granulated sugar

3 tablespoons freshly squeezed lemon juice

4 tablespoons light soy sauce

2 eggs, lightly beaten

1/2 cup coarsely chopped fresh cilantro

1 bunch watercress, tough stems removed

1 or 2 teaspoons sesame oil

Soak the noodles in cold water for 30 minutes. Drain, then cook in a large pot of boiling salted water for 30 seconds to 1 minute, until cooked through but firm. Drain, rinse with cold water, and set aside.

Heat the oil in a large frying pan over medium heat and lightly brown the garlic. Add the tofu and fry until light gold. Transfer to paper towels to drain. Stir-fry the chiles, bell pepper, and broccoli in the pan for 2 to 3 minutes. Add the water chestnuts, sugar, lemon juice, and soy sauce and toss to combine. Add the eggs to the pan and stir until they begin to set, then add the noodles, cilantro, and half the watercress, and toss well. Top with the tofu and the remaining watercress, drizzle sesame oil over all, and serve immediately.

Pasta with Sesame Broccoli and Red Bell Peppers

Serves 6

This uncomplicated dish is full of Asian flavors. It's good hot or cold, and perfect for picnics. If New Mexico red chiles are unavailable, you can substitute other dried chiles, or fresh chiles such as jalapeños, serranos, or Thai red chiles.

1 pound penne

2 tablespoons olive oil

2 large red bell peppers, cut into 1/4-inch-thick strips

2 bunches broccoli florets, cut into bite-size pieces

1/2 cup water

2 dried New Mexico red chiles, stemmed, seeded, softened, and minced (see page 40)

1/4 cup tamari soy sauce

3 tablespoons sesame oil

3 tablespoons red wine vinegar

2 teaspoons granulated sugar

1 teaspoon hot chile oil

2 tablespoons toasted sesame seeds (see page 75)

Cook and drain the pasta, and keep warm. In a large skillet over medium-high heat, heat 1 tablespoon olive oil, then cook the bell peppers until tender-crisp. Transfer the bell peppers to a bowl. In the same skillet over high heat, sauté broccoli in the remaining 1 tablespoon olive oil, stirring quickly and constantly. Stir in the water. Reduce heat to medium-high, cover, and cook 3 minutes. Add the minced New Mexico red chiles and cook, uncovered, 5 minutes, or until the broccoli is tender-crisp, stirring frequently.

In a large bowl, combine the tamari sauce, sesame oil, vinegar, sugar, and hot chile oil. Add the cooked pasta, bell peppers, broccoli, and chiles, and toss to coat. Sprinkle with toasted sesame seeds. Serve warm, or cover and refrigerate to serve cold later.

Fettucini with Sautéed Mushrooms and Wilted Spinach

Serves 4

Inspired by spinach lasagna, this fettucini incorporates similar flavors but with much less fat. (It can also be made in a fraction of the time.) For a richer mushroom flavor, substitute 2 cups of thinly sliced shiitakes or portobello mushrooms for the white button mushrooms. The Gorgonzola cheese sprinkled over the top pulls the flavors together.

1 pound fresh spinach, stemmed and coarsely chopped

1 tablespoon unsalted butter

4 large shallots, minced (about 1 cup)

1 pound thinly sliced white button mushrooms (about 6 cups)

1 teaspoon hot paprika

1/4 cup dry white wine

Salt to taste

Freshly ground black pepper to taste

1/2 pound fettucini

1 tablespoon olive oil

4 large cloves garlic, minced

2 large red bell peppers, roasted, peeled, seeded, and cut into small slivers (1 generous cup)

4 ounces Gorgonzola cheese, crumbled

1/2 cup fresh basil chiffonade, for garnish

1 teaspoon crushed red pepper flakes, for garnish

Rinse spinach leaves and set aside in colander to drain. In a large skillet, melt butter over medium heat. Add shallots, mushrooms, paprika, wine, and salt and pepper. Stir to coat and simmer, uncovered, until liquid has reduced and mushrooms begin to brown, about 10 to 12 minutes. Meanwhile, begin to cook the pasta.

Transfer the mushroom mixture from the skillet to an ovenproof bowl and keep warm, uncovered, in a 300° oven.

In the same skillet over medium heat, add olive oil and garlic and sauté until softened, about 2 minutes. Add all the spinach. (Some water should still be clinging to the leaves, but not an excessive amount.) Using tongs, turn the spinach to coat with the oil and garlic. Continue tossing until the spinach wilts but retains its bright green color, about 2 to 3 minutes.

Drain the pasta and place in a serving bowl. Lift spinach from the skillet, shaking off any excess juice, and place over the pasta. If necessary, reduce the juices in the pan by cooking 1 minute longer, then scrape remaining spinach and garlic bits into the serving bowl. Top spinach with reserved and warm mushroom mixture, then with roasted red bell peppers (reheat the peppers if necessary). Sprinkle cheese over top, then garnish with fresh basil and pepper flakes.

Pasta Gratin with Mustard Greens

Serves 6

The mustard greens give this classic macaroni-and-cheese dish both color and a spicy twist.

1/2 pound egg noodles

2 tablespoons butter

2 large eggs

1 tablespoon Dijon-style mustard

1 tablespoon habanero hot sauce

1 3/4 cups whole milk (see note)

1/4 cup heavy whipping cream

1 tablespoon vegetable oil

2 cloves garlic, finely chopped

1/2 pound mustard greens, tough stems removed, washed and cut into 1/4-inch-wide strips (approximately 4 cups loosely packed)

Salt

3 tablespoons water

1/2 pound sharp Cheddar cheese, coarsely grated

1/2 pound Monterey jack cheese, coarsely grated

Preheat the oven to 350°. Spray a 9 by 12-inch casserole dish with nonstick cooking spray.

Cook the pasta until al dente in a large pot of salted boiling water. Drain in a colander, then return the pasta to the pot and toss with the butter. In a mixing bowl, beat the eggs with the mustard and hot sauce until well mixed, then beat in the milk and cream. Set aside.

Heat the oil in a large stockpot over medium-high heat. Add the garlic and stir for 15 seconds. Add the greens by the handful, allowing each addition to wilt somewhat before adding more (or, if your pot is big enough, put all of the greens in at once). Salt lightly. Add the water, cover the pan, and reduce the heat to medium. Simmer for 5 minutes until wilted. Add the greens to the noodles and stir well to combine.

Fold the milk mixture and the cheeses into the pasta, and transfer the mixture to the prepared casserole dish. Bake for 35 to 45 minutes, until bubbling and browned.

Note: You may substitute lowfat or nonfat milk for the whole milk, but you'll lose some of the richness.

Creamy Polenta with Ancho–Red Wine Sauce

Serves 8

Warm and comforting, polenta is an appropriate companion to spicy foods and, with the addition of cheese, can be quite rich. Serve this polenta as an entrée with a salad and crisp dry flatbread or as a hearty, unusual first course. The earthy Ancho-Red Wine Sauce is also great on semolina.

Ancho-Red Wine Sauce

2 red onions, quartered

2 yellow onions, quartered

2 cups port wine

8 ancho chiles, stemmed and seeded

1 1/2 cups Vegetable Stock (see page 75)

2 teaspoons salt

4 tablespoons butter

Creamy Polenta

2 cups milk

2 cups heavy cream

1/2 teaspoon salt

1 teaspoon freshly ground black pepper

1 teaspoon crushed red pepper flakes

3/4 cup yellow cornmeal

4 tablespoons butter

1/3 cup grated Romano cheese

In a food processor, pulse the onions, wine, and chiles several times, taking care not to overblend (until mixture is the consistency of a relish). Combine in a medium saucepan with the stock and salt, bring to a boil, then reduce heat and simmer partly covered until the sauce begins to reduce and thicken slightly, about 35 to 45 minutes. Slowly swirl in the butter a little at a time, whisking to incorporate.

In a large saucepan, bring the milk, heavy cream, salt, pepper, and pepper flakes to a boil. Reduce the heat and slowly whisk in the cornmeal. Stir continuously, adding the butter and cheese, and cook for 20 minutes over low heat.

Spoon the polenta onto serving plates and top with sauce.

POLENTA

Thought to have originated in Venice or Lombardy, this creamy porridge is one of Italy's oldest dishes. It was traditionally made with a wooden spoon in a large copper pot called a paiolo. In medieval times, polenta was made with millet, chestnut flour, or spelt (corn wasn't introduced to Italy until the early sixteenth century) and was more popular than pasta or bread. Today it is largely made with cornmeal, although you'll find delicious polenta made from chestnut flour in Tuscany, where chopped walnuts and fresh rosemary are added to the pot. Devotees through the centuries have even formed the ranks of gastronomic societies in celebration of the dish. Perhaps the most famous one was the P.P.P.P., which stands for Prima Patria Poi Polenta ("First the homeland, then polenta!"), founded in the early 1800s.

Polenta Biscuits with Borlotti Bean Salsa

Serves 6

This dish boasts a spectacular presentation with its architectural nod to the strawberry shortcake. All similarities end there, as gastronomically it brings together some traditional Mexican ingredients to create a fresh, piquant first course or festive lunch. The biscuits and the salsa can be made a day ahead and the shortcake assembled quickly at the last minute.

Biscuits

1 1/2 cup semolina flour

1/2 cup polenta or cornmeal

4 teaspoons baking powder

1/4 cup kosher or sea salt

1/4 cup unsalted butter, melted

2 eggs

6 tablespoons nonfat sour cream or plain yogurt

2 jalapeño chiles, finely chopped

Ground cayenne pepper for dusting

Pure chile powder for dusting

2 ripe avocados, cut into 12 slices

4 cups Borlotti Bean Salsa (see page 62)

3 cups sour cream

Whole fresh cilantro leaves, for garnish

To make the biscuits, preheat the oven to 425°. Combine the dry ingredients in a medium bowl, then make a well in the center of the ingredients and gradually add the butter, eggs, and sour cream. Fold in the jalapeños. The mixture should be slightly sticky and moist enough to form a ball; if it's too dry, add a few drops of milk or buttermilk. (I prefer polenta for its finer texture, but if you substitute a coarser cornmeal you probably won't have to add the additional milk.) Turn the dough onto a board dusted with semolina flour, roll to 1/2- to 3/4-inch thickness, and cut 6 biscuits approximately 3 to 4 inches in diameter. Place on a lightly greased baking sheet, sprinkle with the cayenne and chile powders, and bake for 15 minutes. Allow to cool.

When ready to assemble shortcakes, slice each biscuit in half horizontally. Reserve the tops. Arrange 2 avocado slices on the bottom layer of the biscuits. Top with approximately 1/3 cup Borlotti Bean Salsa and 1/4 cup sour cream. Place biscuit tops lightly over the sour cream. Add another 1/3 cup salsa and 1/4 cup sour cream over top of biscuits, garnish with cilantro leaves, and serve immediately.

Pan-Seared Stuffed Polenta with Green Sauce

Serves 6

There is no end to the versatility of polenta. By using less liquid you can create a firm polenta that can be chilled, cut into shapes, and pan-seared.

Polenta

2 cups heavy whipping cream

2 cups water or Vegetable Stock (see page 75)

1 teaspoon salt

1/2 teaspoon freshly ground black pepper

1 teaspoon crushed red pepper flakes

2 cups polenta

2 tablespoons chopped fresh basil

4 tablespoons butter

Stuffing

2 roasted poblano chiles, stemmed, seeded, peeled, and julienned

2 roasted red bell peppers, stemmed, seeded, peeled, and julienned

1/4 cup chopped oil-packed sundried tomatoes, drained

1/4 cup lightly toasted pine nuts (see page 73)

1 tablespoon chopped fresh basil

1 tablespoon chopped fresh cilantro

1 tablespoon chopped fresh parsley

2 cups fresh spinach chiffonade

1 cup crumbled feta cheese

1 1/2 cups Green Sauce (recipe follows)

2 tablespoons olive oil

Sprigs of fresh parsley, cilantro, and/or basil, for garnish

To make the polenta, bring the heavy cream, water, salt, pepper, and pepper flakes to a boil in a large saucepan. Slowly stir in the polenta and cook over low heat for 20 minutes. Stir in the basil and butter. Remove from heat and spread 1/4 inch deep in an ungreased baking pan. Chill.

To make the stuffing, combine the chiles and bell peppers with the sundried tomatoes, pine nuts, basil, cilantro, parsley, spinach, and feta cheese.

Remove the polenta from the refrigerator and cut into 2-inch squares. Carefully cut each square in half through the middle to make top and bottom halves. Place enough stuffing on each square to cover the surface. Cover with the top half of the polenta square.

Ladle the Green Sauce onto each serving plate. In a heavy skillet, heat 2 tablespoons olive oil, and brown both sides of each square of polenta. Transfer to plates, placing a square on top of the sauce on each plate. Garnish with sprigs of fresh herbs.

Green Sauce

Makes 1 1/2 cups

1 large poblano chile, stemmed and seeded

1/4 cup milk

2 tablespoons unsalted butter

1 tablespoon all-purpose flour

1 cup heavy whipping cream

1/2 teaspoon salt

2 tablespoons sour cream

2 tablespoons chopped fresh cilantro

1 tablespoon chopped fresh parsley

In a blender, purée the poblano chile and milk. Heat the butter and flour in a saucepan and stir until smooth, then cook for 5 to 7 minutes over low heat, stirring constantly. (You want a light golden color.) Stir in the chile-milk purée. Add the cream and stir over low heat until the mixture thickens. Add the salt and sour cream and stir to combine. Remove from the heat and stir in the herbs.

Buttercup Squash Pizza with Gorgonzola

Makes one 12-inch pizza

Try this intriguing multilayered assembly of flavors and textures: crisp crust, smooth squash, tangy tomato, spicy peppers, resinous rosemary, and salty, earthy Gorgonzola cheese.

Sponge

1 teaspoon active dry yeast

1/2 cup warm water

1/3 cup whole-wheat flour

Dough

1/3 cup warm water

1/4 cup warm milk

1 teaspoon olive oil

1/2 teaspoon salt

1 3/4 to 2 cups unbleached all-purpose flour

Pizza Topping

3 tablespoons olive oil

1 1/4 cups chopped canned peeled tomatoes, with juice

1-pound buttercup squash, peeled, seeded, and cut into 1/8-inch slices

1 yellow onion, peeled and thinly sliced (about 1 cup)

3 cloves garlic, peeled and thinly sliced

1/4 teaspoon crushed red pepper flakes

1 1/2 teaspoons finely chopped fresh rosemary needles

1/2 teaspoon freshly ground black pepper

1/4 teaspoon salt

Cornmeal

1/2 cup crumbled Gorgonzola cheese

1/3 cup freshly grated Parmesan cheese

To make the sponge, dissolve the yeast in the water in a large bowl. Stir in the whole-wheat flour and mix until smooth. Cover and set aside in a warm place for 1 hour until the mixture is bubbling.

To make the dough, stir in the 1/3 cup water, the milk, olive oil, and salt into the sponge. Gradually stir in 1 1/2 cups of the all-purpose flour and mix thoroughly to make a soft dough. Scrape the mixture onto a floured surface and knead vigorously, incorporating additional flour to make a pliable dough. Continue kneading for about 10 minutes until the dough no longer sticks to your hands and coheres in a smooth, elastic mass. Return the dough to the bowl, cover, and set aside to rise for about 1 hour, or until doubled in bulk.

When ready to cook the pizza, preheat the oven to 450°. Spray a 9 by 12-inch shallow roasting pan with nonstick cooking spray. Heat 1 tablespoon of the olive oil in a small saucepan over medium heat. Add the tomatoes and simmer gently until thickened and reduced by half, about 20 minutes. Place the squash, onion, garlic, and seasonings in a mixing bowl and toss well. Drizzle the remaining 2 tablespoons of olive oil over the vegetables and toss to coat evenly. Spread the vegetables in the prepared pan. Place on the top rack of the oven and roast until just barely tender and lightly browned, about 15 minutes. Set aside to cool.

Sprinkle cornmeal on a heavy pizza pan at least 12 inches in diameter. Punch down the dough to remove air bubbles, but do not knead. With floured hands, shape the dough into a 12-inch round and place on the baking sheet. Spread the tomato mixture on the dough, leaving a 1/2-inch margin at the edges. Arrange the roasted squash and onions on top in a single layer. Sprinkle evenly with the Gorgonzola and the Parmesan. Bake for 20 minutes on the top rack of the oven until browned and bubbling. Allow to rest for 1 or 2 minutes before cutting.

Note: You can substitute other types of squash, although the sweetness of roasted buttercup is the best partner for the Gorgonzola.

NEW WORLD FOODS

Chile peppers have been used in Mexico since prehistoric times. It wasn't until Columbus and the Spanish and Portuguese explorers landed in the New World that chiles made their way via the trade routes to Africa, India, and Indonesia. Other foods the New World gave us include:

Allspice

Beans

Chocolate

Corn

Lima Beans

Peanuts

Pineapple

Potatoes

Pumpkins

Squashes

Tomatoes

Vanilla

Focaccia Pizza with Pears, Walnuts, and Gorgonzola

Serves 4

This thick-crusted version of the popular Italian flatbread is substantial enough to serve as supper with soup or a salad. Dense with the flavors of autumn, this focaccia has a tanginess that comes from an onion topping laced with coarsely ground black pepper and Gorgonzola. The full-flavored filling is lent a subtle sweetness by the pears and an herbal aroma from the fresh rosemary.

Sponge
4 1/2 teaspoons active dry yeast
1 cup warm water (110° to 115°)
1 1/2 cups all-purpose flour
1/8 teaspoon salt

Focaccia
1 1/2 cups all-purpose flour
1/2 cup whole-wheat flour
1/4 cup grated Parmesan cheese
8 tablespoons extra virgin olive oil
2 teaspoons coarsely ground black pepper
2 teaspoons kosher salt
1/2 cup dried chopped pears (about 2 ounces)
1 teaspoon minced fresh rosemary needles
1/4 cup warm water
1 cup thinly sliced red onion
1/2 cup walnuts, chopped
3/4 cup crumbled Gorgonzola cheese
3/4 cup grated mozzarella cheese

In a small bowl, mix the yeast with water and stir to dissolve. In a medium bowl, whisk the flour and salt. Make a well in the center of the flour and slowly add the yeast and water, mixing with a fork to incorporate. Cover with plastic wrap and a clean kitchen towel and set aside in a warm, draft-free location for 1 hour or until doubled in bulk.

When the sponge is ready, combine the 1 1/2 cups all-purpose flour and 1/2 cup whole-wheat flour. Place combined flours on a large, clean work surface. Spread the flour into a circle about 12 inches in diameter with a large well in the center. Scrape the sponge into the well with the Parmesan cheese, 2 tablespoons of the olive oil, black pepper, salt, pears, rosemary, and warm water. Using a fork, mix the center ingredients together slowly, gradually working in the surrounding "wall" of flour. When thoroughly mixed, gather into a ball and knead the dough until elastic, about 3 to 5 minutes.

Divide the dough in half. Oil the bottom and sides of two 8-inch round cake pans with straight 2-inch-high sides with 4 tablespoons of the olive oil. Gently roll each dough half to approximately 8-inch rounds and place into the pans. With a fork, poke the dough in several places. (Note: you may substitute one 9 by 15-inch pan for the two 8-inch pans, in which case you would not divide the dough in half.)

In a bowl, toss the onion and walnuts with the remaining 2 tablespoons of olive oil. Add the Gorgonzola and mozzarella cheeses. Divide this mixture between the two pans and distribute evenly over the surface of the dough. (If desired, coarsely grind a little extra black pepper over the top.) Cover the pans with plastic wrap and a kitchen towel. Set aside in a warm place to rise about 1 1/2 to 2 hours. (The dough will rise about 3/4 of the way up the side of the pan.)

Preheat the oven to 400°. Uncover the pans and bake 30 minutes, or until golden and the crust is crisp. (If you are using one large rectangular pan, bake for 30 to 45 minutes.) With the tip of a knife, loosen the edges of the crust from the pan if necessary, and slide the focaccia onto a bread board. Cut into wedges or squares and serve immediately.

The word pizza means to "sting" or "season."

—*Larousse Gastronomique*

Guajillo Cheddar Grits

Serves 4

Far from what you'll find at most diners in the South, these grits provide a well-seasoned blast of heat, as well as a musky sweetness from the cloves. The guajillo is a dried Mexican chile (when fresh, it's known as a mirasol chile), approximately 5 inches long, with a thin brittle skin and an earthy, slightly tannic flavor. Other dried chiles, such as the New Mexico red chile, may be substituted.

1/2 teaspoon cumin seed

1/4 teaspoon coriander seed

1 teaspoon whole black peppercorns

3 whole cloves

1/2 dried guajillo or New Mexico red chile, stemmed and seeded

2 1/2 cups water

1 teaspoon salt

10 tablespoons quick-cooking grits

3/4 cup shredded Monterey jack cheese

1/4 cup shredded Cheddar cheese

4 to 6 pickled tabasco peppers, minced

Preheat a small cast-iron skillet over medium heat. Add cumin, coriander, peppercorns, and cloves and heat until fragrant and lightly toasted, about 2 minutes, shaking pan or stirring seeds to prevent burning. Remove from skillet and set aside.

Flatten the guajillo chile, place in skillet, and toast for a few seconds on each side. Remove from skillet, and grind chile and spices in a spice grinder until coarsely ground.

To make grits, bring water to boil in a medium saucepan. Add salt and grits. Cover and reduce to low heat. Cook 5 minutes, stirring often, until thick. Remove from heat and stir in cheeses. Stir in half of the spice blend, and reserve the remainder. Stir in the Tabasco peppers, taste, and add the remaining spice mix, if desired. Serve immediately.

Note: To adjust the heat, serve the second half of the spice mix in a small bowl at the table or serve the tabasco peppers whole as a garnish. (You can also store the remaining spice blend in a dark, dry place in an airtight container.)

Tortilla, Rice, & Bean Dishes

This chapter is filled with tortillas, casseroles, pilafs, and stir-fries that make hearty meals when accompanied by a salad or vegetable dish or an intriguing lunch or snack when served solo. Indeed, I keep returning to the Spicy Baked Potato Quesadillas year-round, grilling them in the summertime as an appetizer or baking them in the winter for a homey supper.

Tortillas, named by the Spanish conquistadors, should always be served hot. Made of corn or flour, they serve as the bread in Latin cuisines and are often stuffed and filled with numerous ingredients. The rice dishes in this chapter range from a simple pilaf, which is a good companion dish, to an Eggplant Potato Curry with Basmati Rice and Peas, which is a meal in itself. The bean dishes are some of my favorites for a simple meal. As old as the pharaohs, beans are good for you and—with the number of heirloom varieties currently being cultivated—offer home chefs a variety of textures, colors, and flavors.

Spicy Baked Potato Quesadillas

Serves 2

This potato-stuffed flour tortilla is a fusion of Indian paratha and the Southwestern quesadilla. Easy to prepare, it makes a quick supper served with tomatoes, avocado, and sour cream or yogurt. Cut into small wedges and served with a fresh salsa, it also makes a great hors d'oeuvre that will serve 8 to 10.

3 yellow Finn potatoes or other boiling potatoes

1 yellow onion, finely chopped

2 small Hungarian wax chiles, seeded, cut in half, and thinly sliced crosswise

1 jalapeño, seeded, cut in half, and thinly sliced crosswise

2 cloves garlic, minced

2 tablespoons peanut oil

3 tablespoons chopped fresh cilantro (leaves and tender stems)

1/2 teaspoon toasted cumin seed, crushed (see page 73)

1/2 teaspoon freshly ground black pepper

1/2 teaspoon salt

1 tablespoon freshly squeezed lemon juice

6 (8-inch) flour tortillas

2 to 3 tablespoons peanut oil

1 1/2 cups grated Cheddar cheese

Sour cream or plain yogurt, for garnish (optional)

Tomato slices, for garnish (optional)

Avocado slices, for garnish (optional)

Boil the potatoes until tender, then drain and peel. While the potatoes are boiling, cook the onion, chiles, and garlic in the oil in a heavy sauté pan over medium heat until tender, about 10 minutes. Add the cilantro and spices and cook a few minutes longer. Add the peeled potatoes while still warm to the onion mixture. With a fork, crush the potatoes, mixing them into the onion mixture until coarsely mashed. Stir in the salt and lemon juice.

Preheat the oven to 400° and spray a baking pan lightly with nonstick cooking spray. Brush one side of each tortilla lightly with peanut oil. Place 3 tortillas oiled side down on the baking sheet and spread about 1/2 cup of the potato mixture on each tortilla. Sprinkle with 1/3 to 1/2 cup of the cheese and top with the remaining tortillas, oiled side up. Bake the quesadillas until lightly browned and crisp, about 10 minutes. Allow to cool for a few minutes before slicing into wedges. Serve hot, topped with a spoonful of sour cream and slices of tomato and avocado on the side.

Mayan Egg Enchiladas

Serves 6

The Mayans were distinguished by their sophisticated palates and favored robust sauces like the ones in this dish. The combination of the eggs and corn tortillas with these beautiful sauces is unique and a perfect treat for breakfast, brunch, or a special luncheon. This is an easy dish—the sauces can be made ahead.

1 dozen corn tortillas

1/4 cup vegetable or corn oil

6 hard-boiled eggs, chopped well in a food processor

Verde Sauce (see page 288)

Roja Sauce (see page 287)

Sprigs of fresh cilantro, for garnish

Sour cream, for garnish

Preheat the oven to 350°. Heat the oil in a large skillet. Very quickly heat each tortilla in oil to soften (don't let them crisp). Drain on paper towels. Place 2 tablespoons of chopped egg in each tortilla and roll tightly. Place tortillas seam side down on an ungreased baking sheet or dish and bake in the oven for 10 minutes.

While the tortillas are baking, arrange the sauces side by side on individual plates. Remove the tortillas from the oven and place on top of the sauces. Garnish with cilantro and sour cream.

Millet Pilaf with Jalapeños, Ginger, and Tomatoes

Serves 4 to 6

Don't pass up this dish if you're unfamiliar with millet! This golden pilaf with bright orange flecks is a spice-lover's delight, with the toasted whole cumin seeds causing every mouthful to pop with flavor. To serve as a main course, add 2 cups of cauliflower florets to the onions and sauté a few minutes before adding the tomatoes. This pilaf also makes a good stuffing for acorn squash. (See page 209 for more information about millet.)

1 cup millet, rinsed and drained

3 tablespoons vegetable oil

1 1/2 teaspoons cumin seed

1 1/2 teaspoons mustard seed

3 whole cloves

1 bay leaf

1 medium yellow onion, chopped

3 jalapeños, finely chopped

1 tablespoon finely chopped gingerroot

1/4 teaspoon ground turmeric

2 cups peeled, seeded, and diced fresh tomatoes

1 1/2 cups boiling water

1 teaspoon salt

4 tablespoons chopped fresh basil, coriander, or mint, for garnish

Sauté the millet in 2 tablespoons of the oil over medium-high heat, stirring constantly for 6 to 8 minutes, or until the grains crackle and begin to turn golden. Turn the millet into a bowl and set aside.

Return the pan to the heat and add the remaining 1 tablespoon of oil. Add the cumin seed, mustard seed, cloves, and bay leaf and stir until the spices are sizzling, about 30 seconds. Add the onion, jalapeños, and ginger and sauté for 5 to 6 minutes, or until the vegetables begin to brown lightly. Add the turmeric and sauté for 30 seconds more. Add the tomatoes and water and increase the heat to high. Cook, stirring for 3 to 4 minutes until the tomatoes begin to give up their juices.

Return the millet to the pan and add the salt. Bring to a boil, and stir well. Reduce the heat to low and cover. Cook until the millet has absorbed the liquid, about 30 minutes. Remove from the heat and set aside for 5 minutes. Fluff the pilaf with a fork and transfer to a serving dish. Remove the bay leaf and cloves. Sprinkle with fresh basil and serve immediately.

What is it that goes along the foothills of the mountains patting out tortillas with its hands? A butterfly.

—From *Nahuatl Proverbs, Conundrums, and Metaphors*, translated by Thelma D. Sullivan

Curried Fried Rice with Vegetables

Serves 6 to 8

With its Southeast Asian influence, this quickly cooked dish of colorful crisp-tender vegetables lends itself easily to variations. Try diced sweet potato instead of white potato and substitute any of the cabbage clan (napa, green, Chinese, bok choy) for the broccoli. While "curry" often denotes a traditional curry flavor (with cumin, coriander, and cardamom), the word historically refers to a savory dish made with a spicy sauce. Here the pungent flavors are fresh, bright, and spicy, but there is only the faintest hint of curry powder.

3 tablespoons vegetable oil

2 teaspoons minced gingerroot

3 cloves garlic

1 large red onion, peeled and cut lengthwise into 1/8-inch slices

1 red or white potato, scrubbed and cut into 1/4-inch dice

1 red bell pepper, seeded and cut into 1/4-inch dice

1 cup (1/2-inch-diameter) broccoli florets

1 cup quartered fresh white mushrooms

1 teaspoon hot curry powder

1/4 teaspoon hot red chili paste (such as Sambal Oelek)

1 teaspoon brown sugar

3 cups cooked white or brown rice (see page 334)

3 tablespoons light soy sauce

1 cup bean sprouts

1/2 cup thinly sliced scallions

Heat the oil in a large heavy skillet over high heat. Add the ginger and garlic, stir until it's sizzling, then add the onion and potato. Cover and cook 3 to 4 minutes, stirring once or twice until the potatoes are half-cooked. Uncover the pan and add the bell pepper, broccoli, and mushrooms and stir-fry 2 minutes until the broccoli begins to turn bright green. Add the curry powder, chili paste, and sugar and stir-fry 2 minutes longer. Stir in the rice and soy sauce and mix rapidly, stirring until the grains are hot before adding the bean sprouts and scallions. Stir another 30 seconds or so and remove from heat. Serve immediately.

Fried Rice with Bananas

Serves 4

Soy-glazed fried bananas complement this vegetable-studded rice dish from my friend Liz Wheeler. For a variation, add chunks of pineapple, apples, or cashews to the rice, or stir in a few tablespoons of coconut cream for a richer effect. Serve this dish as a main course, followed by a green salad, or as a side dish with grilled vegetables and a cabbage salad.

3 tablespoons vegetable oil

1 yellow onion, peeled and finely chopped

1 cup diced red bell pepper

6 Thai or serrano chiles, finely chopped

3 cloves garlic, finely chopped

1 1/2 teaspoons finely chopped gingerroot

1/4 teaspoon ground coriander (toasting the coriander seeds, then grinding them will increase the flavor)

1/4 teaspoon ground cumin (toasting the cumin seeds, then grinding them will increase the flavor)

1/4 ground nutmeg

1/3 cup raisins

3 cups cooked brown or white long-grain rice (see page 334)

4 firm, ripe bananas, peeled and cut in half crosswise at an angle

1 tablespoon brown sugar

2 tablespoons light soy sauce

2 tablespoons freshly squeezed lime juice

4 tablespoons freshly squeezed orange juice

Watercress or small lettuce leaves (Bibb, romaine, or red leaf), for garnish

Several bananas, cut in half, for garnish

Orange wedges, for garnish

Heat 2 tablespoons of the oil in a large skillet over medium-high heat. Add the onion and bell pepper and stir-fry for 1 minute. Add the chiles, garlic, ginger, and spices and stir-fry 2 to 3 minutes until the vegetables are softened. Add the raisins and rice and toss until heated through. Cover and remove from the heat.

Heat the remaining 1 tablespoon of oil in a small skillet over medium heat. Add the angle-cut bananas and sauté for 30 seconds, shaking the pan constantly until they begin to brown lightly. Add the sugar and fry until it begins to melt, about 30 seconds. Add the soy sauce, lime juice, and orange juice, and shake over the heat until the sugar dissolves.

Arrange the greens on serving plates. Spoon the rice on each plate and garnish with one banana half and an orange wedge. Serve immediately.

Ginger sharpneth the sight, and provoketh slothful husbands.

—William Vaughn, *Directions for Health*, 1600

Rice with Adzuki Beans and Jalapeños

Serves 6

At least once a month, my husband makes a big pot of rice and beans. They are hearty, nutritious, and easy to make (and reheat later in the week). This version is enlivened with olives and spices.

2 tablespoons olive oil

1 large yellow onion, chopped

1 green bell pepper, diced

2 jalapeño chiles, seeded and minced

2 cloves garlic, minced

1 tablespoon pure chile powder

1 teaspoon ground cumin

1 teaspoon annatto powder

1 1/2 cups uncooked white rice

3 cups water

4 cups cooked adzuki or dark red kidney beans (see page 333)

1/2 cup stuffed green olives, chopped

2 tablespoons chopped fresh cilantro

Salt to taste

In a large saucepan, heat the oil over medium heat. Add the onion, bell pepper, jalapeños, and garlic, and cook until the onion and bell pepper are tender, about 8 minutes. Stir in the chile powder, cumin, and annatto and cook 1 minute. Add the rice and water and heat to boiling. Reduce heat to low, cover, and simmer 15 minutes or until liquid is absorbed and rice is tender. Stir in the beans and olives and heat through. Remove from heat, and stir in the cilantro. Salt to taste.

Eggplant Potato Curry with Basmati Rice and Peas

Serves 6

Indian curries have a slow-growing, long-lasting heat that is not for the faint of heart. This dish has a lovely finish from the fresh lime, basil, parsley, and black onion seed and is delicious served with slices of ripe papaya and chutney. Don't let the long list of ingredients scare you; the preparation is simple and your kitchen will smell exotic.

1 large eggplant (approximately 2 pounds)

Salt to taste

1 teaspoon black onion seeds plus 2 tablespoons for garnish (see note)

4 tablespoons olive oil

1 teaspoon black mustard seeds

1/2 teaspoon cumin seeds

1 tablespoon minced gingerroot

2 unpeeled yellow Finn, white, or new potatoes, unpeeled, cut into medium dice

2 carrots, sliced into thin half-moons

1 large yellow onion, cut into medium dice

2 cloves garlic, minced

1/2 teaspoon ground cayenne pepper

3 teaspoons salt

4 tablespoons curry powder

1 tablespoon garam masala (see note)

1 15 ounce can coconut milk

1 15 ounce can stewed tomatoes

1 tablespoon brown sugar

Juice of 2 limes

2 tablespoons hot mango pickle (see note) or hot (not sweet) chutney, or 1 tablespoon apple cider vinegar

2/3 cup fresh basil chiffonade

2 jalapeños, minced

2 cups blanched cauliflower florets

6 cups water

3 cups uncooked basmati rice

1 cup fresh uncooked peas

1/3 cup coarsely chopped flat-leaf parsley

Lime wedges, for garnish

Ripe papaya slices, for garnish

Preheat the oven to 350°.

Cut the eggplant into large cubes and sprinkle with 1 teaspoon salt. Set in a colander for 20 minutes.

Toast the onion seeds in the oven until fragrant. In a heavy saucepan, heat 2 tablespoons of the olive oil. Add the toasted onion seed, mustard seed, cumin seed, and ginger. Cook on low heat until fragrant. Add the potatoes and carrots and brown lightly, stirring frequently. Add the onion, garlic, cayenne, salt, curry powder, and garam masala. Stir and cook on low heat for 5 minutes. Add the coconut milk, stewed tomatoes, and brown sugar. Stir, then cover and simmer for 30 minutes, stirring occasionally.

In a large skillet, heat the remaining 2 tablespoons olive oil. Add the eggplant to the hot oil and brown. Add the lime juice. Remove from heat, and add the eggplant to the curry mixture along with the hot mango pickle, 1/3 cup of the basil leaves, the jalapeños, and the cauliflower. Continue cooking for 15 minutes.

In the meantime, to cook the basmati rice, bring the water to boil in a medium pot, and add the rice. Bring to a boil again, lower heat and cover, and simmer for 10 minutes. Add the peas to the rice and simmer for an additional 5 minutes.

Check the curry mixture and, when the potatoes are tender, turn off the heat. When the rice is ready, place a portion on each plate and create a well in the center. Spoon some curry mixture into the center of the rice, sprinkle with chopped parsley, the remaining basil, and black onion seed, and garnish with the lime and fresh papaya slices.

Note: Black onion seed is available in health food or specialty stores. You may substitute 1/2 teaspoon dried mustard for the black onion seed, but don't use dried mustard as garnish. You may substitute 2 1/2 teaspoons curry powder and 1/4 teaspoon each ground cardamom and ground cinnamon for garam masala. Hot mango pickle is a jarred condiment available at specialty stores and health food stores.

Green Rice Casserole with Tomatillos

Serves 6 to 8

Ever so slightly tart with the addition of tomatillos, this casserole is delicious served with soft flour tortillas, black beans, fresh chopped tomatoes, sautéed zucchini, sautéed corn, and a dollop of sour cream.

Tomatillo Sauce

1 pound fresh tomatillos, husked and rinsed

6 serrano chiles, roasted, peeled, stemmed, seeded (for less heat) and minced (see page 40)

1 cup loosely packed chopped fresh cilantro (leaves and tender stems)

1 tablespoon vegetable oil

1 yellow onion, chopped

1 clove garlic, finely chopped

1/2 teaspoon salt

1/2 teaspoon granulated sugar

Rice

1 tablespoon vegetable oil

1 yellow onion, diced

2 large green bell peppers, roasted, peeled, seeded, and diced

1 clove garlic, minced

1/2 teaspoon salt

1 bay leaf

1 teaspoon oregano

1 1/2 cups long-grain white rice

2 3/4 cups boiling water

Salt to taste

Freshly ground black pepper

1 1/2 cups grated Cheddar cheese

Green peas, boiled carefully with onions, and powdered with cinnamon, ginger, and cardamoms, well pounded, create for the consumer considerable amorous passion.

—Shaykh Nefzawi,
The Perfumed Garden, ca. 1400

Steam or simmer tomatillos about 10 minutes, or until they soften and lose their bright green color. Allow to cool, then place in a food processor or blender with 1/2 cup of the cooking liquid. Add the roasted serrano chiles and the cilantro to the tomatillos in the food processor, and purée.

Heat the oil in a nonreactive saucepan over medium heat. Add the onion and garlic and cook 5 minutes until softened. Add the tomatillo purée, salt, and sugar and cook about 10 minutes, stirring occasionally, until thickened. Set aside.

To make the rice, heat the oil over medium heat in a heavy 2-quart saucepan with a tight-fitting lid. Add the onion and green peppers and cook, stirring until softened, about 5 minutes. Add the garlic, salt, and herbs and cook for 2 minutes longer. Add the rice and cook, stirring frequently, for 5 minutes, until the grains have whitened. Add the boiling water all at once and stir once. Bring to a boil, cover, then reduce the heat to low and simmer without disturbing for 20 minutes. Remove from the heat and set aside, covered, for 10 minutes. Then fluff the rice with a fork, remove the bay leaf, and season with salt and pepper. Fold in the green sauce and 1 cup of the cheese.

Preheat the oven to 350°. Spoon the rice mixture into a lightly oiled baking pan and smooth the surface. Sprinkle the remaining cheese on top. Cover the pan with aluminum foil and bake for 30 minutes until heated through and bubbling. Remove the aluminum foil, bake for a few minutes to crisp the top, and serve.

CHESTNUTS

Although chestnut trees were once common in North America, a blight around the turn of the century wiped out many, and today most chestnuts are imported. Dried chestnuts can be found in Italian markets, usually in the winter months. They are sold shelled and should be soaked before using. Interestingly, chestnuts are the only nut with vitamin C—7 ounces offers 86% of the daily recommended allowance. If you can't find dried chestnuts, buy whole fresh chestnuts and poke them with a fork, put in a 400° oven to roast for about 20 minutes, then cut them in half and put in a dehydrator for about 12 hours.

Paella

Serves 6

Fennel seeds, artichokes, and dried chestnuts stand in for the sausage and shellfish found in this spicy vegetarian version of Spanish paella. A large, shallow, enamel paella pan is most suited to the volume of this dish, but a large skillet or heat-proof serving casserole will work well, too. In the warmer months, you might prepare the paella on the grill outdoors—the wide paella pan shows off the different ingredients and creates a festive (and fragrant!) focal point for an outdoor party.

1/2 cup dried chestnuts

3 whole arbol chiles (or other hot, dry chile pepper)

3 tablespoons extra virgin olive oil (preferably a buttery olive oil from Spain)

1 large yellow Spanish onion (about 2 1/4 cups diced)

1 medium red bell pepper, diced

1 medium green bell pepper, diced

5 large cloves garlic, minced

1 1/2 cups arborio rice

3 large plum tomatoes, peeled, seeded, and chopped

2 teaspoons fennel seed

1 teaspoon dried oregano

1 teaspoon dried basil

1 teaspoon kosher salt

1 teaspoon black pepper

3 cups Vegetable Stock (see page 75)

1 cup water

1/4 cup dry red wine

1 teaspoon saffron threads

1 14-ounce can artichoke hearts, drained and chopped

1 cup manzanilla olives, with or without pimento, drained

1 cup green peas

Chopped fresh parsley, for garnish

Lemon zest, for garnish

Cover the chestnuts with warm water and soak at least one hour, then drain and chop.

In a large skillet over medium-high heat, toast the whole arbol chiles 1 to 2 minutes, turning often until they are fragrant and the skin color deepens. Do not burn. Transfer to a cutting board to cool. Remove the stem end and with a sharp pair of kitchen shears coarsely cut up the chile skins. Set aside with the seeds.

Add 2 tablespoons of the olive oil to the skillet, then add the onion and bell peppers. Sauté until the onion is soft and golden, about 6 to 8 minutes. Add garlic and sauté 1 minute more. Transfer the mixture to a plate or bowl.

Reduce heat to medium, and add the remaining 1 table-spoon of oil and the rice to the skillet, stirring until the grains begin to turn golden, about 3 to 5 minutes. Slowly add the onion and bell pepper mixture back into the skillet with the rice. Add the tomatoes, fennel, oregano, basil, salt, and black pepper.

In a separate bowl, combine the stock with the water and wine. Add 2 cups of the liquid to the mixture in the skillet. Stir the saffron into the skillet. Add the arbol chile and seeds to the paella. Simmer, stirring often, uncovered, until most of the liquid has evaporated, about 10 to 12 minutes. Add an additional 1 cup of liquid and simmer 8 to 10 minutes more. Add the remaining liquid and the chestnuts. Simmer an additional 10 minutes, or until the liquid is more than half reduced and the rice is cooked but not soft and mushy. Add the artichoke hearts, olives, and peas. Stir gently to blend and heat through, about 2 to 3 minutes.

Remove skillet from the heat and cover with a lid or foil and allow to steam about 15 minutes to further blend the flavors. Garnish with parsley and lemon zest.

Couscous Curry Timbales

Serves 6

Couscous is a handy vehicle for many flavors. It also holds up well, so this is a good party dish that can be made ahead. Originally, timbales were silver drinking goblets (like a baby's cup), but today the word is used to describe a metal mold that shapes food into architectural forms—the original jello mold! This dish is good served with a salad of tomatoes and cucumbers tossed with fresh chives and mint.

1 tablespoon olive oil

1 large yellow onion, finely chopped

1 medium green bell pepper, finely chopped

1 cup tomato juice

1/2 cup water

1/4 cup white wine

2 medium carrots, peeled and grated

1 teaspoon salt

1 tablespoon curry powder

1/2 teaspoon ground allspice

1 tablespoon orange zest

1 cup uncooked couscous

1/2 cup currants

Dressing

1 tablespoon freshly squeezed lime juice

1 tablespoon apple cider vinegar

1 tablespoon Dijon-style mustard

4 tablespoons olive oil

1/2 teaspoon salt

2 teaspoons ground cayenne pepper

Freshly ground black pepper to taste

Fresh whole parsley leaves, for garnish

WILD ABOUT RICE

Today, Americans are consuming more rice than ever before. According to the Houston-based U.S.A. Rice Council, consumption in 1995 increased to 25 pounds per person per year (up from 10 pounds per person 10 years ago). We still have a long way to go; the annual per capita consumption of rice in China and Japan is between 200 and 400 pounds per year.

In a medium saucepan, heat oil over medium heat. Add the onion and pepper, cover, and sweat for 3 to 4 minutes, or until slightly softened but not browned. Add tomato juice, water, wine, carrots, salt, spices, and zest and bring to a boil, covered, over medium heat. Add couscous and currants, mix well, cover, and return to a boil. Remove immediately from heat, keeping covered, and allow to sit about 20 minutes. Fluff with a fork and cool, uncovered, at room temperature about 20 minutes.

Meanwhile, make dressing by whisking together all ingredients in a small bowl until smooth and emulsified. Pour dressing over couscous and mix to blend well. Taste for salt.

Pack mixture into six 6-ounce ramekins or timbale molds, or into one large bowl with an interesting shape. For added effect, line the bottom of the molds with fresh parsley leaves. Refrigerate 2 to 3 hours or overnight. When ready to serve, invert onto individual plates and lift away molds.

Red Beans with Chipotles

Serves 4 to 6

The heat of the chipotles in this dish is subtle, but it will sneak up on you. The most memorable sensation, however, is the delightful smokiness. This dish is a good accompaniment to a grill menu, or it can be served as the entrée if presented on a bed of rice. (Since starches absorb the heat of chiles, if you're planning to serve this with rice or if you like the heat, you may want to use 5 to 6 chipotles instead of 2.) For variety, add a handful of chopped celery and green peppers to the cooking pot. Remember to soak the beans overnight and allow time for this dish to simmer for several hours.

1 large yellow onion, diced

Vegetable oil

3 cloves garlic, minced

2 tomatoes, chopped

Freshly ground black pepper

2 teaspoons salt

1 bay leaf

1 teaspoon thyme

2 teaspoons oregano (preferably fresh)

1 pound red kidney beans, soaked overnight

2 to 5 chipotle chiles (depending on desired heat)

In a large saucepan, sauté the onion in a little vegetable oil until tender, about 5 minutes. Add the garlic and sauté for another minute. Add the tomatoes, pepper, salt, bay leaf, thyme, and 1 teaspoon of the oregano. Add the beans and enough water to cover the beans by 2 inches. Bring to a boil, and add the chipotles to soften them. Cover, lower heat, and simmer. Remove the chipotles once they are softened, about 15 to 20 minutes. Stem and chop half of the chipotles, and toss back into the pot. Simmer for 2 hours, or until the beans are tender. Just before serving, add the remaining teaspoon of oregano. Taste, and if more heat is desired, chop and stir in the remaining chipotles (or reserve them in the refrigerator for another use).

People are familiar with the old standbys—pinto, kidney, and black beans—but farmers are increasingly introducing heirloom and specialty beans to the market. Ernie Miller, for example, found ancient Anasazi beans growing wild around ruins once inhabited by Anasazi Indians near Dove Creek, Colorado, and has been cultivating them since 1984. Elizabeth Berry grows heirloom varieties with names such as monk pea and ying-yang on her farm in Abiquiu, New Mexico (see Mail-Order Sources, pages 342-344). These beans are prized by chefs, who find them sweeter, nuttier, and more textured than commercially grown beans. High in fiber and rich in iron, calcium, protein, and B vitamins, beans also offer the vegetarian cook a colorful way to create tasty, healthful, economical dishes. Here's a culinary road map:

Adzuki: Also called aduki or azuki. Long revered for its healing properties in Japan, this small dark red bean resembles a kidney bean, but cooks faster and is tastier. In Asian markets you'll find a red bean paste made from adzukis. Can be substituted for lentils.

Anasazi: Named after the Anasazi Indians, this native American bean has speckled cranberry and white skin. Slightly sweet and mealy, this bean goes well with Southwestern and Mexican ingredients and spices and can be substituted for pintos.

Black (turtle) bean: A small, black, sturdy bean with a suggestion of sweetness and a dense mealy texture. Popular in black bean soup, refried beans, bean burritos, and also in Japanese and Chinese cooking.

Black runner bean: A sweet, shiny pole bean that keeps its color and shape when cooked. Many Santa Fe chefs prefer this variety when they want a large black bean.

Black-eyed pea: Also known as cow peas, these small beans are distinguished by a black dot on the cream-colored skin. Brought to America by African slaves, they are said to bring good luck if served on New Year's Day. Good in soups, stews, and salads.

Borlotti: Also known as rose coco, this tan-colored bean with red flecks is popular in Italy and Portugal. Can be used interchangeably with kidney beans.

Cannellini: This large, white kidney bean is often found in antipasto and other Italian dishes. Starchy, flavorful, and rather fragrant, it is good with olive oil, basil, rosemary, and tomatoes. Navy beans may be substituted.

Christmas lima: A big, flat, cream-colored lima bean with maroon streaks, this heirloom variety has a creamy texture and subtle chestnutlike flavor.

Cranberry: A nutty ovoid-shaped bean (slightly larger than an Anasazi bean) with cranberry speckles on light pink skin. Good in soups, stews, and casseroles.

D R I E D

B E A N S

Dried pea: Also known as soup peas, these green peas look like fresh peas that have shriveled and dried up. Soft and rather sweet, they are used in soups, but are more commonly found split (see split peas).

Fava: Also known as broad beans, these big flat beans have an earthy flavor and mealy potatolike texture. The thick skin needs to be removed before eating. Popular in Italian cooking, they blend well with strong spices.

Flor de Mayo: A small bush bean from Mexico that is still rare in the United States, but was recently made available by Elizabeth Berry. While the color is a challenge (ranging from tan to lilac to purple), the taste is outstanding, with a sweet smoky quality.

Garbanzo: Also known as chick-peas, these yellow, pea-sized legumes have a firm shape and slightly nutty flavor. Popular in many cuisines, they are a key ingredient in falafel and hummus.

Great Northern: This kidney-shaped white bean from the Midwest is quite mild and holds its shape well, making it an old standby in soups and stews. Navy beans may be substituted.

Jacob's Cattle Bean: An heirloom bean from Germany that melds beautifully with other flavors in a dish yet retains its own distinctive character.

Kidney: This versatile kidney-shaped bean has a range of colors from dark red to light red to white. Popular in Mexican dishes, it is favored in chili, soups, and stews.

Lentil: There are many varieties of this small, lens-shaped bean, which ranges in color from red to green to brown. Popular in Middle Eastern, Indian, and Mediterranean cooking, they cook quickly and don't require soaking. Yellow and pink lentils are soft, aromatic, and delicate and work well in purées and sauces. Brown and green lentils are heartier and delicious in side dishes, burgers, and salads. Puy lentils, used in French cooking, are quite flavorful.

Lima: A dried white bean with a sweet subtle taste and creamy, starchy texture. Lima beans are available in two sizes: the big ones are called butter beans or Fordhooks, whereas the small ones are called baby limas. Unlike most beans, lima beans should be cooked in salt water, which keeps their skins intact.

Madeira: A nutty, full-flavored pole bean brought to the Americas by Portuguese and Italian immigrants.

Monk pea: This heirloom pea is the famed pea of pea soup. Grown for centuries by Dutch monks, it is bigger than a regular pea, with a rough brown skin. Elizabeth Berry has a few available for serious growers who would like to help preserve this pea in their own gardens.

DRIED

Mung: This small, green or yellow bean is sold whole, split, or hulled, and is the bean from which bean sprouts grow. Quicker-cooking and more delicate than some beans, mung beans don't require soaking and are some-what sweet. Popular in Indian cooking, they are also known as green gram beans.

Navy: Also know as small white beans or pea beans, these mild, dense, white beans are used for baked beans.

New Mexico Appaloosa: Hailing from Mexico and the Southwest, this ancient bush bean has red and white or black and white markings and is creamy and quick cooking. May be substituted for pinto beans.

Pigeon: Originally from Africa and a staple of Caribbean cooking, these round tan peas are also known as Congo peas or gungoo peas and are popular in the Caribbean dish of peas and rice.

Pinto: This aptly-named bean (pinto is Spanish for painted) has tan-colored skin with reddish-brown flecks. Used in chili and refried beans.

Scarlet Runner Bean: Named after its flower, which is found in English gardens and beloved by hummingbirds, this ancient pole bean grows like a morning glory on walls or trellises and is a favorite among chefs.

Soybean: Rich in pro-tein, this tan colored bean is native to eastern Asia, where it is known as "meat without bones." Soybeans are turned into many prod-ucts, including flour, oil, a milk substitute, cereal, and baby food. In Indian cooking, dal is made from soybeans.

Split pea: This quick-cooking legume (known as channa dal in India) doesn't require soaking and is delicious in soups and purées or tossed with vegetables. Yellow split peas have a slightly nutty flavor and are pop-ular in Europe and India, whereas green split peas are more common in the United States.

White runner: Native to the American Southwest, this large tan-colored bean has a good, simple potatolike flavor; indeed, taking a bite is like eating a mini potato. Also called White Aztec, it is delicious and colorful when served with black beans in a side dish.

Ying-yang: A rare heir loom bean with a half white and half red, yellow, or black shape that curves around the bean like a ying-yang symbol. Even when cooked, the bean keeps its distinctive marking and is a good mate in a three-bean salad.

B E A N S

Étouffée

Serves 4

With a zing from the fresh jalapeño, this fragrant étouffée is a meal in itself served on a bed of basmati rice.

1 pound firm tofu, drained

4 tablespoons vegetable oil

1/4 cup flour

1 yellow onion, chopped

4 scallions, chopped

1 jalapeño pepper, seeded (for less heat) and finely chopped

1 green bell pepper, stemmed, seeded, and chopped

1 stalk celery, chopped

3 to 4 cloves garlic, finely chopped

1/2 teaspoon freshly ground black pepper

1/4 teaspoon ground cayenne pepper

1 teaspoon fresh thyme leaves

1 1/2 cups drained, chopped canned tomatoes

1 1/2 cups Vegetable Stock (see page 75), heated

1 1/2 teaspoons Worcestershire sauce

1/2 teaspoon salt

4 tablespoons chopped fresh parsley

4 cups freshly cooked brown basmati rice (see page 334)

Cut the tofu into 1/2-inch cubes. Put 3 layers of paper towels on a baking sheet and arrange the tofu pieces on top. Cover with another 3 layers of paper towels and put a second baking sheet on top. Set heavy cans or books on top of the second baking sheet to compress the tofu for 30 minutes.

Preheat the oven to 300°. Coat the bottom of an ovenproof 12-inch skillet with nonstick cooking spray (or use an ovenproof nonstick skillet). Heat 2 tablespoons of the oil in the skillet over medium heat. Add the tofu and sauté until lightly browned on all sides. Transfer the tofu to drain on paper towels.

Reduce the heat to medium-low and add the remaining oil to the pan. Stir in the flour and cook, stirring constantly for about 5 minutes until bubbling. Put the pan in the oven and roast the mixture for 20 minutes longer, stirring well every 5 minutes.

Remove the pan from the oven and place over medium heat. Add the onion, scallions, jalapeño and bell peppers, celery, garlic, black pepper, cayenne, and thyme and cook, stirring frequently, until the vegetables are soft, about 10 minutes. Increase the heat to high and add the tomatoes. Cook, stirring until bubbling, then add the stock, Worcestershire sauce, and salt. Cook, stirring, until the mixture thickens. Reduce heat to low and add the tofu. Simmer, partially covered, for 45 minutes.

Stir in the parsley, and taste for seasoning. To serve, spoon the rice onto serving plates and ladle the étouffée over it.

ANNATTO

Annatto adds a subtle flavor and beautiful reddish orange hue to many dishes and is used to color pastries, butter, cheeses—even varnish. The small annatto tree grows throughout the Caribbean, Yucatán, and Central and South America, with pretty pink flowers reminiscent of roses. The dye is extracted from the pulp surrounding the tiny seeds (which look like pebbles and are contained in a spiny pod) and centuries ago was used by the Carib Indians for body paint and to repel mosquitoes. A number of Caribbean recipes call for annatto oil, which is made by heating the seeds over medium-high heat in vegetable oil just until the color is released, about 5 minutes. In the islands, annatto is also known as achiote, bija, and roucou.

Curried Garbanzos Chez Hugo

Serves 4

This simple but tasty dish was a specialty of Hugo Churchill, a dear friend and botanist who had a deft hand in the kitchen. It's great if you're in a hurry and want to fix dinner in a snap, and good with chutney on the side. My special thanks to Audrey Werner for the recipe.

3 cups water

1 1/2 cup basmati or other rice

2 tablespoons olive oil

1 yellow onion, finely chopped

1/2 cup finely chopped red bell pepper

1/2 cup finely chopped green bell pepper

2 tablespoons curry powder

2 15-ounce cans garbanzos (see note)

1 teaspoon salt

In a medium pot, bring the water to a boil. Add the rice and stir, boil again, then lower the heat and cover. Simmer for 15 minutes, then remove from heat.

Meanwhile, place 1 to 2 teaspoons of olive oil in a medium skillet over medium heat. Add the onion and bell peppers and sauté until softened, about 5 minutes. Push the vegetables to the side of the skillet and add the remaining oil near the opposite edge of the pan. Stir the curry powder into the oil until it is dissolved. Let the oil and curry heat together for a few moments, then stir together with the vegetables.

Drain the garbanzos, retaining the liquid. Add them to the skillet, stir, and cook for about 3 minutes. Add the retained liquid and heat through. Salt to taste.

Fluff up the rice with a fork, and serve on individual plates, topped with curried garbanzos.

Note: You may substitute 4 cups cooked garbanzos and reserve a little of the cooking liquid for adding to the skillet.

Southern Black-Eyed Peas with Mustard Greens

Serves 4 to 6

This hearty combination of peas and greens can serve as a main dish with hot crusty bread to soak up the juices or as a robust side dish. Rich in calcium and rather spicy, the frilly mustard greens will turn tender after steaming. Look for leaves that are 6 to 10 inches long—those that are longer with mustard seeds attached are overmature.

2 tablespoons peanut oil

1 yellow onion, chopped

3 large cloves garlic, chopped

1 stalk celery with leaves, thinly sliced

1 small green bell pepper, finely chopped

2 bay leaves

3/4 teaspoon crushed red pepper flakes

1/2 teaspoon coarsely ground black pepper

2 teaspoons sea salt

4 sprigs fresh thyme, stems removed

1 28-ounce can whole tomatoes

3 cups cooked black-eyed peas (see page 333 and note, below)

1 bunch (1 1/2 pounds) mustard greens

Place oil in a large skillet over medium heat. Add the onion, garlic, celery, and bell pepper and sauté about 5 to 7 minutes, until soft and beginning to brown, stirring often. Add seasonings and mix well.

Drain the tomatoes, reserving the liquid. Add the tomatoes to the skillet mixture, breaking them up with a wooden spoon. Simmer gently over medium-low heat, partially covered, for about 15 minutes, adding 1/4 to 1/2 cup of the reserved tomato juice if the mixture becomes too dry. Add the peas and stir well.

Meanwhile, rinse the mustard greens in several changes of water. Trim the stem ends and discard any tough outer, yellow, or bruised leaves. Chop into small bite-size pieces (about 8 cups loosely packed).

In a large stockpot, bring 2 quarts of water and a pinch of salt to a boil. Add the chopped mustard greens, cover, and steam 3 to 5 minutes in simmering water until wilted and bright green in color. Drain in a colander. Add the greens to the black-eyed pea and tomato mixture. Stir well to combine. Remove the bay leaves. Adjust the seasoning and serve.

Note: If using canned black-eyed peas, be sure to rinse and drain well.

Curried Peas

Serves 6 to 8

Yellow or green dried peas or lentils work well in this dense, rewarding dish, which is good served over basmati rice. By decreasing the cooking time and adding more liquid, you can turn this into a delicious soup, too. Either way, top with chopped parsley and mint and a spoonful of yogurt. This dish goes well with the Vietnamese Cabbage Salad with Red Chile–Garlic Dressing on page 194.

2 cups dried split peas or lentils

4 stalks celery, diced

1/2 teaspoon salt

6 cups water

2 tablespoons olive oil

1 tablespoon unsalted butter

1 yellow onion, diced

2 teaspoons minced gingerroot

1/2 teaspoon cumin seed

1/2 teaspoon ground cayenne pepper

2 teaspoons curry powder

2 tablespoons hot mango pickle, finely chopped (see note)

1 cup plain yogurt, for garnish

Chopped fresh parsley, for garnish

Chopped fresh mint, for garnish

Lemon slices, for garnish

Rinse and pick through dried peas. Combine with celery, salt, and water in a pot and bring to a boil. Reduce heat to a simmer and cook for 30 to 45 minutes.

While peas are cooking, heat the oil and butter in a large sauté pan, taking care not to let the butter burn. Add the onion, ginger, cumin seed, cayenne, and curry and cook until onion is wilted. Remove from heat and set aside. Test the peas to see if they are tender. If so, pour off and reserve some of the cooking liquid. Add the sautéed onions and spices. Stir well and simmer until mixture thickens and liquid reduces almost completely, about 10 minutes. During the last 10 minutes of the peas' cooking time, add the pickled mango and stir to combine. Add some of the reserved liquid if you desire a thinner mixture. Garnish with a spoonful of yogurt and a sprinkle of parsley and mint, and serve with lemon slices.

Note: Hot mango pickle is a jarred condiment available in specialty stores and health food stores.

Baked & Grilled Entrées

Many ingredients are used for filling various vegetables and pastries in this chapter. These hearty dishes can be the centerpiece of a meal with rice, a salad, or a vegetable or served as a companion dish.

My husband and I grill year-round in New England. In the summertime, we use an old-fashioned stone grill in the backyard, which is handy and an aromatic focal point when guests are gathered on the lawn on a warm summer night. But we also keep a gas grill on the back porch so that we can have grilled foods in the dead of winter, when the wind is howling and there's three feet of snow on the ground.

Spinach-Stuffed Anchos

Serves 4

My Mexican friend Jose Marmolejo experiments with dozens of chile varieties in the kitchen and also sells them through his company Don Alfonso Foods in Austin. This wonderful dish of his flatters the mild-mannered ancho, with the subtle stuffing allowing the flavors of the chile to emerge in your mouth. It's a mildly spiced dish, easy to make, and quite dramatic with the dark stuffed ancho sitting atop a bed of polenta or rice, dusted with fresh mint leaves. The pod sizes of chiles can vary. If you use smaller pods (under 4 inches), the stuffing makes enough for 8 chiles.

4 ancho or pasilla chiles

1 clove garlic, minced

1 shallot, finely chopped

Dash of olive oil

8 button mushrooms, chopped

2 cups loosely packed spinach leaves

1 cup heavy whipping cream

1 cup grated Parmesan cheese (see note)

Chopped fresh basil or mint, for garnish

Rinse the chiles in running water. Slit them and remove the seeds, leaving the veins intact (they contain a lot of the flavor). Drop the chiles into boiling water and cook for 1 minute. Remove and drain.

Sauté the garlic and shallot in olive oil. When they begin to change color, add the mushrooms and then the spinach. When the spinach is wilted, add the whipping cream to partially cover. Add the cheese and stir until it becomes a uniform paste. Stuff the chiles with this mixture, and garnish with fresh basil or mint.

Note: A young, mild Parmesan cheese works best. If the Parmesan is very sharp, substitute mozzarella for half of it.

The Pythagoreans make a point of prohibiting the use of beans, as if thereby the soul and not the belly was filled with wind!

—Cicero,
De Divination,
44 BC

Roasted Red Bell Peppers Stuffed with Tomatillos and Rice

Serves 6

Mexican, Indian, and Chinese ingredients make this variation on a traditional Eastern European dish a mongrel, but like all great mongrels, what it lacks in pedigree it makes up for in its eagerness and ability to please. Aromatic and spicy, it has the potential to win over the most steadfast purist. Be sure to choose bell peppers that stand upright easily.

6 firm red bell peppers

1/2 cup extra virgin olive oil

Salt

Freshly ground black pepper

2 yellow onions, finely chopped

3 cups cooked basmati rice (see page 334)

1 cup crushed tomatillos (see note)

2/3 cup golden raisins

2 teaspoons hot mustard powder

2 teaspoons Chinese five-spice powder

1 teaspoon pure chile powder

1 teaspoon ground cayenne pepper plus additional, for dusting

1 cup chopped fresh cilantro

Pinch of salt

Preheat the oven to 350°. Wash and carefully core the red bell peppers by cutting around the stem and pulling out the center. With a paring knife, gently loosen the remaining core and seeds, and tap to empty. (Don't worry if a few seeds remain.) Brush the insides and top of each pepper with a little of the olive oil and sprinkle the insides with salt and black pepper. Place peppers on a baking sheet, and roast open side up for 30 minutes.

While the peppers are roasting, in a medium frying pan over low heat, sauté the onions in the remaining oil until softened and translucent. Do not brown them. Remove from the heat and add the remaining ingredients, stirring to mix well.

Remove the roasted peppers from the oven and allow them to cool slightly. Pour any juices that have collected in their bottoms into the rice mixture and stir to mix. The mixture should be moist, with the consistency of risotto. Once the peppers are cool enough to handle, fill them with the rice mixture, dust with a little extra cayenne, and return to the oven for 15 minutes to warm through. Serve hot, whole or neatly halved vertically through the center.

Note: If you can find fresh tomatillos, by all means peel off the papery husk and purée them. Otherwise, look for Goya's canned crushed tomatillos in a Spanish or Mexican market.

CHINESE FIVE-SPICE POWDER

Chinese five-spice powder is a savory blend of flavors—sweet, sour, bitter, salty, and pungent—used in Chinese cooking. The powder is found in most grocery spice sections, but you can easily make your own (see page 310).

Chiles Rellenos with Chipotle-Corn Sauce

Serves 6

There are almost as many versions of chiles rellenos as there are tomato sauces in an Italian household. In New Mexico, the stuffed chiles are typically fried in a simple egg mixture. In Colorado, they are batter-fried. In certain regions of Mexico, the chiles are baked instead of fried and smothered in a walnut sauce. This recipe is closest to the latter in that the chiles are stuffed, baked, and served on a cream sauce of roasted corn and smoky chipotle chiles. The black beans and pumpkin seeds in the stuffing create a rich texture. This makes a colorful appetizer for 12, or serve it as an entrée with a salad of brown rice, peas, and chopped scallions, followed by a green lettuce salad topped with fresh tomatoes.

1 head plus 2 cloves garlic

12 Anaheim chiles or poblano chiles

1 cup grated Cheddar cheese

1 cup grated Monterey jack cheese

1/2 cup queso cotijo or queso fresca (or substitute lowfat ricotta)

1 bunch fresh cilantro, chopped

1 can black beans, rinsed and drained

1/2 cup raw pumpkin seeds or pine nuts

6 scallions, chopped

3 tablespoons puréed canned chipotle chiles in adobo sauce

2 teaspoons ground cumin

3 teaspoons ground coriander

1 teaspoon freshly ground black pepper

1/2 teaspoon ground cayenne pepper

1/2 teaspoon salt

2 cups fresh or canned corn, roasted in a dry skillet or broiled until caramel colored

1 cup heavy cream

1 pint sour cream

Fresh cilantro leaves, for garnish

Roast the garlic according to the instructions on page 35.

To prepare the chiles, lay them flat on a baking sheet and place under the broiler, turning occasionally, until blistered all over. When the chiles are blistered, remove them from the broiler and cover them with a clean towel. After 20 minutes, the skin will separate from the flesh. To peel the chiles, have a bowl of water ready to dip your fingers into, and very carefully pull the skin away from the flesh. Remove the seeds by making a small slit toward the stem end of the chile with a paring knife and reaching in gently with your fingers to remove them. Dip your fingers in the bowl of water to help remove seeds from your fingers. (It's not necessary to remove every last seed.)

When the roasted garlic is cool, squeeze out the cloves and set aside.

To prepare the stuffing, preheat the oven to 325°. In a bowl, combine the cheeses, cilantro, black beans, pumpkin seeds, scallions, 1 tablespoon of the chipotle purée, and the spices. Stuff each chile and arrange in a lightly oiled baking dish. Bake 20 minutes, or until filling is completely hot.

While the chiles are baking, make the sauce in a blender by puréeing the corn with the heavy cream, roasted garlic cloves, and the remaining 2 tablespoons of chipotle purée. Transfer to a sauté pan or skillet and heat through. Place the sour cream in a bowl and whisk or stir to a creamy consistency.

To serve the rellenos, place a small amount of sauce on each plate and lay a chile in the middle of the sauce. With a teaspoon, drop a small dot of sour cream to each side of the chile. Place a cilantro leaf on each of the dots of sour cream for a lovely presentation.

Stuffed Eggplant with Brown Rice, Vegetables, and Chipotle-Almond Sauce

Serves 4

This dish is filled with many flavors and textures—fresh vegetables, rice, and sundried tomatoes—with a sauce that is a marriage of a Spanish almond-garlic sauce and chipotle chiles. If you like cheese, finish the dish by crumbling feta or cotija over the top before serving. Even those who dislike eggplant will love this dish, guaranteed!

1 large eggplant (1 1/2 to 2 pounds)

Salt

1/2 cup olive oil

1/2 cup mushrooms, coarsely chopped

1 clove garlic, minced

Juice of 1/2 lemon

1 cup cooked brown rice (see page 334)

1/2 cup blanched fresh asparagus, cut in half lengthwise and in 1-inch-long pieces

1/2 cup blanched fresh green beans, cut into 1-inch pieces

1/2 zucchini, shredded

2 heaping tablespoons drained and coarsely chopped oil-packed sundried tomatoes

Pinch of salt

1/2 teaspoon dried oregano

Pinch of Parmesan cheese

Freshly ground black pepper

Sauce

2 red bell peppers, roasted, peeled and seeded (see page 40)

12 cloves garlic, roasted (see page 35)

2 cups sliced almonds

2 tablespoons canned chipotle chiles in adobo sauce

2 cups Vegetable Stock (see page 75)

Salt to taste

Chopped fresh parsley, for garnish

Cut the eggplant lengthwise into 1/4-inch-thick pieces. Sprinkle the eggplant all over with salt, and let it sit in a strainer for 20 minutes to pull out the moisture. Pat the eggplant pieces dry before frying.

In a large skillet, heat about 1/4 cup of the oil on medium-high heat and fry the eggplant on both sides just long enough to soften, adding more oil as needed while reserving 2 tablespoons. Drain on paper towels. After all the eggplant is cooked, add the remaining 2 tablespoons of oil to the skillet and sauté the mushrooms and garlic in the same skillet on medium-high heat until they begin to brown. Stir in the lemon juice, brown rice, blanched vegetables, zucchini, sundried tomatoes, salt, oregano, cheese, and black pepper and remove from the heat.

Preheat the oven to 375°. Place a large spoonful of the rice mixture on each slice of eggplant and roll up. Lightly grease a baking dish with olive oil. Arrange the stuffed eggplant, seam side down, in the baking dish. Bake the eggplant for 20 minutes.

Meanwhile, prepare the sauce. Purée bell peppers, garlic, almonds, and chipotles in adobo in a food processor. With the machine running, add the stock and salt and set aside. Pour the sauce over the eggplant and bake for 20 minutes longer. Top with the chopped parsley.

Roasted Sweet Peppers Stuffed with Rice Salad

Serves 2 to 4

Here the smoky heat of the chipotle chile is tamed by the rice, which goes nicely with the roasted pine nuts and raisins. Stuff small peppers for a delicious appetizer, or serve larger peppers as a light dinner for 2 to 4, accompanied by a mixed salad, avocado slices, and fresh ripe tomatoes. You may substitute 2 teaspoons chipotle sauce with a sharp vinegar finish, such as Coyote Cocina Chipotle Sauce, for the chipotle chile in adobo.

1/4 cup raisins (soaked in brandy or hot water)

3 cups cooked rice

1/4 cup pine nuts, toasted (page 73)

4 scallions, thinly sliced

1/2 cup fresh parsley, chopped

Juice of 1 orange

1 canned chipotle chile in adobo sauce, minced

2 tablespoons extra virgin olive oil

1/2 teaspoon salt

Freshly ground black pepper

3 to 3 1/2 cups Orange-Chipotle Dressing (recipe follows)

4 medium to large red bell peppers

Drain the raisins and combine all ingredients except dressing and bell peppers. Roast and peel the bell peppers (see page 40). Cut each pepper into half lengthwise and seed. Spoon some of the rice onto each pepper, arrange on plates, and drizzle with the Orange-Chipotle Dressing.

Orange-Chipotle Dressing
Makes about 3 1/2 cups

The heat of the chipotles is absorbed by the orange juice and honey, so taste as you blend the dressing and add as much chipotle as your palate desires. You may substitute 4 to 5 tablespoons chipotle sauce with a sharp vinegar finish, such as Coyote Cocina Chipotle Sauce, for the chipotle chiles in adobo.

2 oranges, peeled and coarsely chopped

1 shallot, coarsely chopped

3 canned chipotle chiles in adobo sauce

Juice of 1 lime

1/2 cup freshly squeezed orange juice

1/4 cup honey

1 teaspoon salt

1 1/2 to 2 cups olive oil

In a blender, purée oranges, shallot, and chipotle chiles. Add lime juice, orange juice, honey, and salt and blend. With blender running, slowly add olive oil to combine thoroughly into a smooth dressing. Taste to adjust salt, or add a bit more honey or orange juice for a sweeter dressing.

GARLIC

The most pungent plant of the lily family, garlic was considered a hot seasoning by the Greeks (indeed, the Latin word for garlic, *allium*, is derived from the Celtic word for "hot") and has been revered for centuries in various cultures for its medicinal and evil-warding properties. Heroditus extolled garlic's virtues as an energy food, and it is believed that the Egyptian slaves who built the pyramids lived mainly on a diet of garlic and onions. The flavor comes from the oil released when a clove is cut open—mincing releases more, and crushing releases the most oil. The longer garlic is cooked, the more subtle the flavor. Roasted garlic is soft and buttery.

Look for garlic that is firm, compact, and has no green sprouts. (Elephant garlic is milder than the smaller white and pink heads.) Garlic should last for several months when stored in a dry, cool, well-ventilated place. Some favorite uses:

- Rub into a wooden salad bowl before adding greens
- Rub on grilled bread that has been brushed with olive oil
- Mince and add raw to vinaigrettes, pesto, aïoli, and garlic butter
- Crush into a small bowl of extra virgin olive oil and serve for dipping with hot crusty bread
- Serve a roasted head of garlic with a plate of grilled vegetables
- Pickle in vinegar and serve as a condiment

Stuffed Poblanos with Chipotle-Tomato Sauce

Serves 4 to 6

The poblano is a mild-tasting fresh chile that was first cultivated in the Puebla region of Mexico (hence the name). When dried, it is called an ancho chile. The Chipotle-Tomato Sauce can be made a day ahead—just refrigerate it until dinner, and allow to sit at room temperature about 15 minutes before baking. You can also freeze it. Or double the amount and have extra sauce on hand for rice, pasta, or scrambled eggs.

Chipotle-Tomato Sauce

2 tablespoons peanut oil

1 large onion, coarsely chopped

5 cloves garlic, sliced

1 28-ounce can plum tomatoes

2 chipotle chiles, stemmed

1 teaspoon dried thyme

1 teaspoon dried oregano

1 teaspoon kosher salt

Stuffed Poblanos

1/2 cup pumpkin seeds

3 cups cooked and cooled white and wild rice blend
(see page 334 and note, below)

1 cup fresh or frozen corn kernels

1/3 cup currants

1 teaspoon fennel seed

1 teaspoon dried oregano

1 teaspoon ground cumin

1 teaspoon kosher salt

1/2 teaspoon freshly ground black pepper

1/2 cup grated Monterey jack cheese plus additional, for garnish

6 poblano or green bell peppers, about 4 to 5 inches long
(see note)

Sour cream, for garnish

To make the sauce, heat the oil in a large skillet over medium heat. Add onion and sauté until just beginning to brown, about 8 minutes. Add garlic and sauté for an additional minute, stirring often. Add tomatoes and their liquid, chipotles, thyme, oregano, and salt. Simmer partially covered over medium heat for 15 minutes, stirring occasionally to break up the tomatoes. Remove from heat and set aside to cool, about 10 minutes. Blend in food processor until well blended, about 30 seconds. The sauce will have some texture and should yield about 3 1/2 cups.

To prepare peppers, dry-toast the pumpkin seeds over medium heat in a small skillet until they begin to pop, about 1 to 2 minutes. In a medium bowl, mix the rice, corn, currants, fennel seed, oregano, cumin, salt, black pepper, cheese, pumpkin seeds, and 1/2 cup of the Chipotle Tomato Sauce. Set aside. Preheat oven to 350°.

Spread 1 cup of the sauce along the bottom of a 9 by 13-inch ovenproof serving dish. Using the tip of a small, sharp knife, split the poblanos lengthwise from stem end to bottom, being careful not to cut through to the other side. Gently spread open the pepper and remove the seeds and ribs, keeping the stem intact. This is done easily under cool running water. (Bell peppers are not as flexible as poblanos, so if using them you will have to slice off about 1/2-inch of the stem to remove the seeds and then stuff. Save the tops and use as a lid to place over the stuffing.)

Divide the rice mixture among peppers, gently close each pepper around its filling, and place in the sauce-lined baking dish. Cover tightly with foil and bake about 45 to 50 minutes, or until the peppers are soft and the filling is steaming hot.

Meanwhile, over low flame, heat the remaining chipotle sauce in a small pan to pass at the table with the stuffed peppers.

When peppers are baked, uncover and top each with a few tablespoons of Monterey jack cheese and return to the oven for about 5 minutes, uncovered, to melt the cheese. Serve with a dollop of sour cream on the side as well as the Chipotle-Tomato Sauce.

Note: If possible, cook rice in Vegetable Stock (page 75) with 2 bay leaves. If substituting green bell peppers, add a 4.5-ounce can of chopped green chiles to the rice mixture.

Stuffed Tofu in Lemongrass-Sake Broth with Wild Mushroom Sauté

Serves 8

The wild mushrooms add texture to the mellow tofu, while the aromatic ginger and lemongrass highlighted with sake and rice vinegar provide a superb richness. You might serve this dish with steamed snow peas topped with fresh orange zest. The black bean garlic sauce and lemongrass are available in Asian markets and specialty stores.

2 10-ounce packages firm tofu

2 tablespoons olive oil

2 tablespoons sesame oil

2 cloves garlic, minced

2 tablespoons minced gingerroot

3 cups julienned savoy cabbage

Juice of 1 lime

1/3 cup unsalted walnut pieces

3 serrano chiles

1/3 cup roasted peanuts

4 scallions, chopped

2 tablespoons black bean garlic sauce or fermented black beans

1 cup plus 1 tablespoon rice vinegar

1/3 cup water chestnuts, coarsely chopped

1/2 cup chopped fresh cilantro

1/4 cup plus 2 teaspoons tamari soy sauce

2 cups water

1/2 pound fresh lemongrass

1/2 cup sliced fresh gingerroot

1 1/2 cup sake

2 cups sliced leek rounds

1 pound assorted wild mushrooms (such as chanterelles and portobellos), sliced

Pinch of salt

Freshly ground black pepper

Fresh cilantro sprigs, for garnish

Prepare the tofu by cutting each square in half diagonally, then diagonally again (in the other direction) until you have four triangles. With a paring knife, carefully cut small pockets out of the side of each triangle, removing a little of the tofu. Transfer the tofu you have removed to a large bowl and set aside the triangles.

In a wok or large skillet, heat 1 tablespoon of the olive oil and 1 tablespoon of the sesame oil. Add the garlic and 2 tablespoons of the minced ginger. When just fragrant, add the cabbage and sauté quickly, until wilted slightly. Add the lime juice, stir, and transfer to the bowl with the tofu. In a food processor or blender, grind the nuts and chiles, then add them to the cabbage and tofu, setting aside 3 tablespoons of the nut mixture for garnish. Add the scallions, black bean garlic sauce, rice vinegar, water chestnuts, cilantro, and 2 teaspoons tamari; mix thoroughly. Carefully stuff each tofu triangle with 2 teaspoons of this mixture.

In the wok, place the water, the remaining 1/4 cup tamari, the lemongrass, the 1/2 cup sliced ginger, and sake. Place a steamer tray over this broth and set the stuffed tofu pieces on it. Cover and simmer for 30 minutes.

Meanwhile, in a large sauté pan, heat the remaining 1 tablespoon olive oil and 1 tablespoon sesame oil. Add the leeks and brown lightly. Add the mushrooms and sauté until lightly browned. Add the salt and pepper. Cover for 5 to 10 minutes, then remove the cover and deglaze with sake. Sauté for a few minutes more, then remove from heat.

To serve, ladle some of the steaming broth into shallow bowls. Place a triangle of stuffed tofu in the broth and top with some of the mushroom-leek sauté. Garnish with fresh cilantro sprigs and a dash of the chopped nut mixture.

Note: For variety, instead of stuffing the tofu, you can layer the tofu triangles into thin slices (creating a sandwich of tofu, stuffing, tofu, stuffing), then wrap the whole layered piece with napa cabbage, bok choy, or Swiss chard.

When the moon is at the full,

Mushrooms you may freely pull,

But when the moon is on the wane,

Wait ere you think to pluck again.

—Old English rhyme

Moussaka

Serves 6

This fragrant vegetarian version of the Greek classic can easily be made in advance. It tastes best after sitting for about 20 minutes before serving, so this makes a good entree for a buffet. Or make a simple dinner by serving it with warm pita toasts and a salad.

3 medium eggplant (about 2 1/2 to 3 pounds)

4 tablespoons olive oil

3 large eggs, lightly beaten

1 cup nonfat ricotta cheese

1/4 cup grated Parmesan cheese

1/4 cup plain toasted bread crumbs (see page 55)

8 ounces white button mushrooms

8 ounces cremini mushrooms

8 ounces portobello mushrooms

1 large yellow onion, minced (about 2 cups)

3 large cloves garlic, minced

1 16-ounce can plum tomatoes with liquid

2 tablespoons tomato paste

1/4 cup dry red wine

1 tablespoon oregano

1/2 cup chopped fresh parsley

1 tablespoon hot paprika

1/2 teaspoon ground cayenne pepper

1/2 teaspoon ground cumin

1/2 teaspoon ground cinnamon

1 teaspoon salt

1/2 teaspoon coarsely ground black pepper

1/2 cup currants

Sauce

1/3 cup unsalted butter

4 tablespoons all-purpose flour

2 1/2 cups milk

1/2 cup grated Parmesan cheese

1/8 teaspoon freshly grated nutmeg

1/2 teaspoon ground white pepper

Prepare a grill. Trim stem ends of the eggplant. Do not peel. Slice each lengthwise into slices about 1/4 inch to 1/2 inch thick. Discard the outermost slice which is mostly the skin of the eggplant, as it may be bitter or tough. Brush slices lightly with 2 tablespoons of the olive oil. Grill until golden. Set aside on baking sheet in a single layer. (These can be made a day or so ahead, covered, and refrigerated.)

Mix the eggs and ricotta in a small bowl and set aside. Mix 1/4 cup grated Parmesan and bread crumbs in a small bowl and set aside.

Remove stems from mushrooms and discard. Mince all the mushroom caps, or pulse quickly in a food processor, to yield approximately 6 cups. Heat the remaining 2 tablespoons of olive oil in a large skillet over medium heat and sauté onions until softened, about 3 to 5 minutes. Add garlic and sauté 1 additional minute. Add mushrooms to the skillet, stirring with the onions, and cover. Cook about 5 minutes to soften and release liquid.

In a food processor, pulse the tomatoes and their liquid until smooth. Add the tomato paste, wine, and seasonings and pulse to blend. Add the tomato mixture as well as the currants to the skillet with the mushroom mixture. Simmer, uncovered, over medium heat about 45 minutes, stirring often, or until the mixture is thick and the liquid has evaporated. Taste and adjust the seasoning if desired.

To make the sauce, heat the butter in a medium saucepan over medium heat. Melt but do not brown, and whisk in the flour and blend until smooth. Slowly whisk in the milk. Continue stirring with a whisk until thickened and bubbly, about 10 minutes. Stir in the Parmesan cheese, nutmeg, and white pepper. Set aside to cool slightly for 10 minutes. Fold in the egg and ricotta mixture.

To assemble the casserole, preheat the oven to 325°. Lightly coat a 7 1/2 by 11 1/2-inch rectangular baking dish with nonstick cooking spray. Sprinkle half of the bread crumb mixture on the bottom. Lay out approximately 8 slices of eggplant to cover the bottom. Spread half of the mushroom mixture over the eggplant. Top with another layer of bread crumbs, then eggplant, and then remaining mushrooms. Distribute the sauce over all, carefully spreading it to the edges to cover completely. Bake about 1 hour, or until the topping is golden. Remove from the oven and allow to sit for about 20 minutes before serving.

PEPPERCORNS

Known as the King of Spices, peppercorns are the berry from a climbing perennial vine called piper nigrum (not to be confused with the chile pepper plant). A highly prized spice since the time of the Roman Empire, peppercorns were once worth their weight in gold (and used during the Middle Ages as currency to pay taxes), and evidence of their culinary use dates back to the fourth century BC. Native to the forests of India, Java, and the Sunda Islands, peppercorns today account for 25% of the global spice trade.

Since the flavor fades quickly after grinding, freshly ground pepper is preferred to the preground powder sold in supermarkets. Harvesting the peppercorn at different stages of maturity will yield different flavors.

Black peppercorns: Made from unripe green peppercorns that have been sundried, black peppercorns are strong, pungent, and have a bite.

Green peppercorns: Harvested while still unripe, green peppercorns have a mild, somewhat fruity flavor.

Grey pepper: A blend of black and white peppercorns, also known as Mignonette in France.

Pink peppercorns: Though not technically a pepper, this rosy berry from a small South American tree has a resinous taste and is used mostly to add beautiful color to a dish. Use sparingly, however; pink peppercorns can be toxic at high levels.

Szechwan peppercorns: Although unrelated to the piper nigrum plant, Szechwan pepper (also known as fagara) looks like a dark red peppercorn and is the dried berry of a small Chinese ash tree. Szechwan peppercorns are colorful, aromatic, milder than black pepper, and a key ingredient in Chinese five-spice powder.

White peppercorns: Made from berries that are fully ripened on the vine and then skinned to reveal the inner white kernel. As pungent as black peppercorns.

Emeril's Grilled Piri Piri Vegetables

Serves 2 to 4

Piri Piri is a spicy Brazilian sauce (called pili-pili in Africa), which is a takeoff of the Arabic falafel or "strong pepper." This recipe comes from Emeril Lagasse, chef at Emeril's in New Orleans and a man who knows a thing or two about spicy foods. Serve the grilled vegetables with rice, couscous, or pasta drizzled with extra piri piri.

Piri Piri

2 cups extra virgin olive oil

5 jalapeño chiles, coarsely chopped (with seeds)

1 to 2 fresh Anaheim or banana peppers, coarsely chopped (with seeds)

2 teaspoons crushed red pepper flakes

1 teaspoon pure chile powder

1 teaspoon salt

1/8 teaspoon freshly ground black pepper

1/4 cup loosely packed fresh cilantro

2 tablespoons minced garlic

Vegetables

1 baby eggplant, stemmed and sliced vertically in 1/4-inch strips

1 summer squash, stemmed and sliced vertically in 1/4-inch strips

1 zucchini, stemmed and sliced vertically in 1/4-inch strips

1 large red or white onion, peeled and sliced in 1/4-inch rings

2 plum tomatoes, cut in half

1 ear sweet corn, shucked

Salt

Freshly ground black pepper

To make the piri piri, combine all of the ingredients except the garlic and vegetables in a saucepan over medium heat, stirring for 5 minutes. Stir in the garlic, remove from the heat and allow to cool to room temperature, approximately 30 minutes. When cool, pour into a food processor and pulse about 20 times.

Prepare a grill. Season the vegetables very lightly with salt and pepper and drizzle with some of the piri piri. Grill the vegetables for 2 minutes on each side, then arrange them on a serving dish, drizzle with the piri piri, and serve.

Grilled Tempeh Skewers with Pineapple and Chiles

Serves 6

Widely available in health food stores and supermarkets, tempeh is a light, protein-rich soybean product that has been cultivated by farmers in Eastern Asia for more than five thousand years. Sold in dense, ready-to-use "cakes," tempeh is versatile and takes well to other ingredients, sauces, and marinades. Crumbled or cut into shapes, it is good fried, grilled, sautéed, baked, or added to stews. My favorite is three-grain tempeh, made of barley, millet, and brown rice fermented with soybeans. For the kebobs, you may substitute other small vegetables such as baby eggplant, baby squash, or zucchini—just be sure that all vegetables are approximately 1 inch in diameter so everything cooks evenly.

Marinade

3 4-ounce jars all-natural apples & plums baby food (see note)

1 1/2 tablespoons tamari soy sauce

3 tablespoons olive oil

1 1/2 tablespoons umeboshi plum vinegar

1 1/2 tablespoon Tabasco sauce

1 1/2 tablespoons Dijon-style mustard

1/4 cup plus 2 tablespoons freshly squeezed orange juice

3 tablespoons pure chile powder

2 large cloves garlic, crushed

2 8-ounce cakes tempeh

12 cremini or small shiitake mushroom caps
    (about 1 inch across)

6 shallots, split in half lengthwise

6 small tomatillos (about 1 inch across), husked

1 1/2 cups cubed pineapple, cut into 1-inch squares

12 hot red cherry peppers

8 cups freshly cooked brown rice (see page 334)

In a small bowl, whisk together the marinade ingredients and set aside.

Cut each tempeh cake into 1 by 1-inch squares. In a nonreactive baking dish, place the tempeh squares, vegetables, and pineapple. Reserve 1/2 cup of the marinade, and pour the rest over the squares, mixing well to coat with the mixture. Cover and refrigerate several hours or as long as overnight.

To make the kebobs, thread skewers with tempeh and vegetables, alternating.

Prepare a grill. Grill kebobs over hot coals, turning and basting with 1/3 cup of the remaining marinade until tempeh is a deep golden color, about 10 minutes. Or broil in a broiler 1 inch from the heat.

Serve immediately with rice, passing around the remaining marinade as a sauce.

Note: The baby food gives the sauce a nice smooth base, but you may substitute 5 pitted plums processed in the food processor with 3 to 4 tablespoons of apple or orange juice until smooth.

TOFU

Tofu originated in China (Buddhist priests took it to Japan in the eighth century), and Westerners have recorded eating it as early as the 1600s. In the late 1800s, there were two tofu suppliers in the United States; today, there are several hundred making over 65 million pounds a year.

Tofu is made by grinding soybeans with water to make a soy milk that is then coagulated. Rich in vegetable proteins and calcium, tofu is remarkably good for you—recently *The New England Journal of Medicine* reported that soy protein can even reduce cholesterol levels. Tofu is available extra-firm, firm, regular, and soft (silken). Firm tofu is good for grilling or sautéing, as it holds its shape well while cooking; soft tofu can be whipped into a smooth creamy dip or dressing. Tofu should be stored refrigerated in cold water that is changed daily.

Grilled Tofu

Serves 2 to 4

This recipe was developed by Chelsea Sleckman, a vegetarian culinary student at Johnson & Wales University, who was first exposed to spicy foods when her parents started making Craig's Hot Sauce in the family kitchen five years ago.

3/4 cup white wine

1 tablespoon olive oil

5 cloves garlic, minced

1/2 cup coarsely chopped fresh cilantro

Juice of 3 limes

2 serrano or jalapeño chiles, seeded and chopped (select red jalapeños if you can find them)

3 tablespoons Craig's Hot Sauce or other habanero hot sauce

1 pound extra-firm tofu, cut in half and sliced into 10 rectangles

Combine all of the ingredients except the tofu in a bowl and whisk to blend. Add the tofu and marinate for at least 1 hour. Broil or pan-fry tofu on each side until browned, about 2 minutes.

Sandwiches

Sandwiches are a great excuse to mix and match savory ingredients—from spicy chutneys to vegetable salsas. Depending on how they are cut and presented, sandwiches can serve as hors d'oeuvres, snacks, or even a light dinner. Keep a variety of breads—from crusty loaves to tortillas—in your pantry or freezer and use the garden and spice shelves for inspiration.

Spicy Grilled Tomato-Parmesan Sandwiches

Serves 2 to 4

This open-face sandwich makes a good summer lunch served with soup, when tomatoes are at their peak. Or cut into wedges and serve as a snack or appetizer.

1 baguette

Olive oil

3 cloves garlic, minced

2 to 3 ripe tomatoes, thinly sliced and at room temperature

1 tablespoon Jump Up and Kiss Me Hot Sauce with Passion or other Caribbean-style habanero hot sauce

.25 ounces fresh Parmesan cheese

Freshly ground black pepper

Light the broiler. Slice the bread lengthwise into 2 pieces. Brush the inside with olive oil and garlic, then layer with the sliced tomatoes. Drizzle with the hot sauce, spreading it smooth and very thin. Shave the Parmesan cheese lightly over the tomatoes, and sprinkle with freshly ground pepper. Place the bread in the broiler and cook until the cheese is melted, about 3 minutes. Cut into sandwich lengths, and serve hot.

Chutney, Red Pepper, and Grilled Cheddar Sandwiches

Makes 4 sandwiches

The star ingredient of these Indian-inspired sandwiches is the Gingered Fig Chutney, which can be prepared ahead and kept for 2 weeks in the refrigerator.

3 large red bell peppers

1 tablespoon olive oil

8 slices dense, moist bread (pumpernickel or semolina)

16 slices extra-sharp Cheddar or Monterey jack cheese

3/4 to 1 cup Gingered Fig Chutney (see page 298)

2 medium eggs

1/2 teaspoon ground cayenne pepper

2 tablespoons milk

2 tablespoons butter

Core, seed and slice the bell peppers into 1-inch-thick strips. Heat the olive oil in a large skillet and sauté the peppers until soft. Remove them with a slotted spoon and set aside. Reserve the skillet to grill the sandwiches.

Lay out bread slices on a cutting board and carefully assemble sandwiches, layering the cheese, then the chutney, then the still-warm peppers, then another layer of cheese between the bread slices. Tie each sandwich like a present with cooking twine (as if you were putting a ribbon on a gift).

Beat the eggs in a bowl with the cayenne and milk. Dip the sandwich packages into the egg mixture just to coat both sides; do not allow them to become soggy. Melt the butter in the skillet used to sauté the peppers. Add the sandwiches and cook slowly on both sides until the bread is lightly toasted and cheese is melted. Snip and remove the twine from the sandwiches, and serve warm.

SAY CHEESE

Other grilled cheese possibilities include:

≈ Cheddar cheese and Liz's Plum Chutney (see page 297) on hearty peasant bread

≈ Gorgonzola cheese, sliced pears, and watercress on wheat bread

≈ Sundried tomatoes, goat cheese, and fresh basil leaves on toasted French bread

≈ Cheddar cheese, fresh chives, diced jalapeños, and a thin layer of tomato salsa spread between two flour tortillas, then grilled on both sides

≈ Cheddar cheese and roasted red peppers on raisin bread

Grilled Portobello Mushroom Sandwiches with Manchego Cheese

Serves 6

Manchego cheese is a delicious Spanish cheese with a firm texture that melts ever so slightly under the broiler. Its rich flavor pairs well with the hearty portobello. If manchego is unavailable, you may substitute asiago, which is tangier but still combines beautifully with the mushrooms.

1/4 cup balsamic vinegar

1/2 cup olive oil

1 tablespoon crushed red pepper flakes

1 teaspoon salt

Juice of 1 lemon

2 cloves garlic, minced

1 teaspoon freshly ground black pepper

1 pound portobello mushrooms, stems removed, sliced in 3/4-inch-thick pieces

2 baguettes

1 pound manchego cheese, cut in 1/8-inch-thick slices

2 beefsteak tomatoes, sliced (optional)

Prepare the marinade by combining the vinegar, oil, red pepper flakes, salt, lemon juice, garlic, and black pepper. Add the mushrooms and let sit for 20 minutes.

Prepare a grill and grill the mushrooms, or sauté them in a hot, heavy skillet, 3 minutes on each side.

Preheat the broiler. Cut each baguette crosswise into 6-inch lengths, slice the pieces lengthwise, and drizzle the inside with olive oil and any remaining marinade. Broil briefly to brown lightly. Remove top pieces of bread from the broiler and set aside. Arrange mushrooms on the bottom pieces of bread, place a slice of cheese on top of the mushrooms, and broil until the cheese starts to melt. Remove from the oven, top with the tomato slices, close with the remaining slices of bread, and serve.

Avocado and Tomato Sandwiches with Jalapeño Mayonnaise

Serves 4

These hearty sandwiches are lightly but intensely flavored with the jalapeño mayonnaise. The alfalfa sprouts give the sandwich a nice crunch. Substitute watercress or arugula for variety.

Jalapeño Mayonnaise

1/2 cup mayonnaise

3 tablespoons pickled jalapeños, drained and finely minced (see note)

1 tablespoon grated lemon zest

1/4 teaspoon salt

1/8 teaspoon coarsely ground black pepper

8 slices whole-grain bread, toasted

1 large ripe Haas avocado, peeled and sliced

1 large ripe tomato, sliced

1 cup alfalfa sprouts

Prepare the jalapeño mayonnaise by combining the ingredients in a small bowl. Mix until blended, then spread on 4 pieces of the toasted bread. Arrange the avocado and tomato slices on top, and top with alfalfa sprouts and the remaining bread. Cut each sandwich in half and serve.

Note: Pickled jalapeños (sometimes labeled "en escabeche") may be found in Mexican markets and shops that specialize in spicy foods. Minced fresh jalapeños may be substituted for them.

Crepes Stuffed with Poblano Chiles and Spinach

Serves 4

These mildly spicy crepes pack dark greens into each dense serving. You can vary the heat by the amount of hot sauce you sprinkle on top of the crepes. (Without the hot sauce, this mild dish can serve as a great disguise for spinach, because it's as much fun as pigs-in-a-blanket for kids.) The crepes are easy to make; the entire dish can be assembled in about 40 minutes.

Crepes

1 cup polenta or finely ground cornmeal

1/4 teaspoon kosher or sea salt

1/8 teaspoon ground cayenne pepper

4 eggs

1 cup water

Filling

3 fresh green poblano chiles, cored and seeded

3 teaspoons chile oil

1 1/2 teaspoons water

3 cups packed, washed, and dried fresh spinach

3/4 cup ricotta cheese

3/4 cup grated Monterey jack cheese

2 eggs

1/8 teaspoon salt

1 to 2 teaspoons crushed red pepper flakes

Freshly ground black pepper

Topping

1 1/2 cups grated Monterey jack cheese

Cholula Hot Sauce or other Mexican or Louisiana-style hot sauce, such as Bufalo or Tabasco

Combine the polenta, salt, and cayenne in a medium-size bowl. In a separate bowl, beat the eggs with the water until well blended. Make a well in the center of the dry ingredients and add the egg mixture slowly, beating constantly with a fork or whisk to avoid lumps. (The mixture will be thin.)

Lightly grease a large skillet for the first batch of crepes only; after that the surface will be well primed. Warm the skillet over medium-low heat, then pour a little more than 2 tablespoons of the batter into the skillet for each crepe. Smooth the crepe batter with the back of a spoon to form circles 5 inches in diameter. Cook on one side only just until top of the crepe is set. Transfer cooked side down to cool on a sheet of waxed paper , and repeat, until all the batter has been used. You should end up with 16 to 20 crepes, which can cool while you make the filling.

Quarter the poblanos and place in a food processor along with the chile oil and water. Blend until peppers are finely chopped. Add the spinach and process again until the mixture is well blended. Turn the vegetable mixture out into a medium-size bowl and add the cheeses, eggs, and seasonings. Mix well, adjusting salt and pepper to taste.

Preheat oven to 350°. Spread approximately 2 to 3 tablespoons of the vegetable mixture along the center of each crepe. Roll up the crepe and place seam side down in a lightly greased 9 by 13-inch ceramic baking dish. Nestle the crepes closely together in one layer. Top with the 1 1/2 cups Monterey jack cheese. Sprinkle generously (but do not soak) with hot sauce. Bake for 25 minutes. Serve with hot sauce on the side.

Vegetable-Filled Chinese Steamed Buns with Orange Dipping Sauce

Serves 6

Steamed buns hail from northern China, where the climate is more suitable for growing wheat than rice. The wheat is turned into noodles and bread, which—with the lack of ovens in most Chinese households—takes the form of steamed buns. Served hot as a snack or side dish for many meals (even breakfast!), steamed buns can constitute a light meal when filled with vegetables. Although somewhat time-consuming, they are not difficult to make, and the filling can be made a day ahead and refrigerated. Serve these buns by themselves, with hoisin sauce, soy sauce, or the dipping sauce that follows.

Filling

1 tablespoon sesame oil

1 tablespoon minced fresh gingerroot

1 tablespoon minced garlic

2 1/2 cups thinly chopped savoy cabbage (remove vein if too thick)

1/2 cup shiitake mushroom caps, chopped finely

10 snow peas, stems removed, sliced thinly crosswise

1/4 cup shredded carrots

1/4 cup finely chopped celery

2 teaspoons tamari soy sauce

1/4 cup hoisin sauce (see note)

1 teaspoon rice vinegar

1 tablespoon dry sherry

1 teaspoon crushed Szechwan peppercorns

5 scallions, trimmed and sliced thinly

Dough

4 cups all-purpose flour

1 1/2 tablespoons sugar

1/2 teaspoon salt

1/4 ounce (1 package) active dry yeast

1 1/4 cups warm water (110° to 115°)

1 teaspoon canola oil

Orange Dipping Sauce (recipe follows)

To make the filling, heat the sesame oil in a large skillet or wok over medium-high heat. Add the ginger, garlic, cabbage, shiitake mushrooms, snow peas, carrots, and celery. Stir-fry to mix well about 2 to 3 minutes.

In a small bowl, mix the tamari, hoisin, rice vinegar, sherry, and peppercorns. Add the sauce to the vegetables. Cover and simmer over medium heat about 5 minutes to thicken and reduce liquid. Uncover and if necessary continue to cook for a few more minutes to reduce liquid. The mixture should hold together well and be somewhat thick. Stir in the scallions and remove from heat. Set aside, uncovered, to cool thoroughly.

To make the dough, in a large bowl mix the flour, sugar, and salt. In a small bowl, dissolve the yeast in warm water. Make a well in the center of the flour and slowly stir in the yeast and water using a wooden spoon or your hands until a ball forms. On a lightly floured surface, knead the dough until elastic yet firm, about 3 to 5 minutes.

In a clean large bowl, place the canola oil. Turn the dough in the bowl to coat its surface with oil. Cover the bowl with plastic wrap and a kitchen towel. Set aside in a warm place until the dough has doubled in size, about 1 1/2 to 2 hours. Knead the dough again on a floured surface until smooth and elastic, about 5 minutes. Flatten the dough slightly then divide into 24 individual portions. Place about 1 1/2 inches apart on a parchment-lined baking sheet. Cover again with plastic wrap and a kitchen towel and set aside for 20 minutes. Meanwhile, cut 24 squares (2 inches by 2 inches) of waxed paper or parchment.

Take one portion of the dough and flatten it in the palm of your hand to approximately a 4-inch circle, trying to make the edges thinner than the center. Place one generous teaspoonful of filling in the center of the dough, then seal the edges by pulling gently toward the center to form a small bundle. Pinch the edges together; no moisture is needed to seal them. Reshape the dough into a ball and place the tightly sealed dough ball seam side down on a small square of waxed paper. Proceed with the remainder of the dough, keeping them loosely covered with a towel until they are all completed and you are ready to steam them.

Place a large (10-inch) two-level bamboo steamer over boiling water in a wok or large skillet. Carefully lay 6 buns on each rack about 2 inches apart. Be sure they don't touch because they will expand during steaming. Cover tightly and steam the buns about 15 minutes, then remove carefully. Repeat procedure until all buns are steamed, keeping the steamed buns in a warm (200°) oven until ready to serve. Serve with the Orange Dipping Sauce.

Note: Hoisin sauce is a thick, earthy, spicy-sweet sauce made with fermented soybeans, garlic, peppercorns, and chiles. Popular in southern China, it makes a delicious marinade, dipping sauce, or stir-fry seasoning. Like other soy sauces, it can be found in Asian markets or the gourmet section of some supermarkets. For a variation, substitute a sweet filling for the vegetables.

Orange Dipping Sauce
Makes approximately 1/2 cup

The orange preserve sweetens and thickens this sauce nicely. If you prefer a thinner smoother sauce, see note below.

1/4 cup all-natural orange preserve or other fruit preserve
2 teaspoons chile oil
1 tablespoon freshly grated or minced gingerroot
2 tablespoons thinly sliced scallions, green part only
2 tablespoons lemon juice
1 tablespoon tamari soy sauce

In a small bowl, mix ingredients well, then refrigerate until needed.

Note: For a thinner sauce, combine all ingredients except the scallions. Refrigerate overnight, strain, pour into a serving ramekin, and garnish with minced scallions.

FUNGUS AMONGUS

A dozen years ago, markets didn't offer much of a mushroom selection beyond the smooth-capped button mushroom, but many exotic varieties are available today. I prefer fresh ones, although dried mushrooms can be reconstituted by soaking in water (or even Madeira or vegetable stock).

Cèpe: From France, this flavorful, fleshy, large, brown-capped mushroom is very versatile and great grilled. Those grown in Italy are known as porcini.

Chanterelle: With a feathery trumpetlike shape, these revered mushrooms have a subtle, slightly fruity taste reminiscent of apricots. Thick-fleshed and pale yellowish orange in color, they are best served cooked and benefit from slow sautéing. Try them with olive oil and lemon juice. Also known as girolle or pfifferling.

Cloud ear: With a mild flavor, this rather crunchy mushroom is good marinated or cooked in sauces. It should be soaked in boiling water for 30 minutes or so before using.

Enoki: A mild but dramatic-looking mushroom, with many tiny white caps perched on long spindly stems. It is often served raw or sautéed. Also known as enokitake.

Matsutake: From the Orient, this prized mushroom also grows wild on the West Coast. With a slightly tough texture, it's best in stews or sautéed.

Morel: This popular honeycomb-shaped mushroom has a marvelous earthy flavor and chewy texture. Often picked wild in the woods in the springtime, morels complement other spring dishes like asparagus and creamy pastas. Or when picked fresh, simply sauté them in butter.

Oyster: With a smooth tan cap, this wild mushroom is mild and somewhat chewy. Though it can be eaten raw, it benefits from sautéing, braising, or frying. Also known as pleurotus, tree oyster, and sovereign.

Portobello: Enormous caps define this versatile, woody mushroom that is tasty grilled whole or thinly sliced and sautéed.

Shiitake: Originally from Japan, these dense dark-brown mushrooms have a strong, earthy flavor that holds up well to strong ingredients (especially soy, garlic, ginger, and chiles). Good stir-fried, grilled, or in duxelles. Also known as black forest or Chinese black.

Roasted Winter Vegetable Turnovers

Makes 10 turnovers

These savory turnovers are warming on a cold night, especially with soup and a hearty salad. A tip on peeling hard squash with ease: immerse the whole squash in boiling water for 1 minute, then cool under running cold water. The peel will come off easily with a sharp knife.

Filling

1 small butternut or buttercup squash, peeled, seeded, and cut into 1-inch chunks (about 2 cups)

2 carrots, peeled and cut into 1/2-inch chunks (about 1 cup)

2 parsnips, peeled and cut into 1/2-inch chunks (about 1 cup)

1 yellow onion, finely chopped

2 cloves garlic, finely chopped

3/4 teaspoon crushed hot pepper flakes

3/4 teaspoon freshly ground black pepper

2 teaspoons crushed fennel seed

1 1/2 teaspoons oregano or marjoram

2 teaspoons chopped fresh rosemary needles

5 tablespoons chopped fresh parsley

Salt

2 tablespoons olive oil

1 1/2 cups cooked brown rice (see page 334)

1 1/2 cups grated Gruyère cheese

1/2 cup lightly toasted pine nuts (see page 73)

1 large egg, beaten

Pastry Dough

2 1/3 cups unbleached all-purpose flour

1 cup whole-wheat flour

1 1/2 teaspoons salt

1 1/2 cups unsalted butter, cut into 1/4-inch pieces

1 large egg

2 tablespoons milk

Preheat oven to 400°. Put the vegetables, onion, garlic, spices, and herbs in a bowl. Salt lightly and toss to combine. Add the olive oil and toss until the vegetables are evenly coated with the oil. Turn the mixture into a roasting pan or baking sheet and cover loosely with foil. Bake for 25 to 30 minutes until the vegetables are just tender. Remove from the oven and cool. Turn off the oven.

Turn the vegetables into a large mixing bowl. Add the rice, cheese, pine nuts, and beaten egg. Mix thoroughly.

To make the pastry, combine the flours and salt in a mixing bowl. Toss in the butter pieces until they are coated with flour. Using a pastry blender or your fingertips, work the butter into the flour until the butter fragments are about the size of small peas and the flour mixture resembles coarse sand.

Beat the egg and milk together until thoroughly mixed and add all but a few tablespoons to the flour mixture. Toss together with a fork, adding the remaining liquid as needed. Working quickly with your fingers, mix and press the dough lightly until it coheres in a mass. Divide the dough into 10 disks, wrap in plastic, and refrigerate for 2 to 3 hours.

Preheat the oven to 400°. Dust a work surface lightly with flour. To roll out the dough, flatten each portion with your hand and give it a few whacks (smack it briskly) with the rolling pin to make it more malleable. Roll the dough out rapidly, giving the disk a quarter turn between each pass of the rolling pin. Continue rolling to make a disk about 1/8 inch thick. Trim into a 6-inch circle and refrigerate until ready to use. Roll out the remaining portions of dough in the same manner.

To assemble the turnovers, remove pastry circles from the refrigerator and place a heaping, packed 1/3 cup of filling in the center of each circle. Moisten the edges of the dough with water. Fold the dough over gently to make a half circle and seal the edges well with a fork.

Place the pastries on a baking sheet about 1 inch apart. Bake for 10 minutes, then lower the temperature to 375° and bake for 15 to 20 minutes longer, or until browned and crisp.

Adzuki Bean Burgers

Makes 6 burgers

The adzuki is a small, reddish brown bean that has been grown in China and Japan for thousands of years. Light tasting, it lends itself perfectly to these burgers, which can be made ahead and frozen; just be sure to thaw the patties completely in the refrigerator before cooking.

1 cup dry adzuki beans

1/2 cup uncooked short-grain brown rice

3 large portobello mushroom caps

3 tablespoons olive oil

1 large leek, chopped (both white and light green portions)

1/3 cup toasted whole-wheat bread crumbs (see page 55)

2 teaspoons whole dry green peppercorns (not packed in liquid), crushed slightly

1 tablespoon soy sauce

1 teaspoon Thai chile paste

1 teaspoon dry marjoram leaves, crumbled

1/4 cup fresh flat-leaf parsley, chopped

Salt

Freshly ground black pepper

1 to 2 tablespoons cornmeal

Rinse the beans and place in a large bowl with 4 cups of cold water and set aside to soak overnight.

To prepare the burgers, in a medium pot bring 1 cup of water to a boil. Add the rice and stir, boil again, then lower the heat and cover. Simmer until done, about 40 minutes, then remove from heat.

Meanwhile, drain the beans of their soaking liquid and place in a medium stockpot with 4 cups cold water. Cover and simmer over medium heat until beans are tender, about 45 minutes. (They should crush easily when pressed with a wooden spoon or between your fingers.) Drain and set aside.

Prepare a grill. Brush the mushroom caps with 1 tablespoon of the olive oil and grill until tender and well browned, about 12 to 15 minutes, turning often. Set aside until cool, then chop into a small dice to yield about 1 cup. In a large skillet over medium heat, sauté leek in the remaining 2 tablespoons of olive oil until softened, about 2 to 3 minutes. Add the bread crumbs to the skillet, along with the peppercorns, soy sauce, chile paste, and marjoram. Stir well, then remove from the heat and set aside.

In the bowl of an electric mixer, place the beans and rice. With the paddle attachment in place, mix until well blended and the grains begin to break up and stick together, about 2 to 3 minutes on medium speed. (Be sure to start on the lower speed at first.) Add the mushrooms, leek mixture, and parsley. Continue to mix an additional minute or until well blended. (If you don't have a mixer, you can use a large bowl and a potato masher or a wooden spoon and mix until the ingredients bind together.) Add a shake of salt and black pepper.

With your hands (moistened in cold water) and an ice cream scoop or a 1/2-cup measure, pack the mixture tightly and make 6 burgers, setting them on a sheet of parchment paper. With a second sheet of parchment placed over the top, lightly press to compact the mixture and shape the patty. At this point, they can be wrapped and frozen in a single layer.

Preheat oven to 425°. Sprinkle 1 to 2 tablespoons of cornmeal on a baking sheet and place burgers on the sheet, about 1 inch apart. Lightly spray the tops with nonstick cooking spray to moisten. Bake until heated through and golden, about 15 minutes.

Note: Although burgers typically are grilled or fried, without the addition of a binder (traditionally fat), these patties won't hold together on the grill and hence are baked. If you want to grill or fry the burgers, lightly beat 2 large egg whites and add to the mixture when you add the mushrooms. If you grill them, use a grill screen and be sure to flip the burgers very carefully with a wide spatula.

Falafels

Makes about thirty 1-inch balls

The red pepper flakes give this Middle Eastern favorite a slow burn—a perfect partner for garlic-yogurt sauce or tahini.

Falafel Balls

1/2 cup bulgur wheat

2 cups coarsely crumbled stale whole-wheat pita bread

1 16-ounce can garbanzo beans, drained and rinsed

Juice of 1 large lemon

2 large cloves garlic, finely chopped

4 tablespoons chopped fresh cilantro

1 1/2 teaspoons crushed red pepper flakes

1 1/2 teaspoons ground cumin

1/2 teaspoon freshly ground black pepper

1/3 cup finely chopped scallions

1 1/2 teaspoons salt

Vegetable oil for frying

4 rounds pita bread, warmed and halved

2 tomatoes, sliced

1 cucumber, julienned

1 bell pepper, thinly sliced

3 scallions, shredded

1 cup loosely packed finely shredded Bibb lettuce

1/2 cup tahini or yogurt sauce

In a bowl, cover the bulgur with cold water and allow to soak for 30 minutes. While the bulgur is soaking, put the bread in another bowl, cover with cold water and soak for 15 minutes. Drain the bread in a colander, squeezing out the excess moisture. Drain the bulgur well through a fine sieve.

In the bowl of a food processor fitted with the metal chopping blade, combine the garbanzos, lemon juice, garlic, cilantro, pepper flakes, cumin, black pepper, and scallions. Process with an on-off motion until the mixture is finely chopped. Transfer the mixture to a bowl. Stir in the bulgur and bread and mix well. Scoop about 2 tablespoons of the mixture and shape into a ball or patty. Set the patties aside on a plate.

Heat 1 inch of oil in a heavy 12-inch skillet over medium-high heat until very hot but not smoking. Add the patties to the pan without crowding and fry for 2 to 3 minutes, turning once, until golden brown all over. As the patties brown, transfer to paper towels to drain and keep warm while frying the remaining batches.

To serve, tuck 3 to 4 balls in each pita half. Add several slices of tomato, cucumber, and bell pepper, and a sprinkling of scallions and lettuce. Drizzle with the tahini and serve immediately.

Salads
& Side
Dishes

Vegetable Salads

I live on salads and serve them at the end of most dinners to cleanse the palate. I often toss mixed lettuces with whatever herbs are available in the herb garden outside my kitchen door—fresh basil, thyme, oregano, rosemary, lemon verbena, and tarragon—to create a light, all-green salad. I always use a wooden salad bowl, rinsing it out after each meal with hot (but not soapy!) water. As a child, one of my kitchen duties was to rub the salad bowl with a split clove of garlic before dinner, which I still do for extra flavor. (I also do it because I love the scent of garlic in the air.)

Melon, Cucumber, and Apple Salad

Serves 6

A takeoff on a street snack in Guatemala and central Mexico, this *pico de gallo* is presented as a composed salad that is good as a first course or as an accompaniment to a rich, savory dish such as black bean soup. This is a clean salad, with sharp flavors.

1/2 cup thinly sliced red onion

Boiling water

4 tablespoons freshly squeezed lime juice

1 teaspoon salt

1 large clove garlic, crushed

3 small Kirby cucumbers, peeled, cut in half, and sliced thin crosswise (about 1 1/2 cups), or an equivalent amount of English hothouse cucumbers

1 Granny Smith apple, peeled, cored, and quartered, each quarter sliced crosswise 1/4-inch thick

2 seedless oranges, peeled, segmented, and cut into thirds

2 serrano chiles, cut in half, seeded and sliced paper-thin crosswise

2 tablespoons finely diced red bell pepper

2 tablespoons finely shredded fresh mint leaves

1 firm, ripe cantaloupe or other aromatic melon

1 bunch watercress, tough stems removed, for garnish

Put the onion in a heat-proof bowl and cover with boiling water. Allow to sit 2 minutes, then drain and combine with the lime juice, salt, and garlic. Set aside.

Combine the cucumbers, apple, oranges, serranos, and bell pepper in a nonreactive bowl. Add the onion mixture and mint, and mix gently. Cover and refrigerate until ready to serve.

Halve the melon, remove the seeds, and cut lengthwise into crescents 1/2 inch wide at the thickest part. Cut away the rind and arrange 2 to 3 overlapping slices on one side of each serving plate. Garnish with a cluster of watercress and spoon the salad alongside.

To see cucumbers in a dream denotes that you will speedily fall in love. Or, if you are in love, then you will marry the object of your affection. To dream that you are eating garlic denotes that you will discover hidden secrets and meet with some domestic jar. To dream that there is garlic in the house is lucky. To dream of lettuces is said to portend trouble...to dream of mushrooms denotes fleeting happiness, to dream you are gathering them, fickleness in a lover or consort. To dream of olives portends concord, liberty and dignity...parsley portends that you will be crossed in love...if you are eating it you will shortly hear good news.

—Richard Folkard, *Plant Lore*, 1884

CABBAGE

Cabbage is incredibly good for you. Researchers now think that half a head of cabbage a day may prevent certain forms of cancer, and 1 1/2 cups gives you almost 80% of the vitamin C required daily. Just be sure to buy whole cabbage; halved cabbage sometimes sold in supermarkets is not nearly as nutritious, since the cabbage begins to lose vitamin C once the leaves are cut. Varieties include:

Bok choy: Also known as Chinese mustard cabbage, bok choy looks a bit like Swiss chard, with thick white stalks and dark green leafy leaves. High in vitamin A, the leaves and stalks are edible, although the stems take a bit more time to cook than the leaves.

Green Cabbage: With pale green outer leaves, this smooth, tightly bound cabbage ball is a familiar sight in most grocery stores.

Hot-and-Sour Cabbage Salad

Serves 6

Though typically an accompaniment to grilled shrimp or meat satays, this crisp Southeast Asian salad is refreshing on its own and would complement mellow beans or a creamy potato gratin. For variation, substitute crunchy bean sprouts or shredded carrots for a portion of the cabbage. This dish is also pretty garnished with tomato, watercress, and a slice of lime.

1 clove garlic, minced or pressed

2 to 3 serrano chiles, cut in half, seeded, and finely sliced (about 2 tablespoons)

1 teaspoon minced and seeded fresh habanero chile

2 tablespoons freshly squeezed lime juice

2 tablespoons apple cider vinegar

2 teaspoons granulated sugar

2 tablespoons light soy sauce

2 tablespoons dark sesame oil

1 (1-pound) green cabbage, shredded finely (about 6 cups loosely packed)

2 large scallions, cut into 3-inch lengths and shredded (about 1/2 cup)

2 to 3 radishes, cut in half and thinly sliced crosswise

3 tablespoons finely sliced fresh basil leaves

3 tablespoons finely chopped fresh cilantro

1/2 cup finely chopped cashews, for garnish

In a large bowl, combine the garlic, chiles, lime juice, vinegar, sugar, soy sauce, and sesame oil. Add the cabbage, scallions, radishes, and herbs, and mix well. Refrigerate for about 1 hour. Just before serving, sprinkle each serving with cashews.

Roasted Eggplant and Yogurt Salad

Serves 6

This cooling summer salad has the soothing texture and flavor of yogurt combined with the surprise bite of cayenne chiles. Since the heat of chiles varies from crop to crop, add a few chiles, then taste and add more if necessary.

3 to 4 small firm eggplant (about 1 1/2 pounds), sliced crosswise into 1/4-inch rounds

2 tablespoons vegetable oil

2 cups plain nonfat yogurt

2 tablespoons finely chopped red or white sweet onion

1 clove garlic, minced

2 to 3 small fresh cayenne or red serrano chiles, seeded and minced

1/4 teaspoon cumin seed, toasted and crushed (see page 73)

1/4 teaspoon freshly ground black pepper

2 tablespoons freshly squeezed lemon juice

2 tablespoons finely shredded basil or cilantro

1 roasted red bell pepper, stemmed, seeded, and cut into thin 1-inch-long slivers

1 ripe tomato, seeded and diced (about 1 cup)

Salt to taste

Preheat the oven to 425°. Brush the eggplant rounds very lightly with oil on both sides and place on a lightly oiled baking sheet. Roast in the oven for 20 to 25 minutes, or until tender and lightly browned. Loosen the rounds with a spatula and set aside to cool. When cool, cut the rounds crosswise to make triangles.

Combine all of the remaining ingredients except the tomato and salt in a large bowl. Fold the eggplant and tomato into the yogurt mixture and season to taste with salt. Serve immediately.

Napa Cabbage: Also called Chinese cabbage, napa cabbage resembles a celery-colored head of romaine lettuce, with each frilly leaf possessing a wide central vein. Milder, lighter, and less crunchy than common cabbage varieties, it is delicious in salads and slaws.

Red cabbage: Not as densely wrapped as green cabbage, the head of red cabbage opens up a bit like a flowering bud. The leaves are a beautiful dark purply red and have more vitamin C than green cabbage.

Savoy cabbage: With frilly yellowish green leaves, this head is less compact than green or red cabbage. Its milder flavor makes it better suited for salads than green or red varieties.

Tomato, Corn, and Roasted Potato Salad

Serves 6

While the flavors of this dish conjure up the Southwest, the recipe was born of a New England "waste not, want not" ethic in its creative use of leftovers. This salad makes a wonderful summer lunch, accompanied by peasant bread and pâté. And if potatoes weren't on the menu the night before, simply double the amount of corn and tomatoes for a lighter but still spicy summer salad.

4 cups small red potatoes (10 to 12)

3 tablespoons olive oil

4 cloves garlic, crushed

Salt to taste

Freshly ground pepper to taste

2 ears fresh corn

3 to 4 jalapeño chiles, seeded and minced

1 tablespoon sesame oil

3 cups quartered ripe plum tomatoes

1 cup coarsely chopped fresh flat-leaf parsley

Balsamic-Dijon Vinaigrette (recipe follows)

Parboil the red potatoes in salted water for 15 minutes. Remove from heat while still firm and let cool in water to keep skins intact. Cut in half and toss with olive oil, garlic, salt, and pepper.

Preheat the oven to 400°, or light a grill. Roast the potatoes, uncovered, in the oven or skewer and grill until tender and lightly browned.

Blanch the ears of corn in boiling water for 3 minutes. Drain, cool, and cut the kernels off cobs. Toss the jalapeños in a skillet with the sesame oil, and toast lightly. Add the corn just before the peppers are done, stirring vigorously with a wooden spoon to separate the kernels. In a large bowl, combine the cooled roasted potatoes with the corn mixture. Add the tomatoes and parsley and toss with vinaigrette just before serving.

What I say is that, if a man really likes potatoes, he must be a pretty decent sort of fellow.

—A. A. Milne,
Not That It Matters,
1920

Balsamic-Dijon Vinaigrette
Makes 1/3 cup

2 tablespoons balsamic vinegar
2 teaspoons Dijon-style mustard
3 tablespoons extra virgin olive oil
1/2 teaspoon coarsely ground black pepper
Salt to taste (optional)

Whisk ingredients together in a mixing bowl.

Fennel Salad

Serves 8

This sprightly salad takes about 10 minutes to assemble.
For the fire-eaters in the crowd, add a small fresh habanero
or Scotch bonnet chile that's been seeded and finely
chopped.

1 bulb fresh fennel
1 small red onion, julienned
Sprinkle of salt
1 tablespoon balsamic vinegar
Juice of half lime
3 oranges, peeled and sliced
1 bunch watercress
3 tablespoons extra virgin olive oil
Sprigs of fennel tops, for garnish

Finely slice fennel bulb in a food processor. Mix together
all of the ingredients except the oranges, watercress, and
oil. Place on a serving platter and arrange the watercress
around the salad. Place the orange slices over the salad.
Garnish with fennel tops. Drizzle with the oil and serve.

The fennel is beyond every other vegetable, delicious. It greatly resembles in appearance the largest size celery, perfectly white, and there is no vegetable equals it in flavour. It is eaten at dessert, crude, and with, or without dry salt, indeed I preferred it to every other vegetable, or to any fruit.

—Thomas Jefferson,
Garden Book

Green Papaya Salad

Serves 6

This salad almost has the texture of cabbage, but is not as crunchy. It makes a light first course or can be served for dinner with tofu marinated in tamari, ginger, and rice wine vinegar. Be sure to use green, unripe papayas; do not substitute sweet, ripe papaya.

1 large unripe papaya (about 1 pound)
1 red bell pepper, julienned
Juice of 3 limes
2 tablespoons fish sauce (see note)
4 scallions, sliced diagonally
2 jalapeño chiles, seeded and finely diced
2 teaspoons black sesame seeds
1 bunch fresh cilantro, chopped, for garnish

Peel the papaya and finely shred in a food processor. In a large bowl, combine with the bell pepper, lime juice, fish sauce, scallions, and jalapeños, and toss well. Sprinkle with sesame seeds, garnish with cilantro, and serve.

Note: You may substitute a pinch of salt dissolved in 2 tablespoons of water for the fish sauce.

Cabbage, Apple, and Carrot Slaw with Habanero Vinaigrette

Serves 6

This slaw is best made a day ahead, which allows the flavors to blend and the cabbage to soften. It also can be served freshly made; it will simply be crunchier. For the vinaigrette, one habanero provides a subtle zest; two habaneros give it more potency. Any color pepper will do, but red habaneros provide pretty red flecks that contrast with the green and yellow colors of the salad.

Habanero Vinaigrette

1/4 cup light olive oil

2 tablespoons red wine vinegar

1/2 teaspoon salt

1 to 2 fresh red habaneros, stemmed, seeded, and minced

Freshly ground black pepper

Juice of 1 lemon

1/2 small (about 1 pound) green cabbage, chopped

2 carrots, peeled and grated

1 tart green apple

Freshly ground black pepper

In a medium-size bowl, combine the vinaigrette ingredients and whisk until blended. Add the cabbage and carrots and coat gently with the vinaigrette. Refrigerate for 8 hours. Just before serving, peel and grate the apple into the salad, dust the top with freshly ground black pepper, and toss.

> **The carrot serveth for love matters; and Orpheus, as Pliny writeth, said that the use thereof winneth love....**
>
> — John Gerardo, *The Herball*, 1636

Sherry-Pepper-Cucumber Yogurt Salad

Serves 4

Yeaton Outerbridge bottles sherry peppers on the island of Bermuda, following a long island tradition that began during the nineteenth century when Royal Navy sailors fortified casks of sherry with fiery peppers to make an all-purpose seasoning that would improve ship rations. The condiment took off with the locals, and "a cruet of homemade sherry peppers soon became a fixture on many a Bermudian side-board," according to Yeaton. For almost 50 years, the Outerbridge family has been bottling their special sherry pepper sauce with 17 herbs and spices.

Dressing

1 cup plain lowfat yogurt

2 teaspoons extra virgin olive oil

2 teaspoons chopped Outerbridge's Original Vinegar Peppers (see note)

Salt to taste

Freshly ground white pepper to taste

Pinch of minced fresh dill

1/4 to 1/2 teaspoon Outerbridge's Original Sherry Peppers Sauce (see note)

2 (8-inch) cucumbers, sliced

Combine dressing ingredients and let stand 1 hour or overnight in the refrigerator. Toss gently with the cucumbers and serve.

Note: Available from Mo Hotta, Mo Betta (see Mail-Order Sources, pages 342-344).

Spicy Sweet Cucumber Salad

Serves 4 to 6

Quick to make, this salad is surprising in flavor, with the sweet raisins countered by the slivered serranos.

1 large Red Delicious apple

Juice of 1 lemon

1 English hothouse cucumber, peeled, cut lengthwise, sliced into half-moons

1/4 cup walnut pieces

2 serrano or jalapeño chiles, seeded and sliced crosswise

2 tablespoons golden raisins

2 tablespoons extra virgin olive oil

1 lemon, cut into wedges

1 lime, cut into wedges

Freshly ground coarse kosher or sea salt

Finely dice apple, place in a small bowl, and drizzle with lemon juice. Toss to coat.

In a large bowl, combine the cucumber, apple, walnuts, chiles, and raisins. Arrange on a platter, and drizzle oil over the top. Serve with lemon and lime wedges and salt.

Vietnamese Cabbage Salad with Red Chile–Garlic Dressing

Serves 4 to 6

This salad is a perfect barbecue accompaniment to grilled sweet corn, marinated vegetables, and garden burgers. Or, for a healthy alternative to spring rolls, try this salad wrapped in green leaf lettuce with rice noodles and fresh mint. But beware: this Vietnamese salad is fiery! You can moderate the heat by adding less chile-garlic paste.

Red Chile–Garlic Dressing

2 to 3 tablespoons red chile-garlic paste or sauce

1/4 cup rice wine vinegar

2 tablespoons soy sauce

1 tablespoon minced fresh gingerroot

2 tablespoons sesame oil

Salad

1 small head green cabbage, finely sliced or shredded (about 6 cups)

1 carrot, julienned

Leaves of 1 small bunch fresh cilantro

1 teaspoon minced gingerroot

1 cup bean sprouts

1 bunch scallions, thinly sliced

1/3 cup roasted peanuts, finely chopped

To make dressing, in a large bowl combine all the dressing ingredients except the sesame oil. Mix well, then whisk in the oil. Add all salad ingredients except the peanuts. Toss with the dressing, and marinate for at least 1/2 hour. Top the salad with peanuts, and serve.

Tomato and Pita Bread Salad

Serves 6

This light, herbal Middle Eastern salad is a wonderful combination of toasted, crumbled pita tossed with lots of fresh greens and tomatoes. It's best to make the salad in advance to let the flavors mingle, adding the tomatoes and pita just before serving. This salad would serve four for lunch.

1 cucumber, peeled, seeded, and diced
6 scallions, finely chopped
1 bunch arugula, coarsely chopped
1 cup coarsely chopped watercress
1/2 cup chopped fresh flat-leaf parsley
1/2 cup chopped fresh mint

Vinaigrette

2 cloves garlic, minced
1/2 cup freshly squeezed lemon juice
1/3 cup extra virgin olive oil
1/2 teaspoon ground cayenne pepper
1/2 teaspoon ground cumin
1/4 teaspoon salt
2 medium tomatoes, diced
2 large whole-wheat pitas, split, toasted, and cut into
    1-inch squares

In a large bowl combine the cucumber, scallions, arugula, watercress, parsley, and mint. To make the vinaigrette, in a small bowl, combine the vinaigrette ingredients and stir until well blended. Toss the dressing with the cucumber mixture and let stand at room temperature at least 30 minutes. Add the tomatoes and pitas just before serving, and toss until blended.

Tuscan Tomato Salad

Serves 8 to 10

This fresh-tasting tomato salad is a good accompaniment to a rice dish and also makes a lively appetizer served on Bibb lettuce. For variety, if you have some hearty day-old bread, toast it briefly, cut it into 1/2-inch croutons, sprinkle with herbs, and toss into the salad just before serving. (Fire-eaters should try first brushing the bread with olive oil, grilling it, then lightly dusting the toast with ground cayenne pepper before cutting it into croutons. It's heavenly.) Perfectly ripened summer tomatoes make this salad marvelous, but the strong flavors of the capers, vinegar, and olives can also offset the unspectacular taste of any hothouse tomato.

10 diced plum tomatoes
1 cup semipacked chopped fresh basil leaves
1 small bunch fresh cilantro, chopped
1 cup mixed Provençal and kalamata olives, chopped
1/4 cup capers
1 small red onion, chopped

Garlic Vinaigrette
1/2 cup spiced garlic oil (see note)
1 teaspoon minced fresh garlic
1/4 cup balsamic vinegar
1 teaspoon coarsely ground black pepper
2 teaspoons red hot sauce
Parmesan cheese, for garnish (optional)

Combine the tomatoes, basil, cilantro, olives, capers, and onion.

In a separate bowl, whisk together the vinaigrette ingredients. Drizzle the vinaigrette over the tomato mixture a little at a time, tossing it to coat. If the tomatoes are juicy, you may not need all of the vinaigrette. Allow the salad to sit for about 10 minutes before serving. Garnish with Parmesan cheese.

Note: There are several varieties of flavored oils on the market. Or you can easily make your own (see page 322). If you're in a hurry, use extra virgin olive oil and add an extra minced garlic clove.

Leafy Greens with Jicama, Toasted Pine Nuts, and Raspberries

Serves 2 to 3

I'm not generally a fan of fruity salad dressings, but the lightness of the raspberries goes well with the crisp jicama and roasted pine nuts. For variety, add a bit of watercress and parsley, or substitute pomegranate seeds for the raspberries.

1/4 cup pine nuts

4 cups loosely packed mixed greens, rinsed and dried

1 cup jicama, peeled and julienned

Rosemary Serrano Vinaigrette (recipe follows)

16 to 20 fresh (or frozen) raspberries per person (if using frozen, bring to room temperature)

Preheat the oven to 350° (or turn a toaster oven to medium high) and toast the pine nuts on a baking sheet until you can smell them, about 8 minutes. Remove from the oven and set aside to cool. Combine the greens and jicama in a salad bowl, and toss with the vinaigrette. Transfer to individual salad plates, and sprinkle each salad with a handful of pine nuts and raspberries.

Rosemary Serrano Vinaigrette

4 teaspoons Rosemary-Serrano Red Wine Vinegar (see page 321), or substitute balsamic vinegar and 1/2 teaspoon fresh chopped rosemary

4 tablespoons extra virgin olive oil

2 cloves garlic, minced

Freshly ground black pepper

Pinch of salt

Whisk all of the ingredients together in a small bowl.

JICAMA

Big, gnarly, and brown, this bulbous root can be intimidating on first sight. Once peeled, you'll find crisp flesh that is white and moist, with the consistency of a hard pear. It's good in salads and makes a wonderful crudité when cut into thick long strips. Or do as they do in Mexico, serve thick slivers with a dusting of chile powder, a spritz of lime juice, and a shake of salt.

PINE NUTS

Driving in the fall on a mountain road from Albuquerque to Santa Fe, I was struck by the extraordinary smell of roasting pine nuts (*piñons*) in the air. Stopping at a small post office (which turned out to be a room in a woman's house) to buy some stamps, I was given a bagful of piñons by the kind postal clerk, who had collected them from under the trees that morning. My husband and I hunted for more ourselves beneath the branches of native pines, then drove along leisurely, cracking the seeds' hard shells and nibbling on them on our way to Santa Fe. The taste is a bit like that of almonds, though spicier and softer. Pine nuts are used in stuffings, pesto, and various baked dishes. They are delicious roasted (just toast them in the toaster oven for a few minutes) and make a beautiful garnish for soups, salads, and rice dishes.

Herbal Greens with Lemon-Ginger Vinaigrette

Serves 2 to 4

Mix various herbs into a salad to add interest and surprise. The mint lends a clean freshness.

6 cups loosely packed mixed greens
1/2 cup loosely packed fresh basil leaves, torn into pieces
1/4 cup whole fresh parsley leaves
1/4 cup whole fresh cilantro leaves
1/4 cup whole fresh mint leaves
Lemon-Ginger Vinaigrette (recipe follows)

Toss all of the ingredients with the vinaigrette in a large bowl, and serve.

Lemon-Ginger Vinaigrette
Makes 1/3 cup

3 tablespoons extra virgin olive oil
1 tablespoon freshly squeezed lemon juice
1/2 cup balsamic vinegar
1/2 teaspoon minced gingerroot
1 clove garlic, minced
Salt to taste
Freshly ground black pepper to taste

Whisk all of the ingredients together in a small bowl.

Mixed Greens with Fennel and Rosemary-Orange Vinaigrette

Serves 4

6 cups loosely packed mixed greens
1 small fennel bulb, cored and julienned
Rosemary-Orange Vinaigrette (recipe follows)

Toss the greens and enough vinaigrette to coat them in a large bowl and serve.

Rosemary-Orange Vinaigrette
Make 1/3 cup

6 tablespoons extra virgin olive oil
1 1/2 tablespoons balsamic vinaigrette
2 cloves garlic, minced
1/4 teaspoon minced orange or lemon zest
1/8 teaspoon ground cumin
Dash of salt
Several dozen rosemary needles, coarsely chopped

Whisk ingredients together in a small bowl.

Arugula with Roasted Red Peppers

Serves 4

Arugula has a spicy bite that provides a piquant counter-point to the sweet roasted red pepper. Tossed with a balsamic vinaigrette, it's a lively close to a meal.

5 cups loosely packed arugula leaves

1 cup fresh whole cilantro leaves

1 roasted red pepper, julienned

2 tablespoons capers

2 tablespoons balsamic vinegar

1/4 cup extra virgin olive oil

Wash and dry the arugula and cilantro leaves, then tear the arugula into large pieces. Combine greens, red pepper, and capers in a salad bowl. In a separate bowl, whisk together the vinegar and olive oil, then pour over salad and toss.

Bean and Grain Salads

Having spent a lot of time on boats, I'm a big fan of grain and bean salads, which are healthy, portable, and easily served on picnics, as an easy lunch, or as a colorful accompaniment to dinner. All of these salads will keep for several days when refrigerated.

Marinated Garbanzo Bean Salad

Serves 4

I was first served this salad on a brilliant summer afternoon by the sea in Amagansett, New York, where my friend Carol Govan made an elegant picnic with this salad, a bowl of olives, a roasted corn and potato salad, and grilled peasant bread. You can also make a pungent sandwich filling for warm pita bread by adding 1/2 cup plain yogurt to this salad to serve as a binder. Or create a dip with toasted pita wedges by adding the yogurt and running it briefly in a food processor, taking care that the garbanzo beans remain chunky.

2 1/2 cups cooked garbanzo beans (see note)

1/2 red onion, diced

1 1/2 cups loosely packed fresh cilantro leaves, coarsely chopped

4 tablespoons freshly squeezed lime juice

1/3 cup sesame oil

4 teaspoons ground cumin

2 teaspoons pure chile powder

Freshly ground black pepper

Combine all of the ingredients in a bowl, adjusting heat by adding more chile powder if desired. Refrigerate, and allow flavors to combine for at least 30 minutes before serving.

Note: The cooking time for garbanzo beans is found on page 333. You may substitute one 20-ounce can garbanzo beans; just be sure to rinse and drain the beans in cold water before combining with other ingredients.

Black Bean, Tomato, and Roasted Poblano Salad

Serves 6

Cool, colorful, and refreshing, this salad can be assembled quickly. It's ideal with winter grill menus or on a summer picnic. Poblano peppers look like green bell peppers, although they are darker green, sometimes more elongated, and slightly gnarled. They give this dish a pleasant kick without adding fire. (For a hotter salad, include the seeds or add a jalapeño pepper.)

2 poblano chiles

2 cups cooked black beans (see note)

1 cup cooked fresh corn kernels

1 cup coarsely chopped watercress

1 large, ripe tomato, diced

3 scallions, thinly sliced

Chile-Lime Vinaigrette

1/4 cup olive oil

1 tablespoon lime zest

2 tablespoons freshly squeezed lime juice

1 tablespoon Dijon-style mustard

1 teaspoon pure chile powder

1/2 teaspoon ground cumin

1/2 teaspoon salt

1/4 teaspoon crushed red pepper flakes

Snap off the chile stems, then roast the poblanos over a gas flame or under a broiler until the skins are lightly charred all over. Place the poblanos in a paper or plastic bag, cover, and let them steam for 15 to 20 minutes. Peel away the skin, and seed. Dice the peppers, then combine in a large bowl with the black beans, corn, watercress, tomato, and scallions.

In a small bowl, whisk together the vinaigrette ingredients. Pour over the salad and toss to coat. Serve chilled or at room temperature.

Note: The cooking time for black beans is found on page 333. You may substitute two 8-ounce cans black beans; just be sure to rinse and drain the beans in cold water before combining with other ingredients.

Black-Eyed Peas

Serves 6

Sometimes called "Texas Caviar," this is a refreshing, easy side dish for a summer grill menu. It also makes a terrific salad with a glass of white wine and a hunk of crusty bread. If you like yours hot, don't seed the jalapeños.

1/3 cup apple cider vinegar

1/4 cup olive oil

1 tablespoon granulated sugar

1 teaspoon salt

1/4 teaspoon ground cayenne pepper

6 cups cooked black-eyed peas (see note)

1 red onion, finely chopped

2 jalapeño chiles, seeded and minced

2 cloves garlic, minced

1/4 cup chopped fresh cilantro

1 hard-boiled egg, chopped, for garnish

In a large bowl, whisk together the cider vinegar, olive oil, sugar, salt, and cayenne pepper until blended. Stir in the black-eyed peas, onion, jalapeños, garlic, and cilantro, and toss to coat. Cover the bowl and refrigerate at least 2 hours to blend the flavors, stirring occasionally. Just before serving, garnish with the chopped egg.

Note: The cooking time for black-eyed peas is found on page 333. If using canned black-eyed peas, be sure to rinse and drain well.

Spicy Lentil and Feta Cheese Salad

Serves 4

Even those who don't generally like lentils are drawn to this robust salad. It's a perfect side dish or addition to a buffet table. Or turn it into an appetizer by filling endive leaves with it.

3 cups cooked lentils (see page 333)
1/4 cup finely chopped red onion
1 cup fresh parsley, chopped
1 large clove garlic, minced
1 teaspoon ground cayenne pepper
Juice of 1 lemon
1/4 cup extra virgin olive oil
1 cup crumbled feta cheese
Salt to taste (optional)

Combine lentils with red onion, parsley, garlic, cayenne powder, lemon, and olive oil. Mix well, then add the feta. Taste for salt; you may want to omit the salt as some feta cheeses are quite salty.

LENTILS

Native to Asia Minor, lentils have been culti-vated since before 7000 BC. They come from the pod of a small legume plant and are rich in pro-tein, iron, carbohydrates, and B vitamins. Lentils combine well with starches to create a satisfying meat-free meal and can be quite beautiful in color. Indian lentils range from pink to yellow and are more aromatic than brown American lentils. Unlike other legumes, lentils don't have to be soaked before cooking.

If you are using canned lentils, rinse them before combining with other ingredients. If you are cooking with dried lentils, see page 333 for cooking instruc-tions, and be sure to drain and reserve the cooking liquid as stock or broth for other recipes.

Brown Rice Salad with Black Beans and Corn

Serves 6 to 8

This hearty salad is good by itself or as an accompaniment to a grill menu, served with a hunk of watermelon on the side. Remember to allow time for soaking the beans overnight.

1 cup black turtle beans, picked over and washed

1 small yellow onion, cut in half

1 bay leaf

1 chipotle chile

Salt to taste

1/2 cup finely diced red onion

2 cloves garlic, finely chopped

3 tablespoons red wine vinegar

3 to 4 jalapeño peppers, roasted, peeled, seeded, and finely diced (see page 40)

1 1/2 teaspoons toasted cumin seed (see page 73)

1 cup uncooked long-grain brown rice

1 tablespoon vegetable oil

1/2 teaspoon turmeric

Freshly ground black pepper to taste

2 cups fresh corn kernels (4 to 5 ears)

1/2 cup chopped fresh cilantro

2 to 3 scallions shredded (about 1/2 cup)

1 large tomato, cut in half, seeded, and diced

Rinse the beans and soak in cold water to cover overnight. Drain the beans and cover with 1 quart fresh water. Add the onion, bay leaf, and chipotle. Bring to a boil over high heat, then reduce the heat to low and simmer gently for 1 1/2 hours, or until the beans are very tender. Add salt. Remove the chile and discard.

Cover the red onion with boiling water and set aside for 2 minutes. Drain and mix with the garlic, vinegar, jalapeños, and cumin. Drain the beans and add the marinade.

Cook the rice in 2 cups boiling salted water for 40 to 45 minutes until tender. Drain and immediately mix with the oil and turmeric. Add the pepper to taste. When cool, mix in the beans and corn. Fold in the cilantro, scallions, and diced tomatoes, and taste for seasoning.

Hot 'n' Dirty Rice Salad

Serves 6 to 8

This Cajun dish incorporates the "trinity," a revered combination of chopped, fresh ingredients (green bell peppers, celery, and onions) that have been used by bayou cooks for centuries to season gumbos, soups, and other foods. This salad is nutty, flavorful, and great for lunch.

2 tablespoons olive oil

1 yellow onion, diced

1 stalk celery, diced

1 green bell pepper, diced

1 clove garlic, minced

1/2 teaspoon ground cumin

1/2 teaspoon ground oregano

1/4 teaspoon ground cayenne pepper

3 cups cooked brown rice (see page 334)

1/2 pound button mushrooms, sliced

1 bunch scallions, thinly sliced

1/2 cup chopped fresh parsley

2 to 3 jalapeño peppers, seeded and minced

1/2 cup slivered almonds, toasted (see page 73)

1/2 cup coarsely chopped pecan halves, toasted

1/4 cup apple cider vinegar

1/4 cup Inner Beauty or other habanero hot sauce

1/4 cup olive oil

1 tablespoon Dijon-style mustard

1 teaspoon salt

1/2 teaspoon coarsely ground black pepper

Heat the olive oil in a medium skillet over medium-high heat. Add the onion, celery, bell pepper, and garlic and cook until very tender, but not browned. Stir in the cumin, oregano, and cayenne, and cook 1 minute. Remove the vegetables from heat and cool to room temperature.

In a large bowl, combine the cooked rice, mushrooms, scallions, parsley, jalapeños, almonds, and pecans. Stir in the cooled vegetable mixture until well blended. In a small bowl, whisk together the vinegar, hot sauce, oil, mustard, salt, and pepper. Stir the dressing into the rice mixture and toss to coat. Cover and refrigerate at least 1 hour before serving to blend flavors.

Botanically speaking, "grain" refers to several thousand species of grasses that have long been revered as the perfect food. In ancient Greece, all three meals often incorporated barley, which Greeks considered to be the staff of life. No wonder; whole grains contain many of the basic nutrients: water, carbohydrates, fats, protein, vitamins, minerals, and fiber.

When we speak of grains, we also include some pseudograins (like quinoa) that act like grain but are actually from other botanical families. Today, grains such as oats and rice are staples in most pantries, but an increasingly wide range of exotic grains— some the culinary legacy of ancient civilizations— are also available:

Amaranth: With tiny tan kernels about the size of a sesame seed, this ancient Aztec grain is strong, earthy, bitter, and slightly "corny." It is often ground into flour, but can be dry-roasted, then fried with vegetables or cooked into a "porridge" spiced up with ginger or garlic. It is the only grain with a respective amount of calcium; 1/2 cup dried provides 19 percent of one's recommended daily requirement.

Barley: With a subtle earthy flavor, barley is chewier than white rice and a good substitute for it. In health food stores, you'll find it available ground or sold as barley flakes (which resemble rolled oats and can be prepared as hot cereal or in baked goods), hulled barley (where only the outer hull has been removed, which makes it a good source of fiber and perfect for stews or thick soups), and pearl barley (which has been hulled and the bran removed, making it less nutritious than hulled barley, but also good in soups).

Buckwheat: Native to the Himalayas, white, unroasted buckwheat is mild and nutty tasting, and popular in pancakes or hot breakfast cereals. Toasted buckwheat (also known as kasha) is heartier and rather woody tasting. Rich in protein, iron, calcium, and vitamins B and E, kasha is good in croquettes, sauces, or in lieu of rice. Noodles made from buckwheat (called soba or buckwheat noodles) have a similar hearty, somewhat nutty taste.

Bulgur: Made by stripping whole-wheat berries of their hull and bran, bulgur is light and mild, with a wheaty flavor. Sometimes called cracked wheat, it goes well with vegetables, pilafs, nuts, and herbs and forms the basis of the Middle Eastern salad tabbouleh.

Corn: Corn is milled and ground into a meal or flour for baking, polenta, and porridges. The flavors vary; blue corn (sacred to the Hopis) is quite delicate, white corn is somewhat sweet, and yellow corn tastes, well, rather corny. In India and Mexico, masa refers to a finely ground yellow corn, and is used for making tortillas. A flour mix for making tortillas, called masa harina, is also available.

Couscous: A staple of North African cooking, couscous is made by stripping the wheat berry of its bran and germ, then grinding, steaming, and drying this semolina to form tiny round pellets. You'll find plain or whole-wheat couscous in many markets. Unlike other pastas, couscous is cooked like rice in a small amount of water that is completely absorbed by the grain.

Job's Tears: Named for the seed's tearlike shape, this ancient grain has been cultivated in China for four thousand years. The pearly white kernels yield a satiny, somewhat chewy texture. A good source of calcium and iron, and with more protein than brown rice, Job's Tears can be combined with rice or seasoned with strong spices such as ginger, chiles, or allspice.

Millet: Native to Africa, this small, yellow, sweet grain is gluten-free and packed with B vitamins, iron, potassium, phosphorus, and magnesium. Toast it before cooking for a nutty flavor and increased fluffiness, and serve it instead of rice. In India, it is called pearl millet and served as a cereal. Before cooking, be sure to rinse the grains to remove the bitter residue from the outer shell.

Oats: Soft, chewy, and lightly flavored, oats can be baked, marinated, or dry-roasted. Look beyond breakfast; use whole oats instead of rice in salads and soups.

Pasta: See page 97.

Quinoa: Light and tender, quinoa (keen-wa) is a grainlike product that cooks quickly and is high in protein and other vital nutrients. With a mild, slightly grassy taste, this whole protein is good in salads, pilafs, and soups. Uncooked it's about the size of a mustard seed, whereas when cooked, it puffs up and has a little white thread (the germ ring) dangling from the grain.

Rice: Cultivated in China more than three thousand years ago, rice has a rich history—Alexander the Great brought it to Greece, Dutch colonists brought it to West Africa in the 1400s, and the Crusaders introduced it to France. All rice can be divided into two types: long grain, whose chemical composition allows the grains to separate and remain fluffy while cooking (making it ideal for salads or side dishes) and short-grain, which sticks together and works well in soups, puddings, or creamy dishes like risotto. Within those two categories are many styles, including:

Arborio: A plump short-grain rice used for the Italian dish risotto (carnaroli or baldo rice can also be used in place of arborio). Typically arborio rice is not rinsed, which would remove the starch that is released during cooking and makes the dish so creamy.

G R A I N S

Basmati: An aromatic, flavorful, slightly nutty, long-grain variety from India and Pakistan. (A variety grown in Texas is called Texmati, while in California it's called Calmati.) When cooked, it looks white.

Brown rice: More nutritious and slightly crunchier than white rice, medium-grain brown rice has kept its bran coat and germ, with only the outer hull removed. Brown rice is longer and plumper than short-grain brown rice and sometimes stickier and chewier when cooked. Long-grain brown rice looks almost white when cooked and is more slender than the previous two; it works well in pilafs and fried rice.

Camolino rice: A polished rice with a light oil coat.

Puffed rice: In India, rice that is roasted and fried on hot sand.

Sticky rice: Short-grain rice (also called gluten rice or sweet brown rice) with a high starch content, used in Thai, Laotian, and Chinese cooking.

White rice: Brown rice that has been stripped of its germ and outer layers. Also called unpolished rice.

Wild rice: Cultivated from a wild aquatic grass (related to the rice plant) that grows in Minnesota, the Great Lakes region, and Canada. Dark, dense, and nutty, wild rice is expensive (much of it is still harvested by hand) and sometimes blended with brown rice. The grains can measure up to an inch long, and when cooked, they split open to reveal a pearl-colored interior surrounded by the brownish shell.

Wild pecan rice: Neither wild or pecan flavored, this hybrid from Louisiana has a nutty, buttery flavor.

Teff: Tiny ("teff" means lost in Ethiopian) and granular, with a sweet flavor, this grain is good combined with other grains or served as a breakfast cereal. In Ethiopia, it is often made into the flatbread *injera*.

Dry-roast grains by washing them thoroughly, then spreading them evenly on a flat baking sheet, then baking them in a 350° oven, stirring periodically, until the moisture is evaporated and the fragrance is evident. Grains should be stored in airtight containers in the refrigerator, where they will stay fresh about five months. (Left on the pantry shelf in paper bags from the health food store, they will stay fresh about 1 month.) Or freeze grains for an indefinite period of time (with the exception of oats, which have a higher fat ratio and will keep fresh for only 3 months or so). For cooking times of grains, see page 334.

G R A I N S

Bulgur Salad with Corn, Garbanzo Beans, and Walnuts

Serves 8

This is a filling salad with heat from the jalapeños, spicy undertones of sweet fennel seed and cumin, and lots of texture. It is good served on a bed of greens (arugula, romaine, and cress) with thick slices of fresh garden tomatoes and hard-cooked eggs. Here the corn is served raw, but you can also use cooked corn. If you can find red jalapeños, use them instead of green ones for added color.

1 cup bulgur

1 cup boiling water

2 teaspoons cumin seed

1 1/2 teaspoons fennel seed

Kernels of 4 ears sweet corn (about 3 cups)

4 tablespoons freshly squeezed lime juice

1 tablespoon apple cider vinegar

1 teaspoon salt

1/3 cup vegetable oil

4 to 6 jalapeños, roasted, peeled, seeded (if you like less heat), and finely chopped (see page 40)

1 small red onion, finely chopped

1 cup diced fennel bulb

1/2 cup chopped fresh cilantro

2 cups cooked garbanzo beans (see note)

1 cup chopped toasted walnuts (see page 73)

10 cups loosely packed mixed greens (optional)

Tomato slices, for garnish (optional)

Combine the bulgur and water in a large bowl and set aside for 1 hour until the liquid is absorbed. Toast the cumin and fennel in a pan over medium heat, then cool and grind in a spice grinder. Combine the corn, lime juice, vinegar, salt, oil, jalapeños, onion, and fennel in a bowl. Stir in the toasted spices and cilantro.

Add the garbanzo beans to the corn mixture. Add the bulgur and stir well to combine. Set aside to marinate, stirring occasionally, for 30 minutes before serving. Just before serving, stir in the walnuts.

Serve the salad on a bed of the mixed greens and garnish with tomato slices.

Note: The cooking time for garbanzo beans is found on page 333. You may substitute one 15-ounce can garbanzo beans; just be sure to rinse and drain the beans in cold water before combining with other ingredients.

Wild Pecan Rice and Dried Cranberry Salad

Serves 4 to 6

Wild pecan rice has a wonderful nutlike aroma and woodsy taste, which makes it ideal for hearty salads. Toasting the rice before adding the liquid enhances the flavor and keeps grain more separate when cooked. This salad is startling with its sweet-tart pull from the cranberries, followed by a delayed bite from the spicy dressing. As this salad sits, it takes on a beautiful ruby blush coloring. It can be made a day ahead and garnished just before serving. Also, all the components of the salad can be made and stored separately, then blended just before serving for a more vibrant and distinctive flavor. This salad makes a pretty fall dish and is perfect for Thanksgiving.

1 1/2 cups dried cranberries

1 cup apple cider, warmed

1 tablespoon canola oil

1 7-ounce package mild pecan rice

2 cups water

1 1/2 teaspoon mustard powder

1/2 teaspoon ground cayenne pepper

1/4 teaspoon ground allspice

1 teaspoon kosher salt

2 tablespoons brown rice vinegar (unseasoned)

1/3 cup canola oil

2 teaspoons mustard seeds

1 teaspoon coriander seeds

1 teaspoon black peppercorns

1/2 cup coarsely chopped pecans, toasted (see page 73)

1 cup thinly sliced scallions

2 tablespoons orange zest, for garnish

3 tablespoons chopped fresh cilantro leaves, for garnish

In a small bowl, cover the cranberries with warm cider. Set aside for 1/2 hour to soften and plump. Drain and discard liquid.

In a medium stockpot, heat the canola oil over medium heat and add the rice. Stir to coat the grains with oil. Continue to heat, stirring often, until the grains turn golden, about 3 minutes. Slowly add the water, cover, and reduce the heat to medium-low. Cook until the liquid is absorbed and the rice is tender, approximately 20 minutes. Remove from the heat, uncover, and set aside to cool.

In a small bowl, whisk the mustard powder, cayenne, allspice, salt, vinegar, and oil to blend well. In a small cast-iron skillet, heat (without oil) the mustard seeds, coriander seeds, and peppercorns over medium-high heat about 1 to 2 minutes, or until fragrant, shaking constantly to prevent burning. Transfer to a mortar and pestle or spice grinder and crush slightly. Add to the dressing. Taste and adjust seasoning if desired.

In a large mixing bowl, toss the rice with the pecans, scallions, and cranberries. Add the dressing and mix well to distribute the spices. Garnish with orange zest and cilantro. Serve chilled or at room temperature.

SOWING YOUR OATS

Grains have played strong roles in religious ceremonies throughout the ages. German priests incorporated oats into spring fertility rituals to the goddess Nertho, which eventually led to the saying, "sowing your wild oats." And rice is still showered on newlyweds to encourage happiness and babies.

Golden Millet Salad with Lemon-Wasabi Dressing

Serves 6

Millet is a staple grain in many cultures throughout the world, but it is still little known in this country—except for use as birdseed! Cultivated since ancient times, millet has a sweet cornlike flavor that works well in salads, especially because it remains fluffy after cooking when the grains are pretoasted. If you want to make this salad ahead, toss in the beans, radishes, and scallions at the last minute so they remain crisp.

1 cup millet, rinsed and drained

2 cups Vegetable Stock (see page 75)

5 sprigs fresh thyme

1/2 pound fresh green beans (or a mix of green and yellow wax beans), trimmed, blanched, and cut on the diagonal into 1/2-inch lengths

1 bunch scallions, trimmed and thinly sliced

2 bunches radishes, trimmed and sliced into paper-thin rounds

2 tablespoons minced lemon zest

1/2 teaspoon kosher salt

1 teaspoon freshly ground black pepper

Dressing

1 tablespoon wasabi powder

1 tablespoon freshly squeezed lemon juice

1 tablespoon rice wine vinegar (unseasoned)

6 tablespoons safflower oil

1/2 teaspoon kosher salt

1/2 cup toasted sliced almonds, for garnish (see page 73)

Place a medium stockpot on medium-high heat. Add the millet, and shake the pot or stir vigorously at first to keep the grains from sticking. Toast the grains about 3 minutes, or until fragrant and dry, stirring often. Slowly add the stock and thyme. Cover tightly, reduce heat to medium-low and simmer about 20 minutes, or until millet is tender and liquid is absorbed. Remove stockpot from heat and set aside, covered, about 10 to 15 minutes. Then turn into a large bowl to cool further, and stir with a fork to separate the grains. Remove stems of thyme sprigs and discard (the leaves will remain to flavor the salad). Add green beans, scallions, 2/3 of the radishes, lemon zest, salt, and pepper, reserving about 1/3 of the radish slices to julienne and use for garnish. Toss gently.

To prepare dressing, in a medium bowl stir the wasabi powder with lemon juice and set aside for 5 to 10 minutes to mellow. Add remaining ingredients and whisk to emulsify. Cover and refrigerate until using.

To prepare salad, toss dressing with millet mixture. Taste for salt. Julienne the remaining radish slices and sprinkle over salad. Sprinkle with almond slices. Cover and refrigerate until ready to serve. Serve cold or at room temperature.

WASABI

Although sometimes called Japanese horseradish, wasabi is unrelated to horseradish other than that they are both roots that have a pungent kick. From Asia, wasabi has a fierce bite and sinus-clearing aroma, and is often found ground or in the form of a paste.

Quinoa Salad with Ginger, Lemongrass, and Seasonal Fruit

Serves 6

Serve this salad for brunch or as a first course; you'll find that the peppery bite of the watercress complements the fruit's sweetness. For variety, substitute other fruit such as apples, papaya, or pears.

3 stalks fresh lemongrass

1 cup quinoa

1 inch-length gingerroot, peeled and cut in half

2 cups water

2 cups seedless red and green grapes, halved

4 serrano chiles, seeded and minced

2 teaspoons minced lime zest

Juice of 1 large lime

1/4 cup canola oil

1 teaspoon kosher salt

3/4 teaspoon ground white pepper

3/4 teaspoon Five-Spice Powder (see page 310)

1 tablespoon minced gingerroot

2 bunches watercress, rinsed, dried, and trimmed of stems

3 medium bananas, sliced on the diagonal about 1/4 inch thick

3 medium pink or ruby red grapefruit, peeled, seeded, and sectioned, with all white pith removed

2 tablespoons minced fresh chives, for garnish

Remove outermost peel of lemongrass stalks. Trim root end and about 3 inches of the top to remove the tough, dry end. With a kitchen mallet or the dull edge of a chef's knife, gently but firmly pound the stalks to soften the fibers, which will enable the delicate, lemony flavor and fragrance to be released during simmering. Set aside.

In a fine-mesh sieve, rinse the quinoa thoroughly under cool water until it runs clear (about 1 to 2 minutes). Place in a medium stockpot with the 1-inch piece of ginger, lemongrass stalks, and water. Cover. Bring to a boil and reduce heat and simmer, covered, over medium-low heat until the grains are translucent, the germ ring within each grain is visible (it will look like a spiraling white thread), and all the liquid has been absorbed, about 10 to 15 minutes. Do not overcook, or the grains will become mushy. Place in a large

My sister, you grain—

its beer is tasty, my

comfort.

—*Song of Songs*, 2100 BC

bowl, discarding the ginger and lemongrass. Stir to fluff and separate the grains, then set aside to cool.

Add the grapes, serrano chiles, and lime zest to the bowl and mix well. In a small bowl, whisk the lime juice, oil, salt, white pepper, five-spice powder, and minced ginger. Remove 2 tablespoons of the dressing and set aside for garnish. Toss the remaining dressing with the quinoa mix, blending well. Chill thoroughly.

To serve, distribute watercress leaves among salad plates. Place alternating banana slices and grapefruit sections over the leaves. Spoon a portion of quinoa salad onto each plate and garnish with chives. Drizzle the reserved dressing over the fruit pieces and serve. (Or arrange in a similar manner on a large decorative platter.)

THE MOTHER GRAIN

While recently "discovered" in this country, quinoa (pronounced keen-wah) was a staple of the ancient Inca civilization (where it was called the Mother Grain) and has been cultivated for the last five thousand years. Nutritionally it is a superstar and, though not technically a grain, quinoa is a grainlike product and used similarly. With a light, delicate flavor, it tastes good in salads, soups, pilafs, mixed vegetables, or rice puddings. It blends well with hot or cold foods, fluffs up nicely when cooked (particularly good in summer salads), and can be substituted for most grains in your favorite dishes.

Small, oval, and slightly flattened, quinoa has a bitter coating (called saponin) that serves as a natural insect repellent, and must be removed with a strong alkaline solution before cooking. Most quinoa sold in North America has already been cleansed of saponin, although the grains should be rinsed under cold running water for several minutes before cooking to remove any of the rust-colored residue.

Found in health food stores and gourmet shops, quinoa is pricier than other grains, but it bulks up to four times its uncooked volume during cooking. Toasting the grain in a skillet or toaster oven for a few minutes before cooking will impart a pleasing nutty flavor.

Fruit and Vegetable Sides

From Grilled Apricots and Cactus Pear to Turnip, Fennel, and Orange Gratin, this chapter focuses on fruit and vegetable dishes that are tasty accompaniments for the evening meal. Special techniques (such as roasting), enticing ingredients (like chiles and curries), and favorite combinations (like spaghetti squash and roasted peppers) add depth and flavor to fruits as well as a variety of root and vine vegetables. Seasonal favorites are included, such as corn on the cob, which is given a twist with chipotle-enhanced butter, as well as hearty winter comforts like Mustard-Glazed Roasted Root Vegetables.

Grilled Pineapple with Passion Fruit–Habanero Butter

Serves 4

Pineapple is a good addition to grilled vegetables, especially when combined with a bean or grain salad. The Passion Fruit-Habanero Butter provides a fruity heat that is delicious.

6 tablespoons Habanero Butter (see page 312), or 5 tablespoons butter and 1 tablespoon Caribbean hot sauce

1 tablespoon passion fruit syrup, mango syrup, or other tropical fruit syrup

Juice of 1/2 lime

1 large ripe pineapple

Prepare a grill. Melt the habanero butter in a small saucepan and add the syrup and lime juice. Cut the pineapple lengthwise into quarters, keeping the leaves on the pineapple for decoration. Brush each side with the butter and grill, turning after 2 to 5 minutes, and basting occasionally. Place on a serving platter and drizzle any remaining butter over the pineapple.

Note: Passion fruit syrup is the concentrated pulp of the fruit, often combined with sugar or corn syrup. The syrup can be found in Caribbean stores and markets and is increasingly available in gourmet shops.

> The flesh of the pineapple melts into water and it is so flavourful that one finds in it the aroma of the peach, the apple, the quince and the muscat grape. I can call it with justice the king of fruits because it is the most beautiful and best of all those of the earth.
>
> —Père du Tertre, 1595

Grilled Apricots and Cactus Pear

Serves 4

When brushed with hot sauce and then grilled, many fruits are transformed from sweet nothings into a spicy-sweet dish with spine. I like to use colorful, unusual fruit and experiment with what's available at the grocery store. Feijoa is a South American fruit with the flavor of strawberries and pineapple and is sometimes referred to as pineapple guava. The cactus pear, with its gorgeous cranberry red flesh, tastes a bit like sour cherries. Your friends will be impressed by this exotic dish!

2 apricots, pitted and cut in half

4 baby bananas, or 1 regular banana, peeled

2 feijoas, skinned and cut in half

2 cactus pears, dethorned, skinned, and cut in half

2 tablespoons Jump Up and Kiss Me Hot Sauce with Passion
   or other habanero hot sauce

Prepare a grill. Brush the fruit with a very thin coating of hot sauce and grill the fruit 2 to 3 minutes per side. Serve immediately.

I am a great eater of

beef, and I believe that

does harm to my wit.

—Shakespeare

Fried Plantains

Serves 6

A type of banana, plantains are starchier than fruit bananas and always served cooked. Popular in Indian, Caribbean, and South African cooking, they are often fried or mashed and go well with tropical fruit salsas like the Caribbean Sun-Splashed Salsa on page 63. With their greenish yellow mottled skin, plantains are often found hanging in clusters in tropical markets and are worth trying!

1/2 to 1 cup vegetable oil

4 yellow plantains, peeled and cut in 1-inch slices

3 cloves garlic, chopped

2 cups water

Caribbean Sun-Splashed Salsa (see page 63)

Fresh lime wedges

Heat the oil in a heavy skillet. Brown the plantains on each side and drain on paper towels. Once all the plantains are browned, smash them flat with the palm of your hand. Place the chopped garlic in a bowl with the water. Dip the plantains into the garlic water, then fry them again on both sides. Drain on paper towels and serve, still warm, with the salsa and lime wedges.

Braised Winter Greens with Golden Raisins and Walnuts

Serves 6

This is an interpretation of the Indian approach to cooking greens, by which they are puréed and cooked with spices for a long time until silky smooth. In this dish, you'll find a coarsely textured mixture of pungent greens spiked with chiles, tempered with cream, and sweetened with golden raisins. The walnuts added at the end provide a nice crunchy texture. Serve these greens with rice on the side for a savory meal.

3 tablespoons golden raisins (sultanas) or diced apricots

3/4 pound collard greens, stemmed and shredded (about 6 loosely packed cups)

3/4 pound Swiss chard, stemmed and shredded (about 6 loosely packed cups)

3/4 pound mustard greens, stemmed and shredded (about 6 loosely packed cups)

2 tablespoons oil

1 large leek, white and light green parts, finely sliced (about 1 1/4 cups)

4 to 6 serrano chiles, seeded and finely chopped

1 red bell pepper, seeded and cut into 1/4-inch dice

1 tablespoon finely chopped gingerroot

2 cloves garlic

1/2 teaspoon ground turmeric

1 teaspoon ground cumin

1/8 teaspoon ground cloves

1 cup heavy cream

1/2 cup toasted chopped walnuts (see page 73)

Cut the raisins in half and place them in a bowl. Add boiling water to cover and set aside to soak. Meanwhile, steam the collard greens until completely wilted, about 10 minutes. Cool under running cold water, and drain. Squeeze out the excess moisture, chop coarsely, and set aside. Steam the Swiss chard and mustard greens separately until completely wilted, about 5 minutes. Cool and squeeze excess moisture as described above, chop coarsely, and set aside.

Heat the oil in a large, nonreactive frying pan over medium-high heat. Add the leek, serranos, and bell pepper, and sauté until softened, about 5 minutes. Add the ginger, garlic, and spices, and cook, stirring until fragrant, about 2 minutes. Add the greens to the pan, reduce the heat to medium and cook, stirring frequently, until most of the moisture is evaporated, about 10 minutes. Season with salt. Add the cream to the pan and simmer for 10 minutes, stirring occasionally, until it is absorbed. Add the walnuts and serve.

Swiss Chard with Channa Dal

Serves 6

This dish evolved from my friend Liz Wheeler's experimentation with an abundance of greens from the Holcomb Farm Community Supported Agriculture project in Granby, Connecticut. The channa dal (yellow split peas) may require a longer cooking time than is indicated, depending on their age.

Yogurt Sauce

2 cups plain yogurt

1/4 cup heavy cream

1 clove garlic, finely chopped or pressed

Salt to taste

2 teaspoons finely shredded fresh mint (optional)

1 cup channa dal (yellow split peas), picked clean and washed

1 bay leaf

1/4 teaspoon ground turmeric

1/4 teaspoon salt

6 tablespoons olive oil

1 1/2 cups thinly sliced onions (about 2 medium onions)

3 red Anaheim or cubanelle chiles

1 tablespoon chopped serrano or Thai chiles

4 cloves garlic, thinly sliced

1/2 teaspoon ground coriander

1/2 teaspoon ground cumin

2 large bunches (about 2 pounds) Swiss chard, steamed and sliced crosswise into 1/4-inch ribbons

Salt to taste

Freshly ground black pepper to taste

    To make the sauce, drain the yogurt by spooning it into a coffee filter cone lined with a dry paper filter or in a sieve lined with several thicknesses of cheesecloth or a clean linen towel. Allow to drain for about 1 hour; the yogurt will be thickened but still soft. Transfer the yogurt to a bowl and stir in the cream and garlic. Add salt to taste, stir in the mint, and set aside.

    Put the channa dal, bay leaf, and turmeric in a saucepan with enough water to cover by a little less than 3/4 inch. Bring to a boil over high heat. Reduce heat to simmer, partially cover, and cook for 30 minutes. Set aside for 10 minutes, or until the channa dal have absorbed most of the water and are tender but still hold their shape. Add 1/4 teaspoon salt.

Put 2 tablespoons of the oil in a 4-quart heavy saucepan with a tight-fitting lid. Over medium heat, stir in the onion, chiles, and garlic, and cook, stirring, until softened, about 5 minutes. Add the coriander and cumin and simmer until aromatic, about 3 to 4 minutes. Add the channa dal and their liquid and simmer until tender, from 10 to 20 minutes.

Heat 1 tablespoon of the oil in a large skillet over medium-high heat. Add 1/4 of the chard and turn it in the oil to coat the leaves. Salt lightly and continue turning the leaves until they are wilted. Transfer to the dal mixture and mix gently. Cook the remaining chard in the same manner, using 1 tablespoon of oil for each quarter portion of chard; add each batch to the dal and stir to combine. Season the mixture with salt and pepper. Simmer, stirring occasionally, for about 30 minutes. Serve warm or at room temperature with the Yogurt Sauce. Serve a few spoonfuls of sauce with each serving of greens.

Spaghetti Squash with Roasted Peppers

Serves 4 to 6

This spicy, colorful dish is relatively low in fat. For another dimension, serve with a little crumbled feta cheese or firm, crumbly goat cheese. Fresh shredded basil may be used in addition to or in place of the chopped parsley.

1 (3- to 3 1/2-pounds) spaghetti squash

1 red bell pepper

1 green bell pepper

1 yellow bell pepper

3 jalapeño peppers (or 1 jalapeño, 1 serrano, and 1 hot chile pepper of your choice)

2 tablespoons olive oil

1 yellow onion, thinly sliced lengthwise

3 cloves garlic, finely chopped

1 teaspoon finely chopped fresh rosemary needles

1/2 cup dry white wine

1/2 cup finely chopped fresh parsley

1/3 cup pitted and slivered black oil-cured olives

Salt to taste

Freshly ground black pepper to taste

1/2 cup diced fresh tomato or quartered cherry tomatoes, for garnish

Prick the squash in several places with a sharp knife. Place a steamer rack in a large pot with a tight-fitting lid over several inches of boiling water. Steam squash for about 45 minutes, or until the squash can be pierced through with a sharp knife. Set aside to cool. When the squash is cool, slice it lengthwise, scoop out and discard the seeds. With a fork, draw out the squash strands, pulling lengthwise, and pile them on an ovenproof platter or casserole dish. Set the squash aside.

Roast the bell peppers and jalapeño peppers under the broiler or over an open flame until the skins are blackened, then set aside in a sealed paper or plastic bag for 15 to 20 minutes. Remove the charred skin, then core and seed them.

Cut the peppers into 1/4-inch dice, combine in a bowl, and set aside.

Heat the oil in a large frying pan over medium-high heat. Add the onion, garlic, and rosemary and cook, stirring frequently, until softened, about 3 minutes. Add the wine and simmer until it is reduced by half. Stir in the peppers, 5 tablespoons of the parsley, and the olives. Season with salt and pepper, and reduce the heat to low. Cover and simmer gently for a few minutes until heated through, then remove from the heat.

Preheat the oven to 300° and reheat the squash for 10 to 15 minutes, or heat it in the microwave for 1 minute. Toss with the roasted pepper mixture and sprinkle with the diced tomato and the remaining 3 tablespoons of parsley.

And God said: Behold I have given you every herb-bearing seed upon the earth, and all trees that have in themselves seed of their own kind, to be your meat.

Genesis, 1:29

Roasted Pumpkin with Amaranth

Serves 4 to 6

A staple of the Aztec diet eight thousand years ago, amaranth is a tiny grain high in protein and fiber. It adapts to many dishes and retains a crunchy texture and nutlike taste whether ground into flour or simmered as other grains. If you've never cooked with amaranth, don't miss this opportunity—I guarantee you'll love it! Serve this pilaf as a side dish, or tuck it into a warm flour tortilla for a sandwich.

2 ears fresh corn

1 tablespoon unsalted butter

1 tablespoon olive oil

1 tablespoon pure chile powder

1 teaspoon ground cumin

1 teaspoon salt

1 teaspoon dried thyme

2 pound sugar pumpkin, peeled, seeded, and diced into 1/2-inch cubes (about 5 1/2 cups)

1/2 cup amaranth

1 1/2 cups Vegetable Stock (see page 75) or water

1 (3-inch) stick cinnamon

2 teaspoons olive oil

1 red bell pepper, diced small

1 small yellow onion, chopped small

1/2 teaspoon crushed red pepper flakes

1/2 cup fresh whole cilantro leaves

Bring stockpot of water to boil. Add corn and blanch for 5 minutes. Remove ears, shock in cold water, and pat dry. Cut kernels off ears and set aside.

Preheat oven to 375°. In a large roasting pan, place butter and oil. In a small bowl, mix the chile powder, cumin, salt, and thyme. Add the pumpkin cubes and spices to the butter and oil, and stir well to coat. Heat the pumpkin in the oven, uncovered, about 20 minutes. Stir with a spatula, taking care not to break up the pumpkin. Bake an additional 25 minutes until tender and golden.

Meanwhile, place the amaranth grains in a cold medium saucepan. Turn heat to medium-high and toast the grains until they are golden and fragrant, about 4 to 5 minutes, shaking the pan or stirring constantly. (You will hear a crackling sound as the grains heat through, but continue to shake the pan or stir to prevent the grains from popping.) Slowly add the stock as well as the cinnamon stick, cover the saucepan, bring to a boil, then reduce heat to medium-low and simmer about 25 minutes, or until the liquid has been absorbed and the grains are tender. Remove the cinnamon stick.

In a large, nonstick skillet, heat the olive oil over medium-high heat. Add the bell pepper, onion, corn, and pepper flakes. Sauté, uncovered, until tender-crisp, about 3 to 5 minutes. Add the pumpkin and amaranth and stir to blend. Stir in the cilantro and serve. (At this point, the mixture can be placed in a 9-inch ovenproof baking dish and kept warm in a 375° oven until ready to serve.)

Spanish-Style Mushrooms in Green Sauce

Serves 4

This dish is typical of what is served at tapas bars and restaurants in Spain. Tapas translates into "small tastes" and is a perfect snack at sunset with a drink (especially since dinner often is not served until 11 P.M. in Spain!) This is an easy dish that can be prepared ahead of time and reheated when ready to serve as an appetizer or side dish. It can also be served over pasta or hearty bread such as pan de campagne. Big in taste, it has good strong flavors, with a hint of a bite at the end.

4 tablespoons olive oil

2 tablespoons unsalted butter

1 pound small button mushrooms, quartered

1/4 cup finely chopped yellow onion

4 cloves garlic, minced

4 teaspoons flour

1/2 cup white wine

1/4 cup Vegetable Stock (see page 75)

2 tablespoons milk

1/2 cup minced fresh parsley, plus additional, for garnish

1 tablespoon crushed red pepper flakes

2/3 cup oil-cured olives, pitted

1/2 teaspoon salt

Lemon slices, for garnish

In a sauté pan, heat 2 tablespoons of the olive oil and the butter. When butter is melted, add mushrooms and sauté over medium heat until browned all over. Remove mushrooms from pan and keep warm. In same pan, heat the remaining 2 tablespoons of olive oil and sauté the onion until wilted. Stir in the garlic and the flour, and cook for 1 minute. Gradually pour in the wine, stock, and milk. Stir to combine, then add the remaining ingredients. Add the mushrooms, stir, and serve garnished with the additional parsley and lemon slices.

Portobello Mushrooms with Poblano Chiles

Serves 4

Rich in flavor and texture, portobello mushrooms stand out amidst other ingredients. This simple sauté works well served as a side dish or over pasta. Or serve it on French bread, topped with asiago cheese and broiled.

2 tablespoons olive oil

2 large portobello mushrooms, sliced in 1/4-inch slices

2 medium poblano chiles, julienned

1 yellow onion, julienned

1 shallot, minced

Juice of 1 lime

1 tablespoon balsamic vinegar

2 teaspoons crushed red pepper flakes

Salt to taste

Freshly ground black pepper to taste

In a large sauté pan, heat the oil on medium-high heat. Add the mushrooms and cook approximately 5 minutes, stirring and turning constantly. Add the poblanos, onion, and shallot and stir to combine. Cover and cook for another 3 minutes. Remove cover and add remaining ingredients. Stir and cook for 5 minutes, or until mushrooms are tender.

Stir-Fried Sweet Corn with Green Beans and Chiles

Serves 4

Every August, when the corn in the Berkshire Hills gets high, locals eagerly await the arrival of a local farmer's crop and delight when hand-lettered cardboard signs announcing PALMER CORN appear in shop windows, convenience stores, and gas stations. Of course, you can also drive up to Charlie Palmer's farm, pick up a few fresh ears, and leave your quarters in the cigar box on the table at the end of his driveway. The corn is so succulent and sweet that we eat it every night when it's available.

2 tablespoons vegetable oil

2 cloves garlic, minced

1/2 pound green beans, cut at a diagonal into 1-inch lengths

2 to 3 jalapeño peppers, cut in half, quartered, seeded, and sliced thinly crosswise

1 large red bell pepper, cut in half, seeded, and sliced crosswise 1/4 inch thick (about 1 cup)

4 ears fresh sweet corn, kernels cut from cobs

6 tablespoons water

1 teaspoon granulated sugar

2 tablespoons light soy sauce

1 teaspoon cornstarch

1 tablespoons freshly squeezed lemon juice

4 tablespoons shredded fresh basil

Freshly ground black pepper

Heat the oil in a large skillet over medium-high heat. Add the garlic and cook, stirring until pale gold. Add the beans and stir-fry for 1 minute. Add the jalapeños and bell pepper and stir-fry for 2 minutes, until softened but still crunchy. Add the corn and 2 tablespoons of the water, the sugar, and soy sauce. Cook, stirring, for 1 minute. Dissolve the cornstarch in the remaining 4 tablespoons of water, and add to the skillet. Simmer for 30 seconds until a clear glaze forms. Stir in the lemon juice and basil and season to taste with pepper. Serve immediately.

Corn with Poblanos and Cilantro

Serves 4 to 6

The heat of poblano chiles can vary from plant to plant. I've had poblanos that were as mild as a green bell pepper and others that were almost fiery. Removing the seeds and veins will lessen the wallop. This side dish is good served with grilled zucchini and tomatoes.

1 tablespoon olive oil

1 yellow onion, finely chopped

1 clove garlic, minced

2 poblanos, seeded and diced

4 cups uncooked fresh corn kernels

1/4 cup half-and-half

1/2 teaspoon salt

1/4 teaspoon coarsely ground black pepper

3 tablespoons chopped fresh cilantro

Ground cumin (optional)

In a large skillet, heat the olive oil over medium-high heat. Add the onion and garlic and cook until the onion is tender, about 5 minutes. Add the poblanos, corn, half-and-half, salt, and black pepper and heat to boiling. Reduce heat to medium and cook, stirring occasionally, until the corn is tender, 3 to 5 minutes. Remove from heat and stir in the chopped cilantro. Dust lightly with cumin, if desired. Serve immediately.

Corn on the Cob
with Chipotle-Tequila Butter

Serves 4

A summertime favorite, this is good served with a fresh tomato salad, olive tapenade on grilled bread, and big hunks of watermelon.

4 ears fresh sweet corn

4 tablespoons Chipotle-Tequila Butter (see page 311)

Salt to taste

Place the corn in a large stockpot of boiling water and cook until tender, 3 to 5 minutes. Drain and serve immediately, passing the Chipotle Butter and salt at the table. Or cut the kernels off the cooked ears and sauté them for a few minutes with the chipotle butter, salt, and black pepper.

Note: For a variation, boil the ears for 2 minutes, drain, and cook over live coals for a few minutes more to give the corn a roasted flavor, then brush with Chipotle Butter and shake on salt.

Hominy Stir-Fry with Southwest Pepper Confetti

Serves 4

Made by soaking dried corn kernels in a lime solution to remove the germ and skin, hominy on its own is rather bland but takes well to various seasonings. Canned yellow or white hominy is readily available in the ethnic section of most supermarkets and may be labeled posole (or pozole), after the popular Southwestern stew. This very spicy stir-fry also goes well with scrambled eggs and looks great served in a terra-cotta or brightly colored bowl.

1 tablespoon olive oil

1 cup medium-diced green bell pepper

1 cup medium-diced red bell pepper

2 large jalapeños, seeded and chopped

2 large cloves garlic, coarsely chopped

1 tablespoon unsalted butter

1 teaspoon pure chile powder

1 teaspoon ground cumin

2 15 1/2-ounce cans white and/or yellow hominy, rinsed and drained well (about 3 cups)

1 teaspoon salt

1/2 teaspoon freshly ground black pepper

Chopped fresh cilantro, for garnish

Lime wedges, for garnish

Place oil in a large skillet over medium-high heat. Add the bell peppers and jalapeños and sauté, uncovered, until the peppers begin to soften but still retain their color, about 3 minutes. Add garlic and sauté 1 additional minute. (The moisture should also be reduced while stirring.) Transfer mixture to a shallow bowl and keep warm.

Melt butter in the same skillet over medium heat. Add the chile powder and cumin and stir to release their fragrance. Add the hominy and stir to coat the kernels. Very loosely cover the skillet with a piece of foil. With a wooden spoon stir the hominy often until it is heated through and you hear the kernels popping, about 3 to 5 minutes. (The foil keeps the popping kernels in the pan.) Do not allow moisture to build up. Uncover and add the bell pepper mixture. Add the salt and black pepper and adjust the seasoning. Serve garnished with fresh cilantro and a few squirts of lime juice.

Carrots with Jalapeños and Ginger

Serves 4 to 6

Be sure to use sweet, flavorful carrots for this simple salad. As a variation, add 2 cups of nonfat yogurt before serving to make a creamy, Indian-style dish to accompany a curry dinner.

3 tablespoons vegetable oil

2 teaspoons yellow mustard seed

2 tablespoons finely shredded gingerroot

4 jalapeños, seeded and thinly sliced crosswise (about 4 tablespoons)

4 cups peeled, coarsely shredded sweet carrots (about 1 pound)

2 tablespoons freshly squeezed lime juice or apple cider vinegar

1 teaspoon brown sugar

1/2 teaspoon salt

2 to 3 tablespoons shredded fresh mint or chopped fresh cilantro

2 cups nonfat plain yogurt (optional)

Heat the oil in a large skillet over medium-high heat until it is very hot. Remove the pan from the heat, add the mustard, and cover to prevent the seeds from popping out of the skillet. Shake the pan gently over the heat until the popping subsides, about 10 seconds.

Uncover the pan and add the ginger and the chiles. Cook, stirring for about 1 minute until the chiles soften. Stir in the carrots and continue to cook, stirring frequently, until the carrots turn bright orange and are slightly softened. Stir in the lime juice, sugar, and salt and cook for another minute. Stir in the mint, and remove the pan from the heat. Taste and season as desired with more salt, lime juice, and mint. Serve cool, but not cold.

Jump Up and Kiss My Pilaf

Serves 4 to 6

Infused with curry from the hot sauce, this dish goes well with grilled vegetables, a summer tomato salad, or winter greens. If you substitute another Caribbean hot sauce, add a teaspoon of curry before bringing the rice to a boil.

1 small yellow onion, finely chopped

2 cloves garlic, minced

4 tablespoons butter or olive oil

2 cups uncooked rice

4 cups Vegetable Stock (see page 75)

**2 tablespoons Jump Up and Kiss Me Hot Sauce with Passion
   or other habanero hot sauce**

Salt to taste

Freshly ground black pepper to taste

Sauté the onions and garlic in the butter until golden, then add the rice, stirring with a wooden spoon, until rice is well-coated and begins to color. Add the stock and 1 tablespoon of the hot sauce, bring to a boil, then lower heat to simmer, cover tightly, and cook until liquid is absorbed, about 20 minutes. Stir in remaining 1 tablespoon of hot sauce, and add salt and black pepper to taste. Serve immediately.

Mustard-Glazed Roasted Root Vegetables

Serves 6

This dish is spicy-sweet and laden with flavor from the mustard glaze and roasting process. Try a medley of root vegetables for contrasting color and texture or, for variety, use only parsnips. Parsnips, which were popular during the Renaissance, are high in potassium and vitamin C, and sweeter than turnips. This dish is comforting on a winter night and also good served slightly warm at a summer picnic.

1 pound carrots, peeled and trimmed

1 pound parsnips, peeled and trimmed

1/2 pound turnips, peeled and trimmed

2 large russet or baking potatoes, peeled

2 large sweet potatoes, peeled

1/3 cup olive oil

2 teaspoons curry powder

1 teaspoon hot paprika

1/4 cup maple syrup

3 tablespoons Dijon-style mustard

1 teaspoon kosher salt

1 teaspoon dried thyme

1 teaspoon freshly ground black pepper

Preheat oven to 375°. Set out 2 large roasting pans. Cut vegetables into lengths that are approximately the same size and thickness (preferably 3-inch lengths about 3/4 inch thick). You should have about 12 cups of vegetables.

Place all vegetables in a large bowl. In a medium bowl, whisk together the remaining ingredients. Pour over the vegetables and toss to coat well. Spread vegetables between the roasting pans in a single layer. (If they are packed too tightly, the vegetables will steam and not really roast and caramelize.) Roast uncovered for approximately 1 hour. Toss 2 to 3 times during the cooking with a spatula to ensure even cooking and coating with the glaze, taking care not to break up the vegetables.

Scotch Bonnet Turnips

Serves 4

The addition of chiles gives turnips a provocative lift. Scotch bonnet peppers are searingly hot (the heat is contained in the inner membrane and seeds), so always wash your hands thoroughly with soap and warm water after handling them. If you are particularly sensitive to chiles, you might want to wear rubber gloves when working with Scotch bonnets (which are also known as "Mademoiselle Jacques' Behind" in Guadaloupe).

1 pound turnips, peeled and cut into 2-inch cubes

1/4 Scotch bonnet or habanero pepper, seeded and minced

Juice of 1/2 orange

2 tablespoons whole milk

2 tablespoons chopped chives or green onion

1 teaspoon chopped fresh rosemary needles

1 1/2 tablespoons butter

1 clove garlic, minced

Cover the turnips in a pot of water and boil until tender, about 10 minutes. Drain and mash with the remaining ingredients in a large bowl. Serve hot.

Turnip, Orange, and Fennel Gratin

Serves 8

A healthful alternative for those who want to avoid heavy cream or whole milk, this gratin goes well with roasted dishes and could be used as a stuffing. Be sure not to cut the turnip too thick.

2 large fennel bulbs, trimmed (about 1 pound)

2 large seedless oranges

2 tablespoons vegetable oil

1 large yellow onion, peeled and sliced into thinly crosswise

5 cloves garlic

1 1/2 teaspoons ground coriander

1 teaspoon ground cumin

1/4 teaspoon ground cayenne pepper

1/4 teaspoon ground cardamom

1/4 teaspoon ground cinnamon

Salt

2 teaspoons brown sugar

1 1/4 pounds tender white turnips, peeled and sliced into 1/8-inch-thick rounds

3 to 4 tablespoons chopped fresh fennel leaves or mint leaves, for garnish

Preheat oven to 350°. Spray an 8 by 10 by 2-inch earthenware or enameled cast-iron baking pan with nonstick cooking spray. With a paring knife, remove the outer ribs of the fennel, pulling away the strings. Slice the fennel crosswise into 1/4-inch-thick slices. Put the fennel in a bowl, cover with cold water, and set aside.

Remove a thin ribbon of the orange skin with a vegetable peeler or sharp knife, then chop finely. Measure 1 1/2 teaspoons and set aside. Using a sharp knife, cut the peel and pith from the oranges. Cut the oranges in half lengthwise, then cut the halves crosswise into 1/8-inch-thick slices. Set aside the slices and accumulated juice.

Heat the oil in a large, heavy skillet over medium-high heat. Add the onion and garlic and cook, stirring, for about 2 minutes. Add the spices and orange zest and cook, still stirring, for about 2 more minutes or until fragrant. Drain the fennel, pat dry, and add to the pan. Salt lightly and cook, stirring for 5 minutes. Reduce the heat to medium and cook for 5 minutes longer, or until the fennel begins to soften. Sprinkle the sugar over the mixture and stir to combine. Remove the pan from the heat.

Layer the turnip slices, orange slices, and fennel mixture in a single overlapping layer (like dominoes) in the baking pan. Press the turnip, orange, and fennel together as you layer them so they are nearly upright rows. Pour the accumulated orange juice over the vegetables.

Cover the dish tightly with aluminum foil and place in the oven. Bake for about 1 hour, or until the juices are bubbling and the vegetables are tender-crisp. Uncover and bake for another 10 more minutes, or until lightly browned. Sprinkle with chopped fennel leaves just before serving.

GRATINS

Meaning "burnt on top" in French, *au gratin* originally was used to describe a crusty dish browned in the oven. Today, "gratin" denotes a cooking process whereby a dish is cooked in the oven with a protective layer to keep the food moist. That protective layer is often made with cheese, bread crumbs, or cream sauces, although the health-conscious will find a few creamless gratins here. Remember to slice vegetables thinly, with equal widths, and to bake them in a shallow dish to promote even cooking. Use an attractive ovenproof dish, so you can transfer the gratin directly from oven to table.

Spicy Potato Gratin

Serves 6

Instead of heavy cream, this gratin uses vegetable stock—you could also substitute beer, which goes well with the jalapeños, cheese, and spices.

2 tablespoons pure chile powder

2 teaspoons ground cumin

1 teaspoon dried thyme

1 teaspoon salt

4 large (2 1/2 pounds total) baking potatoes, cut into 1/8-inch-thick slices

1/4 cup minced jalapeños

2 tablespoons cold butter, cut into small pieces

3/4 cup Vegetable Stock (see page 75)

8 ounces Monterey jack cheese, shredded

Preheat oven to 375°. In a small bowl, combine the chile powder, cumin, thyme, and salt.

In an 8 by 8 by 2-inch casserole, arrange half the potatoes in one layer. Sprinkle with half the jalapeños and half the chile powder mixture, and dot with 1 tablespoon butter. Layer with remaining potatoes, jalapeños, chile powder mixture, and butter. Pour stock over potatoes and top with cheese. Cover and bake until potatoes are tender but don't fall apart when pierced with a fork, about 45 minutes.

Eating of these roots doth excite Venus and increaseth lust.

—seventeenth-
century writer,
on potatoes

Giant Bakers with Green Chile-Cream Cheese Sauce

Serves 4

Although I'm partial to spooning Green Chile-Cream Cheese Sauce over baked potatoes, this rich, spicy sauce is also good with chiles rellenos, omelets, huevos rancheros, or other egg dishes. It's also delicious ladled over fettucini. This recipe makes 2 1/2 cups of sauce—plenty for potatoes with some left over.

4 large baking potatoes, washed

Green Chile-Cream Cheese Sauce

2 teaspoons olive oil

4 tablespoons chopped yellow onion

1 jalapeño chile, stemmed and minced

2 serrano chiles, stemmed and minced

1/4 tablespoon crushed garlic

1 4.5-ounce can diced green chiles

6 tablespoons chopped fresh tomatoes

6 tablespoons crushed tomatoes

1/8 teaspoon salt

1/2 teaspoon freshly ground black pepper

3/4 cup Vegetable Stock (see page 75)

1 tablespoon dry white wine

4 ounces cream cheese, cut into pieces

Preheat oven to 350°. Bake potatoes 50 minutes to 1 hour, or until soft when pierced with a knife blade.

While potatoes are cooking, heat the olive oil in a medium skillet over medium-high heat. Add the onion, jalapeño, and serranos and sauté until the onion is clear. Add garlic and sauté 1 additional minute. Add green chiles and simmer for 15 minutes. Add tomatoes, salt, pepper, and stock and simmer for 1/2 hour. Add wine and cook for another 15 minutes. Turn off heat and mix in the cream cheese, a few pieces at a time, until thoroughly blended and sauce is smooth.

Pan-Fried Potato Cakes with Leeks, Cayenne, and Sherry Cream Sauce

Serves 6

With a rich savory sauce that complements the leeks and crunchy potato cakes, this is a terrific side dish or appetizer, but it is so delicious that it sometimes ends up as the main course.

6 large yellow Finn potatoes, peeled and grated

2 eggs, beaten

1 teaspoon salt

1 teaspoon ground white pepper

1/2 cup finely grated Parmesan cheese

1/4 cup plus 1 tablespoon olive oil

Sauce

1 shallot

1/2 cup dry white wine

1/2 teaspoon salt

1 teaspoon ground white pepper

2 teaspoons ground cayenne pepper

1 cup dry sherry

4 cups heavy cream

1 tablespoon butter

1 tablespoon olive oil

2 pounds leeks, thoroughly rinsed and sliced crosswise

Freshly ground black pepper, for garnish

Sour cream, for garnish

Fresh chopped parsley, for garnish

In a large bowl, mix the potatoes with the eggs, salt, white pepper, and cheese. Place a heavy skillet over medium-high heat. Add the oil to a depth of 1/8 inch, and heat until very hot (but not smoking). Form several large patties with the potato mixture and place in the pan. (Don't worry about it holding together completely as it will bind during cooking.) Fry on both sides until crisp and nicely browned. Carefully transfer to a plate and keep warm in the oven.

To make the sauce, heat the shallot, white wine, salt, and spices in a saucepan. Reduce down to 1/4 cup then add 1/2 cup of the sherry. Bring to a boil, then whisk in the cream. Cook over medium-high heat, whisking regularly. As soon as it begins to boil, lower the heat and simmer, whisking, until it thickens, about 15 minutes. If the sauce becomes too thick, add more sherry, a little at a time. Add salt to taste.

In a sauté pan, heat the butter and olive oil, and lower heat to avoid browning the butter. As soon as the butter melts, add most of the leeks, reserving a little for garnish. Sauté quickly, stirring constantly, until the leeks begin to wilt. Pour the remaining sherry over the leeks and cover. Simmer, covered, for 10 minutes, then remove cover and cook long enough to reduce any remaining liquid.

To serve, place a potato cake on each serving plate, top with some of the reserved leeks, and spoon the sauce over the top. Garnish with pepper, a dollop of sour cream, and parsley.

YOU SAY POTATO, I SAY POTAHTO

The English name potato is derived from patata, the Native American name for sweet potato. In Italy, it's called *tartufola* ("little truffle"), in Germany *kartoffel*, and in France *cartoufle*. Originally grown by the Incas, it is the world's best-known vegetable and good for you. Half a baked potato provides 22 percent of your daily vitamin C requirement and more potassium than a 6-ounce glass of orange juice. Leave the skin on whenever possible; it's a good source of fiber and has more iron, calcium, and B vitamins than the flesh. As a rule, moist "waxy" potatoes (round reds, new potatoes) are good for potato salads, boiling, and steaming, since they keep their shape after being cooked and diced, whereas starchy "floury" potatoes (Idaho potatoes, long russets) are best for baking and mashing.

Red Potato Pancakes with Collards and Chiles

Serves 6

Potato pancakes are delicious as an appetizer or snack—or serve them as an entrée by making larger pancakes (4 to 6 tablespoonsful each), topping them with soft scrambled eggs and a dollop of hot sauce.

3 cups grated red potatoes (peeled or unpeeled), soaked in water to cover

1 packed cup finely shredded collard greens

1/2 cup shredded carrot

1/2 cup finely shredded yellow onion

2 serrano chiles, seeded and minced

2 cloves garlic, minced

1 teaspoon crushed toasted cumin seed (see page 73)

1/2 teaspoon ground turmeric

1/8 teaspoon sweet paprika

1/4 packed cup chopped fresh cilantro leaves and tender stems

1 teaspoon salt

1/4 cup garbanzo bean flour

2 large eggs, lightly beaten

Vegetable oil for frying

Sour cream (optional)

Drain the potatoes, squeeze them dry by the handful, and spread them on a kitchen cloth. Roll the cloth tightly and press it to remove excess moisture. Put the potatoes back in the mixing bowl and add the remaining ingredients. Mix well to combine.

Place a heavy skillet on medium-high heat. Add oil to a depth of 1/8 inch, and heat until very hot (but not smoking). Test the heat with a small spoonful of the potato mixture (the oil should sputter). For each pancake, scoop about 2 tablespoonsful of the potato mixture into the pan, flattening it into an 1/8-inch-thick cake. The pancakes won't hold together well until browned, so you may want to use two spatulas to handle them. Fry until golden brown, about 2 minutes per side. Drain on paper towels and keep warm while frying the remaining batter. Serve with sour cream on the side.

New Mexico Garlic Mashed Potatoes

Serves 4

In the dead of winter, nothing beats comfort food, especially when enlivened with garlic and New Mexico chiles.

6 medium red potatoes, washed and quartered (skins left on)
1 head garlic, peeled
1 cup loosely packed grated Cheddar cheese
2 tablespoons milk
3 tablespoons unsalted butter
3/4 teaspoon finely minced fresh rosemary needles
Salt to taste
Freshly ground black pepper to taste
2 to 3 teaspoons ground New Mexico chiles, or pure chile powder

Put potatoes and garlic in a large pot and add enough water to cover. Cook over medium heat until potatoes are soft, about 25 minutes. Remove from heat and drain water. Add cheese, milk, and butter and mash until light and fluffy. Add rosemary and salt and pepper to taste. Add ground chiles 1 teaspoon at a time until desired heat is achieved. Serve hot.

MAKING YOUR OWN CHILE POWDER

The chile powder you find in supermarkets, often old and stale, is a blend of black pepper, cumin, and various herbs and spices. Making your own is easy and results in a fresher, deeper flavor. Buy whole dried chile peppers (see Mail-Order Sources, pages 342-344), remove the stem and seeds, and wash and dry them thoroughly. (Don't bother to seed them if you like a hotter powder.) Roast the peppers on a baking sheet in a 350° oven or toaster oven until you smell them, about 2 to 3 minutes—taking care not to leave them in too long, which will make them bitter. Then grind them in a spice or coffee grinder. You can make ancho chile powder or New Mexico chile powder—the varieties are virtually endless—or combine several chiles to make a custom blend.

Golden Potato, Squash, and Lima Bean Sauté

Serves 4 to 6

The warmth of this hearty dish makes it a welcome meal or side dish on a damp rainy day. Cooking your own beans will yield a better texture and flavor than the canned variety; you can make them ahead of time and keep on hand in the freezer for this and other quick menus. The crumble can also be made ahead.

Crumble

1 cup chopped, sliced, or slivered almonds

2 tablespoons dry whole-wheat bread crumbs

1/2 teaspoon salt

1 teaspoon ground ginger

1/4 teaspoon ground cinnamon

1/2 teaspoon pure chile powder

2 teaspoons safflower oil

Lima Bean Sauté

2 tablespoons olive oil

1 1/2 cups chopped yellow onion

1 pound Yukon Gold or yellow Finn potatoes, peeled, and diced small (about 3 cups)

1/2 pound butternut squash, peeled, and diced small (about 1 1/2 cups)

1 teaspoon salt

1/2 teaspoon black pepper

2 cups cooked small (baby) lima beans (see page 333 and note, below)

6 tiny whole red tabasco peppers (in brine), drained

Toss the nuts, bread crumbs, and spices together in a bowl. In a nonstick, large skillet over medium-high heat, heat the oil, then add the nut mixture. Stir well to coat. Continue stirring, or shake the pan, until the almonds are golden and the mixture is fragrant and toasted, about 3 to 5 minutes. Transfer to a shallow bowl and set aside.

In the same skillet, heat the olive oil over medium heat and add the onion. Sauté until translucent, about 3 minutes. Add the potatoes, squash, salt, and black pepper. Stir to coat. Cover and cook over medium heat about 5 minutes, stirring or shaking the pan often to prevent sticking. Add the lima beans and tabasco peppers. Stir well, then cover and cook an additional 5 minutes. Taste and adjust seasoning.

Transfer sauté to a shallow casserole serving dish. Crumble the nut mixture over the top of the sauté and serve.

Note: For added flavor, simmer the lima beans with 2 large bay leaves. If you have made the crumble earlier in the day, reheat it in a dry, nonstick skillet until heated through (about 3 to 5 minutes on medium heat).

Braised Green Chiles

Serves 6

The heat of this creamy chile dish depends on the chiles you use. For extra heat and contrast, add a teaspoon or more of crushed red pepper flakes. Braised chiles are a delicious side dish, especially at a barbecue, or as an accompaniment to a simple grain dish such as rice pilaf, corn pudding, or spoonbread. Or serve them with soft corn tacos with cubed boiled potatoes, cheese, and fresh tomatoes.

12 large green Anaheim or New Mexico green chiles
   (or other mildly hot chiles such as poblanos)

1 tablespoon vegetable oil

3 yellow onions, peeled, cut in half, and thinly sliced
   (3 1/2 to 4 cups)

2 large cloves garlic, lightly crushed

Salt

1 teaspoon dried marjoram

1 cup heavy cream

2 tablespoons chopped fresh cilantro

Roast the chiles on a grill or over a stovetop gas flame until evenly blistered. Put them in a bowl covered with a clean towel to steam while preparing other ingredients.

Heat the oil in a large skillet over medium heat. Add the onions and garlic, and salt lightly. Lower heat and cook, partially covered, for 45 to 60 minutes, stirring occasionally, until very tender and lightly caramelized. Add the marjoram halfway through the cooking time.

Peel, seed, and devein the chiles and tear or cut into 1/2-inch-wide strips. Add to the onions and simmer for 2 to 3 minutes. Add the cream and simmer for 10 to 15 minutes longer, raising the heat if necessary, until the juices are thickened. Season with salt and sprinkle with cilantro.

Breads

Nothing fills a kitchen like the smell of fresh bread baking. Chiles combine particularly well with corn breads and cheese-based breads, as you'll discover when you try the Parmesan-Cayenne Bread and Johnnycakes. Store bread at room temperature in a plastic bag (it will lose its moisture if refrigerated), or freeze if you're not going to eat it promptly. Grilled bread is a savory treat—slice it thick, brush with olive oil and crushed garlic, and grill for a few minutes on either side, then serve with pâtés, tomatoes or vegetable salads.

Johnnycakes

Makes 16 (2-inch) squares

Growing up along the shore in southeastern Massachusetts, we were a stone's throw from Rhode Island, where milkshakes were called "cabinets" and corn bread was called "Johnnycake." (Years later, I learned the word dates back to colonial times, when corn bread was considered suitably sturdy for long horseback trips—a good "journey cake.") In the fall, we'd order Johnnycakes with quahog chowder at the diner in Little Compton or bake it on summer evenings to pack in our picnic hamper before heading out to sail for the day on Buzzards Bay. The mild-mannered ancho chile gives these muffins a warm, rustic earthiness, for a good example of how chiles can add flavor to a dish without driving up the heat.

1 cup all-purpose flour
1 cup yellow or white cornmeal
1/2 teaspoon baking soda
1/2 teaspoon salt
2 teaspoons baking powder
2 tablespoons granulated sugar
1 1/2 dried ancho chiles, stemmed and seeded
2 eggs
1 cup milk
3 tablespoons butter, melted
1 small yellow onion, grated

Preheat the oven to 425°. Sift the dry ingredients into a bowl.

Lay the anchos on a rack in the oven and roast until you can smell them, about 2 to 3 minutes. Allow them to cool slightly, then grind in a spice or coffee grinder until chile particles are the size of confetti, or finer. Add to the dry mix. In a separate bowl, whisk together the eggs, then beat in the milk and butter, and add the onion. Fold the liquid into the dry ingredients and stir gently to combine. Spoon into greased muffin tins or a greased 8 by 8-inch baking pan, and bake for 20 to 25 minutes. Serve piping hot with butter.

I'm Frank Thompson, all the way from "down east." I've been through the mill, ground, and bottled, and come out a regular-built down-east johnny cake, when it's hot, damned good; but when it's cold, damned sour and indigestible— and you'll find me so.

—Richard Henry
Dana, Jr.,
*Two Years
Before the Mast*

Jody's Sundried Tomato–Garlic Bread

Makes 2 loaves

This bread is filled with two of my favorite ingredients: sun-dried tomatoes and roasted garlic. You can experiment with other fillings, such as olive tapenade, roasted garlic, and fresh herbs. Whatever filling you choose, it's a handsome loaf to set out with dinner or present as a late-night snack with a good ale.

2 cups dry-packed sundried tomatoes
4 heads of roasted garlic (see page 35)
1 teaspoon extra virgin olive oil
2 tablespoons active dry yeast
2 1/2 cups tepid water
6 to 6 1/2 cups all-purpose flour
1 teaspoon salt

Steam the sundried tomatoes in a vegetable steamer over boiling water for 8 minutes, or until soft, then chop. Lightly mash the roasted garlic cloves in a small bowl with the olive oil.

Dissolve the yeast in the water and let stand 5 minutes. Place the yeast mixture in a mixing bowl and slowly add the flour. Beat with the paddle of an electric mixer (or work in flour by hand) until dough pulls away from the sides of the mixing bowl. Add 1/4 of the garlic mixture and the salt. Place the dough hook on mixer and knead for 5 minutes (or knead by hand for 15 minutes).

Place the dough in a lightly oiled bowl, and cover loosely with a kitchen towel. Let rise in a warm place 1 to 2 hours, or until doubled in bulk. Punch the dough down and let it rise for 1 to 1 1/2 hours until doubled in bulk again. Punch down and divide the dough in half. Roll each half into a 15 by 7-inch rectangle about 1/2 inch thick. Spread the remaining garlic and chopped tomatoes evenly between the two rectangles. Roll each as for a jelly roll, beginning with the narrow side. Seal the long edge. Grease two loaf pans. Place sealed edge down in the loaf pans. Let rise again until doubled, about 45 to 60 minutes.

Preheat the oven to 450°, and bake bread for 10 minutes. Reduce the heat to 400°, and cook 25 to 35 minutes longer, or until loaves sound hollow when tapped. Transfer to a rack to cool.

> **If the bread is good and plentiful/The rest of the meal can be excused.**
>
> —Bertolt Brecht,
> *The Bread of the People*

Beer—sometimes called *flussiges brot*, or liquid bread, by the Germans—has a long history in North America. Thomas Jefferson brewed his own beer, often asking James Madison to give him a hand, and George Washington had a brewery at Mount Vernon. In the last decade, microbreweries and homebrewers have revived the tradition of craft brewing and are brewing interesting, full-flavored beers that stand up well to spicy flavors. Below are a few favorites:

Belgian ale: Malty, soft, fruity, and accentuated with pear notes, this strong ale has a light color that belies its potent complexity and depth of flavor. Fat Tire Belgian Ale is delicious as an apéritif or served with strong cheeses and fresh fruit.

Bitter: This classic English pub beer is full flavored and hoppy, and goes well with spicy barbecue; Redhook makes a nice one.

Bock: Originally brewed to celebrate the coming of spring, bock beer is a strong, malty lager. Stoudt's Double Honey Maibock has sweet caramel-like undertones and a fresh flavor, and is good with garlicky foods.

Brown ale: Medium bodied, with a rich fruity aroma and full malt flavor, brown ale is a choice autumn beer. Brooklyn Brown Ale goes well with nutty dishes, dark breads, and spicy food.

Oktoberfest: In the days before refrigeration, Oktoberfest lagers, which are malty, roasty, and faintly sweet, were brewed in March, then laid down in caves for the summer, and served ceremoniously in the fall. Samuel Adams makes a deep amber Oktoberfest that is good with chowders, pizza, or spicy stews.

Pale ale: Pale ales are very dry with good malt character and plenty of hop bitterness. Sierra Nevada Pale Ale is a classic American-style pale ale, with overtones of citrus and grapefruit from the Cascade hops grown in the Pacific Northwest. Good as an aperitif or with salty or fried foods.

Pilsner: A crisp, dry lager with a fresh floral bouquet and strong hop aroma and flavor. Pete's Wicked Lager is a good example and a great summertime drink.

Porter: Complex and intensely flavored, this deep, dark ale has a roasted-malt finish with chocolate and coffee overtones and a corresponding hops bitterness that perfectly balances the malt. Catamount Porter is remarkably smooth and great with hearty food.

Steam beer: This soft, crisp, slightly fruity beer is full-bodied, with a wonderful hop dryness. Popular during the Gold Rush, it is uniquely American, with the name allegedly derived from the steam power at early California breweries. Anchor Steam is appealing as an apéritif or all-around beer.

Stout: A black, thick, creamy ale. Samuel Smith is bitter, like all stouts, but also sweet and complex. Good with winter meals, at tailgate parties, or with a late afternoon repast.

Trappist ale: A soft, fruity ale that's been brewed by Trappist monks since the Middle Ages. Chimay is delicious as an apéritif or with nut pâtés.

Wheat beer: This bright, golden ale is light and dry, and slightly tart from the wheat. With an aroma of cloves, Pyramid Wheaten Ale is a refreshing summer drink and sometimes garnished with lemon and a shot of fruit syrup.

LIQUID BREAD

Irish Soda Bread

Makes one 9-inch loaf

This untraditional soda bread is dense and nutty from the walnuts and loaded with flavor from the spices and chiles. Easy to make, this recipe yields a big, beautiful, round loaf, which is delicious served fresh from the oven. It also makes a thoughtful weekend house gift.

4 cups plus 1 tablespoon all-purpose flour
1/4 cup sugar
2 tablespoons pure chile powder
2 teaspoons baking powder
1 teaspoon ground cumin
1 teaspoon ground cayenne pepper
1/2 teaspoon baking soda
1/2 cup cold butter, cut into small pieces
1 cup walnuts, chopped
1/4 cup chopped scallions
1/4 cup minced jalapeños
1 1/2 cups buttermilk

Preheat the oven to 350°. In a large bowl, combine 4 cups flour, sugar, chile powder, baking powder, cumin, cayenne, and baking soda. Cut in the butter until mixture resembles coarse crumbs. Stir in the walnuts, scallions, and jalapeños. Stir in the buttermilk until ingredients are moistened.

Turn out dough onto a lightly floured surface. With floured hands, knead lightly for 5 minutes. Transfer dough to an ungreased baking sheet and shape into a 9-inch round. Sprinkle with the remaining 1 tablespoon flour. With a knife, cut a 1/4-inch-deep cross into top. Bake 1 hour and 15 minutes. Transfer to a wire rack to cool.

> There is a communion of more than wine or body when bread is broken and wine is drunk.
>
> —M. F. K. Fisher, *The Gastronomical Me*

Parmesan-Cayenne Bread

Makes 2 loaves

Nestled along the shore of Buzzards Bay in southeastern Massachusetts, Mattapoisett is a small village that was a shipbuilding center centuries ago (Herman Melville went to sea in a ship made there). Today, it's a quaint harbor and popular haven for sailors on their way to the Vineyard or down east. The launch brings sailors ashore, where their noses lead them to the Shipyard Galley, a bakery on the wharf that serves sweets and breads, including Parmesan-Cayenne Bread, which baker Jan Spark adapted from *Eating Well* magazine. Soulful with the flavor of freshly grated Parmesan, the bread is also spicy from the cayenne pepper. For a "hotter" loaf, add more cayenne.

4 1/2 teaspoons dry active yeast

1 1/4 cups tepid water

2/3 cup nonfat dry milk

1 cup plus 1 tablespoon fresh Parmesan cheese

1 large egg, lightly beaten

1 tablespoon extra virgin olive oil plus additional for coating

2 teaspoons granulated sugar

1 1/2 teaspoons salt

3/4 teaspoon ground cayenne pepper

1 tablespoon Jump Up and Kiss Me Hot Sauce with Passion

3 3/4 to 4 cups all-purpose flour

1 egg white, lightly beaten, for glazing

Dissolve yeast in warm water. Stir in the milk, 1 cup of cheese, egg, oil, sugar, salt, cayenne pepper, hot sauce, and 3 cups of the flour. Beat well. Stir in remaining flour until dough pulls away from the side of the bowl. Knead the dough by hand for 5 minutes on a floured surface or in a mixer with a dough hook until smooth and elastic, adding more flour if necessary.

Oil a large bowl and add the dough, turning to coat it lightly and thoroughly with oil. Cover loosely with a kitchen towel and let rise 1 1/2 hours, or until doubled in volume.

Punch down the dough and divide in half to form 2 balls. Place balls on a greased baking sheet. Cover loosely and let rise in a warm place until doubled in size, about 30 to 40 minutes.

Preheat oven to 350°. Slash breads, brush with the egg white, and sprinkle with remaining Parmesan cheese. Bake for 25 to 35 minutes or until crust is golden brown.

Jalapeño-Onion Corn Sticks

Serves 4 to 6

Bits of fresh corn and minced jalapeños make these lively corn sticks perfect for nibbling. Spoon the batter into a round pan and you have fresh corn bread.

1 tablespoon olive oil

1/2 cup finely chopped onion

1/3 cup fresh or frozen corn kernels (thawed if frozen)

3 jalapeño chiles, stemmed and minced

1 clove garlic, minced

1 1/4 cups all-purpose flour

1 cup cornmeal

1/4 cup firmly packed brown sugar

2 1/2 teaspoons baking powder

1/2 teaspoon salt

1/4 cup vegetable shortening

1 cup shredded Cheddar cheese

1 1/4 cups milk

1 large egg

Preheat the oven to 400°. Grease 14 cast-iron corn stick molds (2 pans, 7 molds each) or an ovenproof 10-inch skillet. Place molds in preheating oven while preparing batter.

In a small skillet, heat the olive oil over medium heat. Add onion and cook over medium-low heat until very tender, about 8 minutes. Stir in corn, jalapeños, and garlic, remove from heat and set aside.

In a large bowl, combine flour, cornmeal, brown sugar, baking powder, and salt until blended. Cut in shortening until mixture resembles coarse crumbs. Stir in the onion mixture and Cheddar cheese. In a small bowl, whisk together the milk and egg until well blended. Stir into dry ingredients until batter is just blended. Spoon the batter into preheated corn stick molds (batter will fill molds completely). Bake 10 to 15 minutes or until toothpick inserted into the center comes out clean. Cool corn sticks in molds on wire racks for 10 minutes. Remove from molds and serve warm.

Big Red Garlic Bread

Makes 1 loaf

Baking garlic bread fills a winter kitchen with wonderful smells. Experiment with other herbs or different kinds of chile powder—ancho chile powder, for example, lends a warm, woody flavor.

1 loaf seeded Italian bread (see recipe below)
2 cloves garlic
1/2 cup butter, softened
1/4 cup finely chopped fresh parsley
1 tablespoon pure chile powder
2 teaspoons dried oregano
1/2 teaspoon crushed red pepper flakes
1/2 teaspoon coarsely ground black pepper
1/4 teaspoon salt

All sorrows are less

with bread.

—Spanish proverb

Preheat the oven to 450°. Cut bread in half lengthwise. Peel and mash garlic with the side of a large knife. In a small bowl, combine the garlic, butter, parsley, chile powder, oregano, pepper flakes, black pepper, and salt until well blended. With a pastry brush, spread butter mixture on all sides of the bread. Loosely wrap in foil and bake until hot and toasted, about 20 minutes.

Italian Bread

Makes one 14-inch loaf

2 tablespoons granulated sugar

1 teaspoon salt

1 packet quick-rise yeast

3 cups all-purpose flour

1 cup milk

1/4 cup unsalted butter

Olive oil

1 egg

1 teaspoon water

1 tablespoon sesame seeds

In a large bowl, combine the sugar, salt, yeast, and flour. In a small saucepan, heat the milk and butter over medium heat until very warm (about 125°).

With a wooden spoon, gradually stir the warmed liquid into the dry ingredients, adding more flour by the tablespoon, if necessary, to make a soft dough. Turn dough out onto a lightly floured surface and knead until smooth, about 10 minutes. Shape the dough into a ball, and place in a large greased bowl. Brush lightly with olive oil, then cover with plastic wrap and let rise in a warm place until doubled, about 30 minutes.

Preheat the oven to 375°. Grease a large baking sheet. In a small bowl, beat the egg and water until blended. Punch down the dough and place on the baking sheet. Shape into a 14-inch-long loaf. Brush the top of the bread with the egg mixture and sprinkle with sesame seeds. Cut two diagonal slashes on top of the loaf. Bake 25 to 30 minutes, or until the bread sounds hollow when tapped on the bottom. Cool on a wire rack.

Margarita Muffins

Makes 12 muffins

The lime is evident in these chewy muffins, which are a welcome addition to Sunday brunch or breakfast with huevos rancheros or other egg dishes. Pass the margaritas!

2 1/2 cups all-purpose flour

1/3 cup granulated sugar

2 teaspoons baking powder

1 teaspoon baking soda

2 large eggs

1 tablespoon gold tequila

1 tablespoon Triple Sec

2 tablespoons freshly squeezed lime juice

1 cup buttermilk

1 tablespoon lemon zest

2 teaspoons lime zest

Kosher salt

Preheat the oven to 400°. Whisk or sift together flour, sugar, baking powder, and baking soda in a large bowl. In a medium bowl, lightly beat the eggs. Add remaining wet ingredients and mix well.

Make a well in the center of the dry ingredients. Add liquids, lemon zest, and lime zest. Stir gently just to blend the wet and dry mixture. Spoon into greased muffin containers. Sprinkle kosher salt lightly over tops of muffins. Bake 15 to 20 minutes. Remove from pan and cool on rack.

Variation: Coarsely chop 1/2 cup golden raisins. Soak the raisins in the tequila, triple sec, and lime juice for 1/2 hour, then combine with other wet ingredients.

Whole Wheat Popovers with Scallions and Black Pepper

Makes 8 popovers

As Bernie Clayton once remarked, a popover is "an ungainly-looking device for getting butter, jams, jellies, and honey into the mouth." While you may want to forego the jam with this peppery popover, it is always appreciated as a brunch item (especially with Bloody Marys), with hot soup, or as a late-night snack.

1/3 cup whole-wheat flour

2/3 cup unbleached white flour

1 cup milk

2 large eggs

1/2 teaspoon salt

2 tablespoons vegetable oil or melted butter

2 teaspoons freshly ground black pepper

3 scallions, sliced thinly crosswise

2 teaspoons black mustard seed

Preheat the oven to 425°. Coat 8 muffin cups with nonstick cooking spray, then brush with vegetable oil or softened butter.

Put the flours in a mixing bowl. In a separate bowl, beat together the milk, eggs, salt, and oil with a whisk. Beat the liquid mixture into the flour until blended thoroughly and smooth. Stir in the black pepper, scallions, and mustard seeds.

Spoon the batter into the prepared cups. Bake for 20 minutes. Reduce the heat to 375° and bake for 10 to 15 minutes longer, until the popovers are puffed and golden brown.

Desserts
&
Drinks

Desserts

Nothing brings a spicy meal to a close better than a cool, refreshing dessert. Hence this chapter includes tropical fruit sorbets that will soothe the palate. Incredibly easy to make, they look elegant when presented in crystal glassware. Pick pretty garnishes to emphasize their pastel frothiness—fresh mint sprigs, a perfect blackberry or peach slice, or a fresh hibiscus flower.

Others like to bring a meal to a close with a hearty dessert loaded with big flavors. Ginger, in particular, is a zesty ingredient that pairs well with blueberries and cream. This chapter also includes one of my personal favorites, Mt. Riga Blueberry Tart with Ginger Cream, as well as Blueberry-Ginger Compote, Coconut-Rum Rice Pudding—even spicy dessert wontons. These desserts are welcomed at the end of the meal or several hours later, accompanied by a fine Spanish port.

Blueberry-Ginger Compote

Makes 3 1/2 cups

Not too sweet or tart, this compote makes a terrific dessert topping for cake, ice cream, or yogurt, and it's also a savory addition to a summer buffet. It will keep well for 1 to 1 1/2 weeks if chilled.

1/2 cup water
1/8 cup balsamic vinegar
1/8 cup apple juice
2 (3-inch) sticks cinnamon
1/2 teaspoon ground coriander
1/8 teaspoon ground cloves
3 tablespoons minced gingerroot
1/3 cup dried blueberries, cherries, or cranberries
1 tablespoon minced lemon zest
2 pints fresh blueberries, washed and picked over
1 cup granulated sugar

Combine the water, vinegar, apple juice, cinnamon, coriander, cloves, ginger, dried blueberries, and lemon zest in a medium saucepan. Bring to a boil over medium-high heat. Add the fresh blueberries, lower the heat, and simmer very gently (taking care not to boil) until berries release their juices but still retain their shape, about 8 to 10 minutes.

Remove berries from pan with a slotted spoon and set aside in a heat-resistant bowl. Leave cinnamon sticks in the pan with the juices. To the juices, add 1 cup sugar. Stir well and bring to a simmer over medium heat. Simmer until liquid is reduced by half, stirring often, about 10 to 15 minutes. Remove from heat, discard the cinnamon sticks, and add the syrup to the reserved blueberries. Set aside to cool thoroughly, then refrigerate before serving.

Mt. Riga Blueberry Tart with Ginger Cream

Serves 10

In the summertime, we often visit a family camp atop a mountain in New York. At this camp is a pristine lake, dotted with a small island that is covered with high- and low-bush blueberries. Called Blueberry Island by generations of camp-goers, the island yields its plentiful fruit in August, and it is then that we canoe over and pick berries in the late afternoon sun. The kids race to see who can fill their coffee cans first, with the pleasing "ping" of the first berries hitting metal giving way to a soft "pppppffff" as berries accumulate. With full cans, we paddle home and make pies, tarts, and always blueberry pancakes the next morning. Try this tart with wild blueberries, which are a juicy contrast to the strong ginger cream.

Crust

1 1/2 cups all-purpose flour

3 tablespoons firmly packed brown sugar

1 teaspoon ground ginger

1/4 teaspoon ground nutmeg

1/4 teaspoon salt

1/2 cup unsalted butter, softened

1 egg white, slightly beaten

Ginger Pastry Cream

1/2 cup crystallized ginger

1/4 cup granulated sugar

3 tablespoons all-purpose flour

1 envelope unflavored gelatin

1/4 teaspoon salt

1 1/2 cups milk

4 egg yolks

1 teaspoon pure vanilla extract

1/2 teaspoon pure almond extract

1/2 cup heavy or whipping cream

1 pint blueberries

1/4 cup apricot jam, melted

Preheat the oven to 375°. In a medium bowl, combine the flour, brown sugar, ginger, nutmeg, and salt. Cut in butter until mixture resembles coarse crumbles. With hands, knead mixture until blended. Pat pastry onto the bottom and along the sides of an ungreased 10-inch tart pan with a removable bottom. Bake 20 minutes, or until pastry is golden. Transfer to wire rack. Brush the hot pastry with egg white, then cool in the pan on a wire rack. Remove the sides of the pan and set aside.

To make the Ginger Pastry Cream, process the crystallized ginger and 1 tablespoon of the granulated sugar in a food processor until ginger is finely ground. Set aside. In a 2-quart saucepan, stir the remaining 3 tablespoons of granulated sugar, the flour, gelatin, and salt. In a medium bowl, beat the milk and egg yolks until well blended, then stir into the sugar mixture. Cook over medium-low heat, stirring constantly, until gelatin is dissolved completely and mixture thickens and coats the back of a spoon, about 15 minutes. (Do not boil or custard will curdle.) Remove saucepan from the heat. Stir in the crystallized ginger, vanilla extract, and almond extract until blended. Refrigerate about 1 hour, or until the mixture mounds slightly.

In a small bowl at medium speed, beat the heavy cream until soft peaks form. Fold the whipped cream into the custard and spoon the mixture into the cooled pastry shell. Generously cover the custard with blueberries and brush with apricot jam. Refrigerate tart until custard is set, about 1 hour.

"Hot" Chocolate Biscotti

Makes 48 biscotti

For those who want to finish a meal with a spicy twist, here's a dessert that one guest described as having a "sweet chocolate burn." Sounds bizarre, but it's tasty, with the straightforward cocoa laced with a faint suggestion of heat. One-quarter teaspoon of cayenne contributes a whisper of warmth, whereas 1/2 teaspoon of cayenne will generate a slight tingle. Serve biscotti with tea in the late afternoon or in the evening with strong coffee and fresh fruit.

3 tablespoons butter, at room temperature

1/3 cup granulated sugar

1/3 cup packed light brown sugar

2 large eggs

1 teaspoon ground cinnamon

1 teaspoon baking powder

1/2 teaspoon baking soda

1 1/2 cups all-purpose flour

1/2 cup unsweetened cocoa

1/4 teaspoon dry mustard

1/2 teaspoon freshly ground black pepper

1/4 teaspoon ground cayenne pepper

Preheat the oven to 350°. Grease an 11 by 17-inch baking sheet or line with parchment paper. Cream together the butter and sugars. Add eggs and beat until smooth.

In a separate bowl, whisk or sift together dry ingredients. Add slowly to egg and sugar mixture and mix thoroughly with a wooden spoon. (Dough will be stiff.) Divide dough in half. With floured hands, shape each half into a slightly flattened log about 12 inches long by 2 inches wide. (This can be done on the baking sheet.) Place logs about 3 inches apart from each other.

Bake 25 minutes, or until firm but not dry. Remove from the oven and cool 15 to 20 minutes on the baking sheet. While still warm, slice logs on a slight diagonal into 1/2-inch-wide slices. Lay the slices on their sides on the baking sheet and bake an additional 15 to 20 minutes or until crisp and dry. Remove cookies from pan and cool thoroughly on racks. Store in tightly sealed container.

Coconut-Rum Rice Pudding

Serves 6 to 8

Although rice pudding is typically served as comfort food, here it is transformed by the rum-soaked raisins, toasted coconut, and freshly grated mace or nutmeg.

1/2 cup golden raisins

1/4 cup dark rum

1/2 cup uncooked short-grain brown or white rice

4 large eggs

1/2 cup granulated sugar

2 3/4 cups whole milk (see note)

1 cup unsweetened coconut milk

1/2 cup shredded unsweetened coconut (packaged or fresh)

Freshly grated mace or nutmeg

Soak raisins in rum for at least 1/2 hour or up to several hours. Meanwhile, cook rice according to the directions on page 334. Drain if necessary but do not rinse. Set aside to cool slightly.

Preheat the oven to 350°. In an ovenproof 2-quart serving bowl or casserole, whisk eggs and sugar to blend. In a separate bowl, mix the milk and coconut milk, then warm slightly on stovetop or in microwave (1 minute on high power). Meanwhile, spread the coconut on a baking sheet and toast in the oven, stirring often, until lightly browned, about 10 minutes.

Add the milk slowly to the egg and sugar mixture in the casserole, stirring well. Add rice, raisins, and rum, and toasted coconut. Stir again to mix well. Generously dust the top with freshly grated mace.

Place the casserole in a large ovenproof pan and add water to 1-inch depth in the outer pan to create a water bath. Bake casserole in water bath for 1 hour. Test doneness by inserting a knife in the center; custard should be set and residue on the knife moist. Remove from water bath and cool on rack, then refrigerate.

Note: Lowfat (1% or 2%) milk may be substituted if desired.

THE CRACKED NUT

Years ago, after sailing for two weeks on a forty-foot sailboat from northern Maine to the British Virgin Islands, our crew was eager to step ashore, take hot showers, and go out for breakfast. The waiter must have seen it in our eyes, because after we sat down he whipped out a machete, whacked off the tops of a few green coconuts, inserted straws in the openings, and presented the nectar to us.

I still remember the pure taste of fresh coconut milk and now crack my own "nuts" when I'm in the Caribbean. If you find a big green coconut on the beach or in a tree, shake it to make sure there's milk inside, then either whack it with a machete or drop it on a big rock to loosen the shell (you want to get to the brown fibrous nut inside). Puncture the brown nut with a nail or ice pick and a hammer, and drain the liquid, which you can either drink, freeze, or refrigerate for up to 24 hours. Gently crack open the nut lengthwise using the hammer, and cut away the firm meat with a small paring knife. Coarsely grate the meat by hand or in a blender with a little hot water to facilitate blending, straining afterward.

MACE

Mace and nutmeg hail from the same hard-shelled fruit found on an evergreen tree in the Spice Islands. Inside is a hard seed—nutmeg—which is surrounded by a lacy red covering called mace. Although gourmet stores charge exorbitant prices for a few whole nutmegs in pretty packages, it's worth hunting for them in health food stores (where they are sold in bulk) and picking up a few, because freshly grated nutmeg tastes much better than packaged grated nutmeg. Store the seeds in an airtight container, and grate them with a tiny nut-meg grater or a kitchen grater. Mace, which is more difficult to grate and is commonly sold already grated, tastes a bit like cinnamon and black pepper. Both nutmeg and mace enhance desserts, soufflés, omelets, and sauces. Freshly ground nutmeg is also delicious sprinkled on rum drinks.

Creamy Dessert Wontons

Makes 56 wontons

With a filling that resembles cheesecake, these wontons are best served warm or at room temperature, either alone or with fresh fruit or chocolate ice cream.

8 ounces cream cheese, at room temperature

1/4 cup sour cream

1 tablespoon dark brown sugar

1 tablespoon ginger brandy

1 teaspoon pure chile powder

1/3 cup chopped dried apricots

2 tablespoons chopped crystallized ginger

2 teaspoons minced lemon zest

56 wonton wrappers

1 tablespoon granulated sugar

1/2 teaspoon ground cinnamon

1/2 teaspoon pure chile powder

Nonstick cooking spray

In a medium bowl, with an electric mixer beat cream cheese, sour cream, brown sugar, brandy, and chile powder until smooth (about 1 minute). Add apricots, ginger, and lemon zest and stir to blend well.

Place approximately 1 teaspoon of the cheese mixture in the center of each wonton wrapper. Moisten edges with a bit of water and fold the edges together and seal tightly to form a triangular shape. Flatten the bottom slightly and place on a parchment-lined baking sheet. (Wontons can be made to this point early in the day or the day before if kept loosely covered and refrigerated.)

When ready to serve, preheat oven to 400°. In a small bowl, combine the granulated sugar, cinnamon, and 1/2 teaspoon chile powder. Lightly coat the tops of the wontons with the cooking spray and sprinkle surface with the cinnamon sugar mixture. Bake until golden and slightly puffed, about 6 minutes. (Do not overbake or they will split open and the cheese will ooze out.) Transfer to a serving plate and allow to cool, about 5 minutes.

Spicy Carrot Cake

Makes one 9 by 13-inch cake

Many have claimed this is the best carrot cake they've ever tasted, which I can heartily attest to since the recipe comes from Scott Avery, a baker in town who makes inspired desserts. It has a pleasant spiciness and even the faintest suggestion of heat, which is soon eclipsed by the sweetness of this dense moist cake. The papaya-based hot sauce in the frosting creates a delightful fruity buzz (and conversation starter!), but is indeed optional.

4 eggs

2 cups granulated sugar

1 1/3 cups vegetable oil

3 cups all-purpose flour

1 teaspoon baking powder

1 teaspoon baking soda

1 teaspoon ground cinnamon

1 teaspoon ground ginger

1/2 teaspoon ground nutmeg

1/4 teaspoon ground cloves

1/2 teaspoon ground cayenne pepper

4 cups grated carrots

1/2 cup raisins or chopped dried fruit

1/2 cup chopped pecans

Cream Cheese Frosting

2 8-ounce packages softened cream cheese

6 tablespoons honey

2 tablespoons Jump Up and Kiss Me Hot Sauce with Passion or other hot sauce with tropical fruit (optional)

Preheat the oven to 350°. Grease and flour a 9 by 13-inch pan. Using an electric mixer with a whisk attachment, combine eggs and sugar and whip until light in color and slightly thick. Reduce speed and add the oil slowly. Stop, scrape bowl, and change to the paddle attachment.

In a separate bowl, combine and sift the flour, baking powder, baking soda, cinnamon, ginger, nutmeg, cloves, and cayenne. Gradually add the dry ingredients to the egg mixture while beating on low speed. Fold in the carrots, dried fruit, and pecans. Fill the pan with the batter and bake until the cake springs to the touch, about 30 to 35 minutes.

Meanwhile, to make the frosting, combine the cream cheese, honey, and hot sauce and beat until smooth. When cake has cooled, decorate with frosting.

> Give me books, fruit, French wine, fine weather and a little music out of doors, played by somebody I do not know.
>
> —John Keats in a letter to Fanny Keats, 1819

Mango-Tequila Sorbet

Serves 4

The taste of fresh mangoes is prevalent in this easy recipe, which provides an exotic close to dinner. Serve in tall stemware, garnished with either lime slices and pomegranate seeds or simply with sprigs of mint from the garden.

1 cup mango purée (about 2 large mangoes)
1/2 cup chilled simple syrup (recipe follows)
1/4 cup tequila
Juice of 1 lime
2 tablespoons milk
Lime slices, for garnish
Pomegranate seeds, for garnish (optional)

Combine all ingredients thoroughly with a whisk or in a blender. Pour into a large bowl and freeze for at least 6 hours. Garnish with fresh lime slices and pomegranate seeds.

Simple Syrup

Makes 8 cups

Used in sorbets, this simple syrup will keep for months in the refrigerator.

4 1/2 cups water
5 1/2 cups granulated sugar

Combine the water and sugar in a medium saucepan and place over high heat. Bring to a full boil, stirring occasionally. Remove from heat and pour into a bowl and chill.

Each tree

Laden with fairest

   fruit, that hung to

   th'eye

Tempting, stirr'd in me

   sudden appetite

To pluck and eat.

—John Milton,
Paradise Lost

Passion Fruit Sorbet

Serves 8

This light dessert is also foolproof. You can pop the bowl of mix in your freezer while at work or the theater, and when you return home you will have a delicious sorbet waiting.

1 cup chilled simple syrup (see page 272)
1 3/4 cups chilled passion fruit nectar
Fresh fruit, for garnish
Fresh mint sprigs, for garnish

Combine the syrup and passion fruit nectar and freeze for at least 6 hours. When ready to serve, scoop it into dishes and garnish with fresh fruit and mint leaves.

Guava Sorbet

Serves 4

To refresh your palate after a fiery dinner, there's nothing like a sweet, cold fruit sorbet. You may substitute your favorite fruit juice, or even add a few tablespoons of rum if you desire.

1 cup chilled simple syrup (see page 272)
1 1/2 cups cold guava juice
Fresh fruit, for garnish
Fresh mint sprigs, for garnish

Combine the syrup and guava juice in a bowl and freeze for at least 6 hours. When ready to serve, scoop it into dishes and garnish with fresh fruit and mint leaves.

TETON DE VENUS

Cultivated since the fifth century BC, peaches have long been prized as a table fruit and dessert ingredient. Indeed, during Louis XIV's reign, so many delectable varieties were grown that the peach was nick-named *teton de Venus* (Venus's breast).

Harvested from June through September, peaches are prized for their succulent flesh and fragrant aroma. White peaches have a fruitier flesh than the common yellow peach variety and are juicier. If you're lucky enough to live near an orchard, eat peaches within two days of pick-ing and don't refrigerate them. Include the skin in your desserts, as that's where most of the vita-mins are contained.

Peach Sorbet

In high summer, try this refreshing dessert, which is also very pretty with its peachy color and dark pink flecks. It takes minutes to make and can be dressed up with lime sliv-ers, fresh peach slices, mint sprigs, or a sprinkling of wild blueberries.

1 cup peach pulp (including skins), chopped
Juice of 1 lime
1 cup chilled simple syrup (see page 272)
Fresh mint sprigs, for garnish
Fresh wild blueberries, for garnish

Combine peaches, lime, and syrup in a bowl and freeze for 6 to 8 hours. When ready to serve, scoop the sorbet into dishes and garnish with fresh fruit and mint leaves.

Drinks

My husband hails from Oklahoma, where his family always welcomes guests into their home with a big, refreshing drink. "What'll I get you, Jen?" my father-in-law asks, and I know I will receive a perfect concoction, served in a tall glass with lots of ice. Drinks needn't be alcoholic—what's important is the highest quality ingredients, plenty of ice, and fresh garnishes. Think of the color, too—a simple dash of Angostura bitters in tonic creates a pale pink drink that is elegant topped with a sliver of lime.

Bright drinks made with fruit provide a soothing accent to spicy foods. In Mexico, you'll find sweating pitchers of flavored waters on sideboards, offering relief from the sweltering sun and chiles. This chapter includes such drinks, good for summer afternoons, tropical winter holidays, or with any spicy dish. It also includes tangy drinks laced with chiles, such as Pepper Vodka, which will take the chill out of a cold winter night.

Pineapple-Lemon Water

Makes 2 drinks

Not too sweet, this light pineapple drink will rejuvenate you after a day at the beach.

2 cups chopped fresh pineapple
Juice of 2 lemons
2 cups water
2 teaspoons granulated sugar, or more to taste
Sprigs of fresh mint, for garnish

Purée pineapple, lemon, and water in a food processor or blender. Strain and pour into glasses filled with cracked ice. Stir in sugar to taste, and garnish with fresh mint.

Pepper Vodka

Makes 1 bottle

This neutral spirit benefits from the addition of chiles, citrus, or herbal flavorings. In Poland, they even add bison grass to vodka, which English author Somerset Maugham claimed created a drink that "smells of freshly mown hay and spring flowers." The longer the chiles steep, the hotter the vodka will become.

4 jalapeños, habaneros, or other chiles small enough to fit through neck of bottle
1 bottle good-quality vodka

Clean chiles thoroughly and add to bottle of vodka. Seal and store in cool, dark place.

Hibiscus Cooler

Makes 2 drinks

In the West Indies, there is a beautiful Jamaican hibiscus flower (sometimes called sorrel) that blooms every December, at the end of the rainy season and the beginning of the dry season. Natives steep the calyx in water to make a popular beverage that is the color of rubies and tastes a bit like cranberry juice. Popular at Christmastime, these sorrel drinks are presented with much ceremony, similar to our treatment of eggnog. Indeed, a Panamanian botanist told me that sorrel is such a popular beverage in Central America that highway crews widening the roads in the 1950s would cut down all the bushes except the sorrel, which flourishes now by the roadsides. While Jamaican hibiscus flowers may be difficult to procure, sorrel syrup is available in Caribbean or Mexican grocery stores, or by mail order from Caribbean Spice Company (see Mail-Order Sources, pages 342-344). With a bit of club soda, it makes a refreshing, slightly acidic drink. It also soothes weak stomachs.

2 cups club soda
4 tablespoons sorrel syrup
2 slices fresh lime, for garnish

Pour the club soda and sorrel syrup into a tall glass over ice, stir, and garnish with the lime.

Note: For variety mix 1 ounce of rum, ice, a sliver of lime, and a few splashes of sorrel syrup.

PASSION FRUIT

Serve it for Valentine's Day! Passion fruit (*fruit de la passion*) is the fruit of the passionflower. It grows throughout the tropics and resembles a thick-skinned plum. Unlike most fruit, it is ripe when the skin is shriveled and puckered. Inside, there are many small black seeds and a tart yellow pulp. You can eat the fruit raw; it's sharp, a little sweet, and has a hint of apricots and berries. Or strain the juice and use it in sorbets, sauces, drinks, jellies, and vinaigrettes.

Passion Fruit Tropic

Makes 2 drinks

Tropical fruit syrups are just starting to catch on in the United States and are becoming available in specialty stores. Made from the concentrated pulp of the fruit (and often combined with sugar and corn syrup), they can be found in most grocery stores in the Caribbean and are tasty combined with seltzer. This recipe calls for passion fruit syrup, but you might also experiment with other syrups, such as guava or tamarind. Serve in tall glasses over ice, decorated with a few plump blackberries or slices of tropical fruit.

4 tablespoons passion fruit syrup

2 cups seltzer or club soda

2 slices lime, for garnish

4 blackberries or a thin wedge of papaya, for garnish

Pour the syrup and seltzer into a tall glass over ice and stir. Garnish with fresh lime and blackberries.

Note: Passion fruit syrup is sold in Caribbean markets or can be purchased through the mail (see Mail-Order Sources, pages 342-344). Other tropical syrups may be substituted.

Passion Fruit-Lime Cooler

Serves 10

Bright and slightly tart, this drink will cool you on a hot day. For a fizzy drink, use half water and half seltzer.

1 1/2 cups freshly squeezed lime juice

3 cups passion fruit syrup (see note)

5 cups cold water

Freshly grated nutmeg, for garnish

10 mango slices, lemon wedges, or blackberries, for garnish

Combine lime juice, syrup, and water in a pitcher, then stir and taste, adding more syrup or sugar if a sweeter taste is desired. Pour into glasses filled with ice, and decorate with nutmeg and a piece of fruit.

Note: Passion fruit syrup is sold in Caribbean markets or can be purchased through the mail (see Mail-Order Sources, pages 342-344). Other tropical syrups may be substituted.

Watermelon-Lime Cooler

Serves 4 to 6

This beverage is a bit like drinking watermelon with a zing. You don't have to boil the sugar water, but it will taste better if you do.

3 cups chopped seeded watermelon
4 cups water
3/4 cup granulated sugar
3/4 cup freshly squeezed lime juice (or more to taste)
Mint sprigs, for garnish
Grated fresh gingerroot, for garnish

In a food processor, purée the watermelon with half of the water, then run through a sieve to extract juice, pressing hard on the pulp. In a saucepan, boil the remaining water and sugar until dissolved, about 5 minutes. Allow to cool, then stir all of the ingredients in a pitcher. Pour into tall glasses filled with ice, and garnish with the mint and a pinch of grated ginger.

Men and melons are

hard to know.

—Benjamin Franklin,
*Poor Richard's
Almanac*, 1733

Peach Lemonade

Serves 4 to 6

Peachy with a hint of lemon, this is one of my favorite drinks—serve it at a summer brunch or to your grandmother. Show off the pink liquid with dark red flecks with a beautiful cut-glass pitcher and glassware.

1 cup granulated sugar
2 fresh peaches, peeled, pitted, and chopped
4 cups water
3/4 cup freshly squeezed lemon juice
Sprigs of mint or peach slices, for garnish

In a saucepan, bring the sugar, peaches, and water to a boil, and then simmer until the sugar is dissolved, about 10 minutes. Allow the mixture to cool, then strain through a sieve, pressing to extract as much juice as possible. Stir in the lemon juice, and serve in tall glasses over ice. Garnish with mint or peach slices.

Mauby

Makes 2 drinks

Made from the bark of the algaroba (carob) tree, mauby is popular in the West Indies. Up until a few years ago, you could still find the "mauby ladies" in Barbados, walking along the docks with jugs of mauby on their heads, selling cupfuls that were as popular with kids as Coca-Cola is in the United States. The flavor is slightly bitter, giving the drink an edge that is welcoming on the hottest days. Mauby syrup is available from the Caribbean Spice Company (see Mail-Order Sources, pages 342-344).

2 cups club soda
2 to 4 tablespoons mauby syrup

Divide the soda between 2 tall glasses filled with ice. Stir in the mauby syrup and sauce.

The man who called it "near beer" was a bad judge of distance.

—Philander Johnson/
Luke McLuke,
Cincinnati Enquirer

Ginger Cooler

Makes 2 drinks

Heading out for a day on the ocean, some sailors pack a big jug of ginger coolers, loading down the jug with crushed ice and floating half-dollars of fresh lime. Not only is it a tonic on a hot day, but it's also good for *mal de mer* ("ocean sickness" in French). I know one sailor who even packs ginger coolers for road trips with her kids. This drink can be made with tap water or given a lift by using—as the ladies of Panama used to call it—"charged water."

6 tablespoons ginger beer syrup (see note)
3 cups water or seltzer
Pinch of freshly grated nutmeg or cinnamon (optional)
Slice of lime, for garnish

Combine ingredients in a pitcher. Pour into tall glasses filled with ice, stir, and serve with lime slices for garnish.

Note: Ginger beer syrup is available from Caribbean Spice Company (see Mail-Order Sources, pages 342-344).

Iced Ginger Tea

Makes 20 cups

On a summer afternoon, impress guests with this marvelous tea, which is pungent and noncaffeinated. It has a distinct taste of fresh ginger, which both soothes and revives.

1 (3- to 4-inch) length gingerroot, peeled and grated
5 quarts of water
2/3 cup pure maple syrup
4 sprigs fresh mint

Combine ingredients in a large pot and bring to a boil. Simmer for 15 minutes, then remove from heat. When cooled, taste and add more water or maple syrup if you desire a milder or sweeter tea. Remove mint sprigs, and refrigerate if not serving immediately. Serve in tall glasses over cracked ice, garnished with additional mint if desired.

Agua de Jamaica

Makes 11 cups

Found in big frosty pitchers in Mexican restaurants, *agua frescas* (fresh waters) are made with water, fresh fruit, and granulated sugar. Quite colorful, they are a great way to use overripe fruit. Dried Jamaica flowers (also called hibiscus) are available in Mexican or Caribbean markets and grocery stores. If you're lucky enough to be in the Caribbean littoral, garnish this drink with a fresh hibiscus blossom.

2 cups dried Jamaica blossoms (or substitute ripe fruit of choice)
10 cups water
Juice of 2 oranges
3/4 cup granulated sugar
2 oranges, sliced, for garnish

Rinse the flowers and place in a pot with 6 cups of the water. Bring to a boil, reduce heat to simmer, and cook for 10 minutes. Remove from heat and let stand for 10 minutes. Strain out the flowers, add the remaining water, orange juice, and granulated sugar, and serve chilled, garnished with orange slices.

GINGER

Used in Asian cooking for over three thousand years, fresh ginger adds effervescence to many dishes. It was also used extensively by the ancient Greeks and Romans, and like many spices, made its way around the world via the trade routes; the Portuguese took it to Africa, and the Spanish introduced it to the West Indies (where Jamaican ginger became a prized commodity). In the islands, it's still a home remedy for stomach ailments, and freshly grated or sliced ginger adds zest to curries, stews, chutneys, stir-fry dishes, and various desserts, the most famous being gingerbread. Avoid powdered ginger; its flat taste is nothing like the punch of fresh gingerroot. Look for the knobby tan roots at the market, peel or slice off the skin, and grate into various dishes.

Jenny

Makes 2 drinks

This is a perfect drink when you'd like a cocktail but prefer to go nonalcoholic. My husband developed it for yours truly.

2 cups tonic water
A few dashes Angostura bitters
2 fresh lime slices, for garnish

Divide tonic water between two glasses filled with ice. Stir in bitters, and top with a slice of lime.

GARNISHES

Forget the umbrella and maraschino cherry. Garnishes for drinks include:

* Freshly grated nutmeg
* Freshly grated gingerroot
* Springs of mint
* Lemon, orange, or lime zest
* A slice of starfruit or other tropical fruit
* A few plump blackberries or raspberries, or a tiny ripe strawberry

Tomato-Serrano Juice

Makes 3 cups

Campbell's Soup now markets a spicy tomato juice—a sure sign that the U.S. is embracing fiery foods. You can easily make your own spiked juice, which is invigorating by itself or in Bloody Marys. Serrano chiles have a clean vegetable flavor that goes well with tomato juice, or you can substitute jalapeños, Thai peppers, cayenne chiles, or—if you dare— habanero peppers. Blend in the seeds if you like your drink extra hot.

3 cups chilled tomato juice
1 to 2 serrano chiles, stemmed and seeded
1/2 bunch fresh cilantro leaves
Juice of 1 lemon
1/2 teaspoon salt
Freshly ground black pepper
3 tablespoons freshly ground horseradish

Blend all ingredients in a blender or food processor.

Mojito

Makes 2 cocktails

Strong and uncompromising, the mojito is an old-fashioned
Cuban cocktail, with the mingling of rum, mint, and soda
sure to get your mojo working, or at least get you fantasizing
about the glory days of Havana.

2 teaspoons sugar
Juice of 1 lemon
2 sprigs mint, plus extra leaves, for garnish
2 jiggers rum
Club soda

Stir together the sugar and lemon juice. Divide evenly
between 2 glasses. Crush a few mint leaves against the
inside of each glass, reserving sprigs. Fill glasses with ice,
and top each with a jigger of rum and a splash of club soda.
Decorate with mint sprigs.

Rum Punch

Makes 2 drinks

When you land in the Caribbean and feel the caressing
breeze on your skin, nothing greets you better than a rum
punch. This drink echoes an old island ditty that spells out
the ingredient proportions: one of sour, two of sweet, three
of strong, four of weak. Freshly grated nutmeg is eminently
better than powdered. Garnish with a fresh hibiscus flower
or mint sprigs.

1/4 cup (2 ounces) freshly squeezed lime juice
1 cup (8 ounces) simple syrup (see page 272)
1 1/2 cups (12 ounces) light or dark rum
2 cups (16 ounces) guava juice
Freshly grated nutmeg, for garnish

Combine lime juice, simple syrup, rum, and guava juice
in a cocktail shaker, shake, and serve in glasses over cracked
ice. Grate fresh nutmeg over the top of each drink.

Basics

Sauces, Chutneys, & Relishes

The easiest way to add zing to a meal is with spicy condiments. They are particularly handy when everyone in the crowd is not a spice-lover and the food is tamer than the fire-eaters desire. I usually keep a dozen hot sauces on my kitchen table, which I add to breakfast omelets, winter soups, grilling marinades, sandwiches, and salads. And by no means limit chutney to curried dishes—try it in a grilled cheese sandwich. The sweet heat of the relishes in this chapter will also dress up the simplest dishes—a generous dollop of Green Mango Relish, for example, in the center of sliced fresh garden tomatoes creates an appetizer that is pleasing to both the eye and the taste buds.

Roja Sauce

Makes 4 cups

Throughout Mexico and South America, you'll find *roja salsa* ("red sauce" in Spanish) on most restaurant tables. Served with tortilla chips or spooned onto eggs, enchiladas, vegetables, or soups, it brightens many meals.

6 ripe tomatoes

1 small white onion

4 cloves garlic

1/2 teaspoon salt

2 habanero chiles or 4 jalapeño chiles, seeded

1/4 cup water

Place the tomatoes and onion on a broiler pan and broil until the vegetables are charred on all sides. Transfer to a blender, skins on, and purée with the remaining ingredients, adding water as needed for a smooth consistency.

Verde Sauce

Makes 2 cups

Although this fresh, pungent green sauce is dense with basil and cilantro and tart with fresh lime juice, the truly unique flavor comes from the raw pumpkin seeds, a staple in Mexican cooking since pre-Columbian times. They are also called *pepitas* and can be found in most health food stores. Spicy but not hot, this sauce has many uses. Serve it as a dip with tortilla chips, or pour it over eggs, or toss with pasta instead of pesto. To make an easy hot appetizer, spread it in a baking dish, top with feta cheese, and bake for a few minutes.

1 cup raw pumpkin seeds

4 fresh tomatillos, husked

1/2 cup fresh basil leaves

1 bunch fresh cilantro

1 poblano chile, seeded

1/4 cup freshly squeezed lime juice

2 cloves garlic

1 teaspoon salt

1/2 to 1 cup olive oil

Purée all of the ingredients, except the oil, in a food processor. Transfer to a blender and add enough oil, while blending, until you have a smooth consistency.

Note: If you're serving this as a dip, you might only need 1/2 cup oil to achieve a guacamole-like consistency. If you're serving it as a sauce over pasta and want a thinner consistency, add 1 cup olive oil. If it's still too thick, thin it with some vegetable stock.

Green Tomatillo Sauce

Makes about 1 cup

Tomatillos have a slightly sour taste that contribute a lively tartness to this sauce, especially when used as a topping for thin-crusted pizza. This sauce is spicy-hot, but not blisteringly so, especially since tomatillos (and other acidic ingredients) counteract the heat of chiles. If you want a fiery condiment, double the amount of jalapeños or serranos. Some of the most daring use one jalapeño for every long green New Mexico chile. When refrigerated, the sauce will keep 2 weeks.

4 tomatillos, husked, or 2 fresh tomatoes

2 tablespoons olive oil

1/2 yellow onion, chopped

2 large cloves garlic, chopped

1/4 teaspoon ground cumin

1/2 cup Vegetable Stock (see page 73)

1 cup water

1 cup (about 10) roasted green New Mexico chiles (long green), finely chopped (see page 40)

3 roasted jalapeño or serrano chiles, finely chopped (see page 40)

1/2 teaspoon salt

1/8 teaspoon freshly ground black pepper

1/4 teaspoon oregano

Parboil the tomatillos for 5 minutes, then chop and set aside. Heat oil in a heavy skillet. Add the onion, cooking over medium heat for about 5 minutes. After the onions have wilted, add the garlic and cook for another minute. Add all remaining ingredients and cook over medium heat until the mixture comes to a boil. Reduce the heat, and simmer for 30 minutes, stirring occasionally. When done, the sauce should stick to the spoon; add an additional 1/4 cup of water if the sauce becomes too dry during cooking. (If you'd like a smoother consistency, allow to cool, then purée the sauce in a food processor or blender with a few short pulses.) Serve hot or at room temperature.

GREEN SAUCE

Green hot sauces made with tomatillos are a fundamental component of Mexican and Southwestern cuisines, both as a basic ingredient in enchiladas and huevos rancheros and as a side dish and ever-present table condiment. Green sauces are rarely just green. I've seen versions that are bright red (especially when tomatoes are abundant in the summer), as well as ones whose pale celerylike color belied a fierce heat. Particularly in the Southwest, green sauces are usually hotter than the basic red sauce (Chile Colorado)—opposite of what one might expect.

CHIPOTLE CHILES

Robust and smoky, with undertones of dried fruit and chocolate, chipotles are extraordinary chiles, and one of my favorites. They are made by smoking jalapeños slowly— a technique devised by Aztecs centuries ago to preserve the thick-fleshed pepper. In the Nahuatl language of the Aztecs, chil means "chile" and pochilli means "to smoke," and the two combined into "chipotle" mean "smoked chile."

Buy chipotles from a reputable source, as the smoking process will influence the outcome. Smoking fires that are too hot turn chipotles bitter, and the type of wood used in the fire is important; I've sampled some chipotles that tasted as though they were smoked over old tires! The best chipotles are smoked over grapevine cuttings, applewood, cherrywood, mesquite, or other fragrant cuttings. For more information about chipotles, I recommend *The Chipotle Chile Cook Book* by Jacqueline Higuera McMahan.

If you find chipotles too powerful, experiment with morita chiles, which are jalapeños (and sometimes serranos) that have been lightly smoked—the flavor is softer, with a hint of berries. Whether cooking with chipotles or moritas, smoked chiles will transform many dishes.

Chipotle-Tomatillo Sauce

Makes 4 cups

This spicy sauce from Lalo Garland at El Rinconcito in Austin, Texas, is very versatile: try it as a dipping sauce with grilled foods, drizzled over mashed potatoes, or added to your favorite sauce. The smokiness from the chipotle chiles is countered by the tartness of the tomatillos and the sweetness of the tomatoes.

3 pounds tomatillos, husked and chopped

1/2 large yellow onion, finely chopped

1/4 bunch fresh cilantro, chopped

4 serrano chiles, minced

2 cloves garlic, finely chopped

Freshly ground black pepper

Salt

1 teaspoon ground cumin

1/2 teaspoon minced garlic

4 tablespoons puréed canned chipotle chiles in adobo sauce

3 tablespoons tomato paste

Place all of the ingredients, except the chipotles and tomato paste, in a large stockpot. Barely cover with water, and bring to a boil. Cook 5 minutes, or until the tomatillos are soft to the touch. Allow the mixture to cool, then transfer to a blender or food processor. Add chipotles and purée. Return the sauce to the stockpot and add the tomato paste. Bring to a boil, then reduce heat and cook for 2 minutes. If the sauce is too thick, add more water until sauce consistency is achieved.

Chipotle Sauce

Makes 2 cups

With their sweet smokiness and woody fragrance, chipotle chiles form the base of this sauce, which I drizzle on everything from grilled mushrooms to fritters.

1 ancho chile

5 chipotle chiles

5 cloves garlic, roasted

1/4 cup chopped yellow onion

1/2 cup aged white wine vinegar

1/2 cup water

1 cup freshly squeezed orange juice

1 teaspoon Dutch-process cocoa

1/4 teaspoon ground cloves

1/4 teaspoon ground cumin

4 teaspoons honey

Preheat the oven to 400°. Puncture the ancho chile with a sharp knife and roast until you smell it, about 3 minutes. Submerge ancho and chipotle chiles into hot water for 15 to 20 minutes, or until softened. Stem, and remove and reserve seeds. Combine chiles with remaining ingredients in a blender or food processor. Blend until smooth, then taste. If you want a hotter sauce, add some or all of the seeds. Blend again. Transfer to a saucepan and heat until just boiling. Remove from heat.

Pepper Rum Sauce

Makes 2 cups

A few drops of this simple island sauce will enhance chowders, soups, chutneys, and vinaigrettes. Fill pretty bottles with it and give them as holiday gifts. The longer the sauce sits in the bottle, the better it becomes.

10 small whole chiles (pequins, tepins, machos, or other slim chiles)
1 cups light rum or dry sherry

Place the peppers in a sterilized bottle or jar and fill with rum. Cover and allow to stand at room temperature for a few days before using.

Papaya-Habanero Hot Sauce

Makes 2 cups

Caribbean sauces often feature tropical fruits such as papayas or mangoes, as well as scorching Scotch bonnet peppers. This sauce is quite hot, with the tropical freshness and fruity aroma derived from both the papayas and the chiles. I use it as a table condiment or blend it chunky and serve it as a hot dipping sauce. The sauce will keep for months in the refrigerator.

1 ripe papaya, cut in half and seeded
2 Scotch bonnet chiles or habaneros, stemmed
1 small yellow onion
1 cup white distilled vinegar
1 clove garlic
1 (1-inch) length fresh gingerroot, peeled and coarsely chopped

Spoon out the papaya flesh, combine with the remaining ingredients in a food processor, and purée. Pour the sauce into a nonreactive saucepan and heat until just boiling. Remove from the heat, let cool, and then bottle.

Amongst sauces I consider Harvey's the best for general use; Sutton's "Empress of India" is a strong sauce with a real flavour of mushrooms; Moir's sauces and "Reading sauce" are very trustworthy, and there are others which, no doubt, commend themselves to different palates, but I denounce "Worcester Sauce" and "Tapp's Sauce" as agents far too powerful to be entrusted to the hands of the native cook.

—Colonel A. Kenney-Herbert, *Culinary Jottings for Madras*, 1855

Tamarind Sauce

Makes 1/2 cup

With a distinct bite, this sauce will enliven boiled potatoes or rice dishes and can also serve as a dip for vegetables and fritters. Tamarind paste may be purchased at Indian or Middle Eastern markets.

1 tablespoon tamarind paste
1/2 teaspoon ground cayenne pepper
1/2 teaspoon salt
1/2 cup warm water

Combine the tamarind paste, cayenne, and salt in a small bowl. Pour the water slowly over the mixture, working the lumps out of the tamarind. Stir until smooth and serve at room temperature. Refrigerated, the sauce will keep for 3 weeks.

TAMARIND

Native to West Africa, tamarind is the fruit from a tree that grows in tropical regions of India, Africa, the Caribbean, and South America. The long bean-shaped pods have a sticky interior pulp that is sour, fruity, and studded with hard seeds. Tamarind makes a delicious, albeit messy, candylike snack and is used in jams, chutneys, sorbets, drinks, and condiments such as Worcestershire. Used sparingly, it will enhance dishes with its fragrance and tart taste. Indian cooks use dried tamarind pulp to season salads and vegetables, while the Chinese garnish sweet-and-sour dishes with crystallized tamarind. At ethnic markets, you can find blocks of dark brown tamarind pulp, tubes of tamarind paste, or bottles of tamarind syrup.

ALLSPICE

Also known as Jamaican pepper, this hard, unripened berry has the aroma of nutmeg, cinnamon, and cloves (hence the name) and has been used for centuries by natives in Mexico and the Caribbean for seasoning. (It was also purportedly sprinkled in the boots of European soldiers during World War I to keep their toes warm in the snow.)

The berry comes from the pimento tree, which grows throughout Mexico and the Caribbean and—like many New World ingredients—was introduced to Europe by Spanish explorers in the 1500s. This lovely tree produces aromatic white flowers, and the allspice berry is a key ingredient in jerk seasonings. Like black pepper, the taste is freshest if you can find whole berries and grind them yourself. Look for Jamaican allspice (sometimes called pimento), which has a high oil content and is believed by many to be the best in the world.

Jerk Sauce

Makes 2 cups

"Jerk" is literally a method of wrapping meat or fish in a spicy seasoning and cooking it over an open fire. Scholars theorize the technique was introduced to Jamaicans by African slaves as early as the 1600s in an effort to preserve pork. Some think the name may be derived from the process of flipping (or jerking) the meat repeatedly over a pit fire, while others contend it reflects the way the meat is ripped from the bone when served. Regardless, the essence of jerk cooking is in the seasoning, which is a blend of spices, herbs, and chiles. This Jerk Sauce can be used as a dipping sauce with fritters, or as a vegetable marinade, or even taken straight up at the table as a multipurpose condiment.

10 scallions, finely chopped
1/2 teaspoon ground cinnamon
1 teaspoon ground coriander
4 habanero chiles, stemmed and seeded
1/4 cup extra virgin olive oil
1/4 cup tamari soy sauce
1/4 cup apple cider vinegar
1/4 cup tamarind syrup (see note)
3 tablespoons ground allspice
1/2 teaspoon freshly grated nutmeg
1 teaspoon chopped fresh oregano
2 tablespoons dark rum
1/4 cup balsamic vinegar
1/4 teaspoon freshly ground black pepper
2 cloves garlic, minced

Combine all ingredients in a food processor and blend until smooth. Allow the flavors to marry overnight.

Note: Tamarind syrup is available at Latin, Caribbean, and Asian markets. If unavailable, use 2 tablespoons of tamarind pulp combined with 2 tablespoons brown sugar.

Aji Picante

Makes 1 heaping cup

Fragrant with cilantro, *aji picante* ("hot pepper" in Spanish) is a popular table condiment in the Dominican Republic. Serve it as a condiment for grilled vegetables or as a fresh-tasting dip with warm tortillas, or add a spoonful to soups, pasta sauces, and sandwich spreads. For less heat, omit the serranos. When refrigerated, this aji picante will keep several weeks.

2 bunches fresh cilantro (about 1 cup packed leaves and tender stems)

1 small tomato, cut into quarters

1 small yellow onion, cut into quarters

1 teaspoon apple cider vinegar

Juice of 1/2 lime

1/4 teaspoon salt

1 clove garlic

2 serrano chiles, stemmed

2 jalapeño chiles, stemmed

2 tablespoons olive oil

Pulse all of the ingredients in a food processor, taking care to not overblend, until mixture is semichunky.

SPICE ISLAND

When you sail into the port of Grenada, the first thing you notice is the smell of spices in the air. Aptly called the Spice Island, Grenada is in the windward chain of the Grenadines, close to Venezuela. Unlike some Caribbean islands to the north, the foods there are rarely just boiled or fried. Instead, you'll find dishes richly infused with the heady ingredients that come from the island, including:

★ Chile peppers

★ Nutmeg

★ Mace

★ Cashews

★ Arabica coffee

★ Vanilla bean pods

Found in kitchens throughout the South and Caribbean, hot sauces are snappy flavor enhancers. Many are salt- and sugar-free and add zip to sandwiches, soups, pizzas, salads, and rice dishes. Even people who don't like hot foods are startled at how, used judiciously, hot sauce will season (but not inflame) many dishes. Here's a round-up:

Asian sauces: A variety of chiles and ingredients define this broad category, which includes Indonesian sambals (relishes) and Asian "chilli" sauces. With ingredients such as fresh chiles, vinegar, garlic, and often curries or soybean paste, brands include Mida's Chilli Sauce, Noh Korean Hot Sauce, and Huy Fong Sriracha Hot Chili Sauce.

Caribbean hot sauces: These scorching sauces are distinguished by the use of the Scotch bonnet pepper or its cousin, the habanero—the world's hottest pepper—which is often blended with tropical fruits and spices to create a fruity, full-bodied, piercingly hot sauce. Delicious in fruit salsas or as an all-around condiment, brands include include Inner Beauty, Spitfire, Isla Vieques, as well as the homemade Papaya-Habanero Hot Sauce on page 292.

Louisiana hot sauces: A simple blend of vinegar, salt, and cayenne or tabasco peppers. Thin and sharp, these sauces have been a Southern tradition for centuries— even Thomas Jefferson had his own hot sauce recipe. Brands include Crystal, Panola, and McIlhenny's Tabasco.

Mexican sauces: These sauces often highlight a particular pepper—be it the smoky chipotle chile or the fresh pequin—that is blended with earthy vegetables (tomatoes, carrots, onions) and herbs born of the hot sun (oregano, sage, thyme). Sauces from the Yucatán often feature the habanero. Examples of Mexican sauces include Cholula (a pequin sauce), Bufalo Chipotle Sauce, El Yucateco (habanero sauce), and the Chipotle-Tomatillo Sauce on page 290.

Piqué: A simple sauce of chiles steeped in vinegar. Still found on Spanish islands in the Caribbean, they are better known in the United States as chile vinegars, and are great drizzled on steamed vegetables, mashed potatoes, or coleslaw.

HOT STUFF

Liz's Plum Chutney

Makes 2 pints

This sweet-hot-sour chutney is a variation of many fall fruit chutneys that my friend Liz Wheeler makes. You can use green tomatoes, fresh pears or apples, or mixtures of the three with various dried fruits such as raisins, dates, currants, and figs. Try a spoonful with baked beans or a baked sweet potato, or mix a little into a creamy coleslaw.

2 cups granulated sugar

1 cup apple cider vinegar

1/2 large lemon, seeded and thinly sliced crosswise, then quartered (about 1/3 cup)

1 1/2 pounds ripe, firm Italian prune plums, pitted and quartered lengthwise (about 4 cups)

4 ounces pitted dried apricots, sliced crosswise 1/8-inch thick

2 tablespoons peeled, shredded gingerroot

2 habanero chiles, seeded and shredded (about 2 tablespoons)

4 teaspoons mustard seeds

2 teaspoons salt

12 cloves garlic, peeled and lightly crushed

Place the sugar and cider vinegar in a heavy, nonreactive 2-quart saucepan. Bring to a boil over medium heat, stirring to dissolve the sugar. Add the lemon, plums, apricots, ginger, chiles, mustard seed, and salt, and stir to combine. Simmer for about 20 minutes, then add the garlic. Simmer gently for another 30 to 40 minutes until the juices are thickened.

Stored in the refrigerator in a covered glass container, the chutney will stay fresh for 1 month. For longer storage, spoon into sterilized pint-size glass jelly jars and seal according to canning jar manufacturer's instructions.

Gingered Fig Chutney

Makes 1 cup

Tart, pungent, and with a hint of heat from the ginger and chiles, this chutney from my friend Carol Govan is so good that I've been known to eat it in front of the refrigerator from the jar. Serve it with roasted red peppers as a sandwich spread, spread some atop cream cheese and serve with crackers as an appetizer, or set it out as a condiment with curried dishes.

1/2 large Bermuda onion, coarsely chopped

4 tablespoons coarsely chopped gingerroot

2 red serrano, jalapeño, or other hot chiles, seeded and coarsely chopped

2 teaspoons grated lemon zest

1/2 cup golden raisins

2/3 cup white wine vinegar or Chile Vinegar (see page 317)

2/3 cup firmly packed dark brown sugar

2 teaspoons ground cardamom

1/2 teaspoon salt

1/4 teaspoon ground cayenne pepper

4 fresh figs, peeled and cut in 1/4-inch dice

Combine the onion, ginger, and chiles in a food processor until the consistency of rice. Spoon the mixture into a deep skillet and add the lemon zest, raisins, vinegar, brown sugar, and spices, and cook over low heat for 1 to 2 minutes. Add the figs and bring the mixture to a slow boil, stirring often until the juices thicken. Remove from the heat and allow to cool completely. Refrigerate before serving.

Now sing of the fig,

Simiane,

Because its loves are

hidden

I sing the fig, she said

*Whose beautiful loves

are hidden,

Its flowering is folded

away

Closed room where

marriages are made:

No perfume tells the

tale outside.

—André Gide

Cranberry-Orange-Habanero Relish

Makes 3 cups

This twist on the classic Thanksgiving cranberry relish is a lively medley of color and tastes. Ingredients that are highly acidic, like cranberries, tend to counter the heat of chiles, so you may want to spike the dish with an additional habanero, especially if you don't plan to serve it for a few days. But be sure to taste it first. The heat will sneak up on you.

1 seedless orange, washed and quartered, with skin
4 cups fresh cranberries, washed and picked over
1/4 cup granulated sugar
1 habanero chile, seeded and minced

Place the orange quarters in a food processor. Add the cranberries and pulse until the ingredients are chopped; do not overblend. (You may have to chop some of the orange peel by hand.) Transfer to a nonreactive bowl and combine with the sugar and habanero. Taste, and add more sugar or chiles if necessary. The flavors will be best if you allow the relish to sit refrigerated for a day or two before serving.

Green Mango Relish

Makes 1 pint

This pretty yellow relish can be served as an appetizer or as a side dish to rice and beans or curried dishes. Be sure to use green, unripe mangoes. When refrigerated, this relish will keep for 1 week.

1 unripe mango (about 1 pound)
1 teaspoon minced yellow onion
1 clove garlic, minced
1 serrano or other hot chile, seeded and minced
2 teaspoons extra virgin olive oil
Salt to taste
Freshly ground black pepper to taste

Peel the mango, and grate it down to the seed. In a mixing bowl, combine the mango with remaining ingredients. Refrigerate until chilled before serving.

Fresh Chiles de Agua

Makes 2 cups

This is a versatile condiment—purée it into a sauce for soups, stews, or vegetable dishes, or chop the ingredients coarsely, add a few diced tomatoes or tomatillos, and serve as a fresh salsa with chips. I usually keep a jar in the refrigerator as a basic flavor enhancer and leaping-off point for other dishes. The chile de agua (literally, "water chile") is a local chile from Oaxaca, Mexico. It's large (6 inches long) with a fresh flavor and intense heat. Any large, green hot peppers can be substituted—I often use a combination of New Mexico chiles and poblano chiles. Mixing red and green chiles will also add color to the dish.

6 fresh chiles de agua or other chiles (unseeded if you want it extra hot)

1/2 white onion

1 clove garlic

Juice of 1 lime

Pinch of salt

1 small bunch scallions

1 small bunch fresh cilantro

Combine all the ingredients in a food processor and either pulse coarsely or purée.

Note: For variety, add a few diced tomatillos or tomatoes, or char the chiles under a broiler and peel and seed them before adding to food processor.

Kim Chee

Makes 4 cups

Kim Chee is a delicious Korean side dish that is salted, spiced, and set aside for a few days before eating. Crisp and tangy, this pickled cabbage can be enjoyed like any relish or pickle and is the perfect accompaniment for picnics and buffets. While piquant, this Kim Chee is not a flame-thrower; for a hotter dish, double the jalapeños and don't seed them.

1 head bok choy cabbage (about 2 pounds)

1 daikon (see note)

2 tablespoons sea salt

3 tablespoons rice wine vinegar

1 teaspoon honey

2 teaspoons dark sesame oil

1 teaspoon lightly crushed Szechwan peppercorns

4 cloves garlic, peeled and sliced very thin

3 red jalapeños, seeded and julienned

1 (1-inch) length gingerroot, peeled and minced

1/2 cup thinly sliced scallions

Trim the root end of the bok choy and discard any yellow or bruised outer leaves. Rinse the cabbage well. Stack the outer leaves together and cut into thirds lengthwise. Cut across into 1-inch-wide strips. Cut the inner cabbage leaves in half lengthwise and also cut across into 1-inch-wide strips. Set aside in a medium bowl. (You should have about 8 cups.)

Peel and slice the daikon in half lengthwise. Thinly slice it into half-rounds. Add the daikon to the cabbage along with the sea salt and mix well. Place a small plate on the cabbage and top with a weighted object such as a full tea kettle (about 3 pounds). Set aside at room temperature for an hour. Rinse slightly under cool water in a colander.

Meanwhile, mix the vinegar, honey, and oil. Add the peppercorns. Place the garlic, jalapeños, ginger, and scallions in a large bowl. Add the cabbage (with some moisture) and dressing. Pack in a nonreactive bowl or jar and cover tightly. Refrigerate for 3 to 4 days before eating.

Note: Daikon is a large, tan, carrot-shaped radish. Also known as a Japanese or Oriental radish, it is spicier than round red radishes.

Canning fruits and vegetables is serious business. Canning jar manufacturers include instructions in every box of jars and lids, but you should check out a more thorough source, such as *Preserving Today* (by Jeanne Lesem, Knopf, 1992) or *Keeping the Harvest* (by Nancy Chioffi and Gretchen Mead, Storey, 1991), to learn the intricacies of the craft. You'll find the time was well spent when your pantry is stocked with tightly sealed jars of colorful vegetables.

Pickled Hot Chiles

Makes 8 cups

An elderly Italian lady from the Little Italy section of Hartford makes this spirited concoction and claims that everyone in her house eats it up right away. Use a mixture of hot and sweet chiles, including Hungarian wax, jalapeño, serrano, Anaheim, and cayenne peppers. Choose a few bright red and yellow chiles for color. Allow to mellow at least two weeks before serving.

2 pounds mixed hot and sweet peppers, seeded and sliced 1/2 inch thick crosswise or in strips

6 tablespoons kosher or sea salt

6 tablespoons peanut oil or light olive oil

12 large cloves garlic, thickly sliced

2 lightly packed cups coarsely shredded fresh mint

2 lightly packed cups coarsely shredded fresh basil

4 cups apple cider vinegar

Put the peppers into a nonreactive bowl and toss with the salt. Set aside for 2 hours, tossing occasionally. Drain and rinse well to remove the salt. Heat the oil in a heavy skillet over medium heat until very hot. Add the garlic, stir until sizzling, then stir in the chiles and herbs. Sauté for 2 minutes until the herbs wilt and the chiles are softened but still crisp. Pack the seasoned chiles into sterilized pint canning jars. Bring the vinegar to a boil and pour over the chiles just to cover. Seal the jars and process according to the canning jar manufacturer's instructions.

Seasonings, Butters, & Spreads

For the spice-loving cook, a pantry of fresh seasonings and spreads offers the tools for creating bright, distinctive meals. Make your own curry by roasting and grinding exotic spices. Bottle your own habanero honey to give to friends and family as gifts. Add zest to the simplest condiments—mayonnaise, ketchup, mustard—with tropical herbs, spices, and chiles. Each of these recipes is easy to make and will add emphasis and originality to the dishes you serve.

Simple Curry Powder

Makes 4 tablespoons

Spice seeds can be bought in bulk at most health food stores. Take advantage of this and make your own curry, which may be stored in a cool, dark place for up to several months.

4 teaspoons coriander seeds

4 teaspoons cumin seeds

2 teaspoons fenugreek seeds

2 bay leaves

1 teaspoon black peppercorns

1 teaspoon ground turmeric

1 teaspoon pure chile powder

Dry-roast the coriander, cumin, and fenugreek in a skillet until lightly browned, 1 or 2 minutes, then grind in a spice grinder with the bay leaves and peppercorns. Shake with the turmeric and chile powder in a small, airtight container.

MAKING HOMEMADE CURRIES

Curry powder refers to a blend of whole or ground spices—including those that are native to India (ginger, pepper, coriander, cumin, turmeric, cloves, fenugreek, and cinnamon) as well as spices brought from the New World (chiles and allspice). In India, there are as many curry blends as there are cooks, and these spice blends are also known as masalas. (Curry was a term coined by British colonials in India to describe savory dishes served in a spicy sauce.)

There's some confusion in the West regarding what curry is exactly. In Indian markets you'll also find curry leaves, which are from an aromatic Indian plant called murraya koeniggi, whose leaves (called kari in India) have been used in Indian cooking since ancient times. According to Indian cooking authority Julie Sahni, this curry leaf is the basis of the original curry powder, and you can now find fresh or dried curry leaves in Indian grocery stores. Curry blends sometimes include the curry leaf, but not always, and can be mild or strong. In the West Indies (where curries were brought from India in the seventeenth and eighteenth centuries), you'll find fiery curries in Trinidad and milder ones in Virgin Gorda and Tortola. Thai and other Southeast Asian cooks use colorful curry pastes—green (made with green chiles), red (colored with paprika and red chiles), and yellow (from the addition of turmeric and yellow chiles).

Curry powders are easy to make and better in flavor and aroma than the ones you'll find pre-blended in supermarkets. Buy the seeds or berries whole, and roast them before cooking, which will bring out the natural oils and give them an intense, roasted flavor. (When raw, the seeds can be rough and catch in your throat.) Grinding them yourself will give you a fresher, more pungent curry. (If you don't have a grinder or mortar and pestle, purchase an inexpensive coffee grinder for this purpose.)

Trinidadian Curry

Makes 1 1/2 cups

This recipe comes from Steve Cobble, chef at the Green Street Grill in Cambridge, Massachusetts, who seasons his food with this powerful curry.

4 tablespoons cumin seeds

2 tablespoons whole coriander seeds

1 tablespoon cloves

1 tablespoon poppyseeds

1 tablespoon mustard seeds

2 tablespoons ground cayenne pepper

2 tablespoons ground cinnamon

2 tablespoons star anise

1 tablespoon fenugreek seeds

1 tablespoon black peppercorns

4 tablespoons ground turmeric

4 tablespoons ground ginger

Roast the cumin and coriander in a dry sauté pan until fragrant, just a few minutes. Grind all of the ingredients, except turmeric and ginger, in a spice grinder. Combine all of the ingredients. Place in an airtight container and store in a cool, dry place for up to several months.

Masala

Makes 4 heaping tablespoons

You can use this basic recipe as a jumping off point to experiment with your own blends, adding mustard seeds, ground cinnamon, even nutmeg. Wrapped in an attractive tin box, masala makes a warm holiday gift for friends.

1 tablespoon coriander seeds
1/2 tablespoon cardamom seeds
1 tablespoon fenugreek seeds
1 tablespoon pure chile powder
1 tablespoon ground turmeric
1 tablespoon ground cumin
Freshly ground black pepper
A few pinches of ground cloves

Toast the coriander, cardamom, and fenugreek seeds in a dry cast-iron skillet until lightly browned. Mix with the remaining ingredients and grind to a powder. Store in an airtight container in a cool, dark place up to several months.

Garam Masala

Makes 8 teaspoons

Garam masala refers to a spice blend from northern India (garam means hot and masala means spices). Traditional ingredients include cumin, coriander, cardamom, and cinnamon. Dry-roasting the spices will fill your kitchen with a perfume that is as rich as the earth, as aromatic as an open fire, as fragrant as an Indian spice market.

4 teaspoons cumin seeds

4 teaspoons coriander seeds

1 teaspoon ground cardamom

1/4 teaspoon whole cloves

1/2 teaspoon black peppercorns

2 (2-inch) sticks cinnamon

1/4 teaspoon ground cayenne pepper

Dry-roast the cumin, coriander, cardamom, and cloves in a skillet until lightly browned, 1 or 2 minutes. When cool, combine with the black pepper and cinnamon in a spice grinder and grind to a powder. Mix with the cayenne pepper and pour into an airtight container. Store in a cool, dry place for up to several months if not using immediately.

Note: To make a paste, stir a bit of tepid water into the spice mixture.

Creole Seasoning

Makes 4 heaping tablespoons

According to Albert Veille, Creole cooking is "a mixture of Caribbean, African, and Hindu recipes, in which there is a blend of subtlety and violence, embellished by the scent of herbs, spices, and peppers." This all-purpose seasoning is good in soups, stocks, and grilled dishes.

2 tablespoons paprika

2 teaspoons dried oregano

2 teaspoons dried thyme

1 teaspoon ground cumin

1 teaspoon ground cayenne pepper

1/2 teaspoon salt

1/2 teaspoon freshly ground black pepper

Combine all of the ingredients in a mixing bowl. Store in an airtight container in a cool, dry place for up to several months.

Mexican Mustang Powder

Makes 6 2/3 tablespoons

A friend once gave me a box of spices she'd found in a small museum shop in Arizona. Called "Mexican Mustang Powder," it was a pepper-driven spice blend, used for making chili. Here's my interpretation of that chile blend, which I find myself shaking on rice and beans, turnovers, grilled tomatoes—even pizza.

4 tablespoons pure chile powder

3 teaspoons ground cumin

3 teaspoons dried oregano

1/2 teaspoon ground clove

1 1/2 teaspoons freshly ground black pepper

Combine all ingredients and place them in an airtight container. Store in a cool, dry place for up to several months.

Five-Spice Powder

Makes a heaping 1/4 cup

This Chinese seasoning was brought to Europe by English sailors in the late 1500s. Widely used in Chinese cooking, it's a savory blend of five popular Asian spices.

1 tablespoon ground fennel
1 tablespoon ground cloves
1 tablespoon ground cinnamon
1 tablespoon pure chile powder
1 tablespoon ground anise

    Combine all ingredients in a small bowl, mixing well. Store in a cool, dry place for up to several months.

Serrano Butter

Makes 1/2 cup

Seasoned butter is tasty on toasted bread, steamed vegetables, baked yams, or sweet potatoes. I especially like it drizzled over steamed asparagus with salt, ground pepper, and fresh-squeezed lemon. The butter should be used within several days, or it can be frozen for a few weeks.

1 tablespoon freshly squeezed lime juice
1 clove garlic, minced
1/2 teaspoon chopped fresh cilantro
2 serrano chiles, seeded and finely chopped
Pinch of salt
1/2 cup unsalted butter, softened

With a fork, beat the lime juice, garlic, cilantro, chiles, and salt into the butter, then transfer to a small crock or ramekin for serving. Cover and refrigerate until firm.

Chipotle-Tequila Butter

Makes 1/2 cup

I first tasted chipotle-flavored butter at the historic La Posada Hotel in Albuquerque and serve it with grilled vegetables or rice, or brushed on corn on the cob.

1 to 2 small chipotle chiles (depending on desired heat)
1/2 cup unsalted butter, softened
1/2 teaspoon freshly squeezed lime juice
2 teaspoons tequila
1 teaspoon chopped fresh cilantro
Pinch of ground cumin

Submerge the chipotles in hot water until soft, about 15 minutes. Remove the seeds, dry thoroughly, and mince. In a mixing bowl, combine with the remaining ingredients. Beat with a fork until blended. Transfer to a small bowl or ramekin for serving, cover, and refrigerate until firm. Use within a few days, or wrap tightly and freeze for up to several weeks.

Curry Butter

Makes 1/2 cup

This pretty copper-colored butter can be dabbed on rice, steamed or grilled vegetables, polenta, or baked potatoes.

1/2 cup unsalted butter, softened
1 1/2 teaspoons curry powder
1 teaspoon freshly squeezed lime juice
1 clove garlic, minced

In a mixing bowl, beat all of the ingredients together with a fork until blended. Transfer to a small bowl or ramekin for serving, cover, and refrigerate until firm. Use within a few days, or wrap tightly and freeze for up to several weeks.

Habanero Butter

Fire-lovers, ignite! This butter is terrific brushed on cheese sandwiches before grilling, tucked into baked squash, or served with bread. Although habaneros of any color will suffice, the orange and red ones provide flecks of color. (Some people also contend that red habaneros are the hottest.) The habanero contributes a fruity, back-of-the-mouth heat, while the cayenne lends a lip-smacking quality to this butter.

1/2 cup unsalted butter, softened
1 fresh red habanero chile, stemmed, seeded, and minced
1 fresh red cayenne or jalapeño chile, stemmed, seeded, and minced

With a fork, mash the chiles into the butter. Transfer to a small bowl or ramekin for serving, cover, and refrigerate until firm. Use within a few days, or wrap tightly and freeze for up to several weeks.

Mango Mustard with Habanero

Makes about 1/2 cup

On the small Caribbean island of Vieques, our friends Jim and Diana Starke have initiated an unusual recycling program. Locals collect empty rum bottles for 5 cents each, and the Starkes fill the bottles with their extraordinary hot sauces, with ingredients ranging from *recao* (a long-leafed coriander) to Vieques honey. The Starkes also make tropical mustards and were nice enough to share this recipe with me. Spoon it into your favorite vinaigrette or mustard cream sauce, or spread on grilled Cheddar cheese sandwiches.

1/2 cup whole yellow mustard seed

1/2 cup apple cider vinegar

5 tablespoons water

1 tablespoon honey

2 tablespoons vegetable oil

1 mango, peeled, pitted, and chopped (1/2 cup)

1/8 to 1/4 fresh habanero chile, seeded and chopped

1/4 teaspoon salt

Finely grind the mustard seed in a spice or coffee grinder. Place all of the ingredients in blender and purée until smooth, scraping down the sides and mixing thoroughly. Adjust the amount of habanero chiles to taste. Spoon the mustard into a covered jar, and refrigerate. Allow it to cure for one week before using. (If the mustard thickens during refrigeration, add more water to achieve the desired consistency.)

Jim's Chipotle Ketchup

Makes 1 1/2 pints

This ketchup isn't blazingly hot, just spicy hot, and infused with a smoky flavor. Store ketchup in the refrigerator for up to 1 month.

2 cups tomato sauce

1 cup white distilled vinegar

1 teaspoon dry mustard

1/2 cup honey

2 stalks celery with leaves, cut into 8 pieces

1 yellow onion, quartered

6 chipotle chiles, stemmed, seeded (seeds reserved), softened, and finely chopped

1 (1-inch) stick cinnamon

1/2 teaspoon whole cloves

In a 1 1/2-quart saucepan, combine the tomato sauce, vinegar, mustard, and honey. Add the celery and onion. Add the chipotles to the saucepan and bring to a boil over medium heat. Combine the cinnamon, cloves, and chipotle seeds in a spice (cheesecloth) bag and place it in the pot. Reduce the heat to simmer, cooking for 2 1/2 hours to reduce volume and infuse with the spices. Remove the celery, onion, and spice bag, and bottle.

Chipotle Mayonnaise

Makes 1 cup

You're tired of the same old sandwich and want one that
tastes different, but you're in a rush, don't feel creative,
and have exactly five minutes to make it. This is the time
to reach for the hot sauce; here the chipotle sauce lends
a pleasant spiciness and faint woodiness to an otherwise
ordinary condiment. Serve this piquant mayonnaise on a
sandwich of fresh tomatoes, sprouts, thinly sliced cucumbers, and whole-grain bread, or with roasted vegetables
tucked into a pita pocket for a taste treat.

1/2 cup good-quality mayonnaise
1/2 cup plain yogurt
**1/2 to 1 tablespoon Jump Up and Kiss Me Chipotle Sauce or
    other chipotle sauce**

Stir together ingredients in small bowl and serve or
refrigerate.

Habanero Honey

Makes 1 cup

Give honey a buzz with a habanero pepper. Although any
color habanero is suitable, a red chile will look beautiful
suspended in the golden liquid. I first tasted habanero honey
on Vieques, where the Isla Vieques Condiment Company
experiments with island honey and homegrown peppers.
Infused with the king of peppers, this honey is sweet, but
with the slightest tingle.

1 whole fresh habanero chile
1 cup honey

Clean habanero chile thoroughly and place in sterilized
jar. Fill with honey.

> The use of Honey is so
> soveraigne that noth-
> ing in our cold coun-
> tries comes neare it for
> goodnesse and perfec-
> tion: insomuch that it
> is rightly called Flos
> Florum, the flower of
> flowers, or rather their
> quintessence. It makes
> old men young, pre-
> serving their naturall
> heate, if they know
> how to use it.
>
> —William Vaughn,
> *Directions for
> Health*, 1617

Vinegars & Oils

Vinegars and oils can be infused with herbs and spices to create flavored seasonings. The vinegars and oils in this chapter also make pretty gifts for housewarmings, birthdays, or the holidays. In Italy, it's even a tradition to celebrate the birth of a baby with a gift of olive oil.

Chile Vinegar

Makes 2 cups

Homemade vinegars make attractive gifts any time of the year, especially if you choose a decorative glass bottle. I've even seen chile vinegars in recycled Amaretto bottles, which look spectacular. The longer the chiles steep in vinegar, the hotter the vinegar will become. If you prefer a milder vinegar, taste after a few days and strain the vinegar into a sterilized bottle when you've reached the desired strength.

2 serrano chiles
2 sprigs fresh thyme
1 clove garlic, slivered
2 cups white distilled vinegar

   Place the chiles, thyme, and garlic in a saucepan of boiling water for 1 minute. Remove, drain, and pat dry. If there's no tear at the stem of the chile, cut a thin slice on one side so the chile will sink to the bottom of the bottle. Put all of the ingredients in a sterilized 10-ounce glass bottle. Heat the vinegar in a nonreactive saucepan to just below boiling point, then pour it into the bottle, and seal. The vinegar will keep for several months in a cool, dark place.

And Boaz said unto her, "At mealtime come thou hither, and eat of the bread, and dip thy morsel in the vinegar."

—*The Book of Ruth*

Vinegar (which means "sour wine" in French) was discovered at the same time as wine, more than ten thousand years ago. As early as the thirteenth century, Parisian vendors sold flavored vinegars on the streets, and during the Middle Ages, pepper vinegar was all the rage in France because wine containing pepper was not taxed.

Good-quality vinegar should be clear as water—cloudy vinegar is the result of bad grapes, poor filtration, or age. Vinegars vary greatly; they can be rich, sharp, mellow, or sweet. Varieties include:

Apple cider vinegar:
An inexpensive, fruity vinegar made from apple pulp or cider. With a hint of apples, it's good for pickling or cooking.

Balsamic vinegar:
A rich, sweet, slightly tart wine vinegar made from white Trebbiano grapes in Modena, Italy. Exceptional in flavor, some balsamic vinegars have been aged in wooden barrels for decades and are as fine as good wine (as costly, too). Balsamic vinegar is excellent drizzled over salads, garden tomatoes, and even fresh fruit.

Champagne vinegar:
A light golden vinegar made from Champagne wine, with the taste and perfume of champagne.

Distilled white vinegar:
Strong and rough as moonshine, distilled white vinegar is made by distilling alcohol from grain. Good for pickling and making Caribbean hot sauces.

Herbal vinegars: Made by infusing wine vinegar (usually white) with fresh herbs.

Malt vinegar: A mild vinegar made from malted barley. Good in chutneys, pickled vegetables, and fruit salads.

Raspberry vinegar:
A subtle, fruity vinegar infused with raspberries.

Red wine vinegar:
A poor man's balsamic vinegar, with a strong, sharp taste, made by fermenting red wine. Good for dressing up salads, steamed vegetables, and sauces.

Rice wine vinegar:
Made from fermented and soured rice wines, Japanese rice wine vinegar has a beautiful amber hue with a subtle oaklike flavor. Chinese rice vinegar can be sharp and even sour.

Sherry vinegar:
Matured in casks and resembling sherry in color, this vinegar is mellow and smooth.

Umeboshi plum vinegar: A light plum-colored vinegar made from the liquid of pickled umeboshi plums. Sweet, sour, and very salty, it's delicious sprinkled on steamed vegetables or salads. Sometimes it is labeled Ume Plum Vinegar.

White wine vinegar:
Made by fermenting white wine; the quality of the vinegar is dictated by the quality of the wine. Used to season salads, marinades, and sauces.

VINEGARS

Spicy Herbal Vinegar

Makes 4 cups

This piquant vinegar can be drizzled on steamed green vegetables or baked beans, stirred into sauces, or sprinkled on piping-hot samosas.

3 small, slender fresh chiles, such as tabasco or cayenne
1 clove garlic
Several long sprigs fresh oregano or thyme (or other herbs)
8 whole black peppercorns
4 cups white distilled vinegar

Place the chiles and garlic in a saucepan of boiling water for 1 minute. Remove, drain, and pat dry. With a sharp knife, cut a single fine line in the chiles so they will sink to the bottom of the bottle. Cut the garlic into slivers, and drop the chiles, garlic, herbs, and peppercorns into 1 or 2 sterilized bottles with a lid.

Heat the vinegar in a nonreactive pan to just below boiling point. Pour the vinegar into the bottle, and seal. Set aside for 1 week to allow the flavors to penetrate the vinegar. The vinegar will keep for several months in a cool, dark place.

HOMEMADE VINEGARS

Any kind of vinegar can be used to make homemade vinegars. To emphasize the delicate flavor of just one herb, select a high-quality wine or cider vinegar with good flavor. If you're making a big batch of vinegar that's loaded with chiles, herbs, and garlic, take a tip from the ladies in the Caribbean and use an inexpensive cider or distilled white vinegar. You'll never notice the difference. At native homes and restaurants in the Caribbean, bottles of chile vinegars chock-full of chiles and garden herbs are on most tables and frequently are refilled with white vinegar when the liquid gets low. The chiles and vegetables (I've seen carrots, celery, and onions) float languidly in the vinegar like tropical sea creatures, creating firewater that is delicious sprinkled on deep-fried fritters. For a decorative touch, stab a large pepper with a sprig of rosemary, and drop it in the vinegar.

Once the vinegar has steeped and absorbed the herbal flavors, you can either strain it or leave the chiles and herbs in for decoration (and intensified taste). If the vegetable matter left in the bottle breaks down or discolors (especially common with garlic), strain the vinegar through cheesecloth or a fine sieve, pour it into another sterilized bottle, and pop a few fresh, clean herbs and chiles into the bottle before sealing. If the peppers have been picked ripe, there should be a tear at the stem end. If not, you will need to cut a slit in them so they'll sink to the bottom of the bottle. Make sure you don't overload a bottle with vegetables and thus diminish the preservative effects of the vinegar.

Rosemary-Serrano Red Wine Vinegar

Makes 2 cups

The color of rubies, this zesty vinegar is fragrant from the fresh rosemary.

2 serrano chiles
1 clove garlic, sliced
1 sprig fresh rosemary
8 whole black peppercorns
2 cups red wine vinegar (or enough to fill bottle)

Place the chiles, garlic, and rosemary in a pot of boiling water for 1 minute, then drain and pat dry. With a sharp knife, make a small slit in the chiles so they will sink to the bottom of the bottle. Drop the chiles, garlic, rosemary, and peppercorns into a clear bottle with a lid. Heat the vinegar in a nonreactive pan to just below boiling. Pour the vinegar into the bottle and seal. Store in a cool, dry place for 1 to 2 weeks, depending on desired strength.

When desired flavor is achieved, strain the vinegar and pour it into a sterilized bottle. Add a long sprig of fresh, cleaned rosemary for decoration, and seal. The vinegar will keep for several months in a cool, dry place.

Flavored Olive Oil

Makes 4 cups

Although olive oil is good on just about anything, I particularly enjoy it at dinner with loads of garlic in a shallow bowl for dipping hot, crunchy bread.

4 cups extra virgin olive oil
4 cloves garlic, peeled and coarsely chopped
1 sprig fresh rosemary, rinsed and dried
1 sprig fresh thyme, rinsed and dried
10 black peppercorns

    In a saucepan, heat the olive oil until warm to the touch. (Be careful not to boil it.) Remove the pan from the heat. Combine the garlic, herbs, and peppercorns in a sterilized bottle or jar, and pour in the oil. Seal, and store in a cool, dark place.

Note: If you're not using the oil within a few days, it's important to strain it and keep refrigerated to prevent bacterial growth.

Spicy Garlic Oil

Makes 2 cups

Make this sprightly oil in small batches and drizzle it over salads or tomatoes, or whisk it into a vinaigrette.

2 cups extra virgin olive oil
2 tablespoons dried Japanese chiles, pequins, cascabels, or other dried chiles (optional)
6 garlic cloves, peeled and coarsely chopped

    In a saucepan, heat the olive oil until it is warm to the touch. (Be careful not to boil it.) Remove the pan from the heat. Combine the chiles and garlic in a sterilized bottle or jar, and pour in the oil. Seal, and store in a cool, dark place.

Note: If you're not using the oil within a few days, it's important to strain it and keep refrigerated to prevent bacterial growth.

The whole Mediterranean, the sculpture, the palms, the gold beads, the bearded heroes, the wine, the ideas, the ships, the moonlight, the winged gorgons, the bronze men, the philosophers, all of it seems to rise in the sour, pungent taste of these black olives between the teeth. A taste older than meat, older than wine. A taste as old as cold water.

—Lawrence Durrell,
Prospero's Cell

Oils are delicious in vinaigrettes, seasonings, salads, and rice dishes. Not only do they season food beautifully, but they also bind the ingredients and pull the dish together. The following oils are made by extracting oil from nuts, seeds, fruit, and grains. Nut and seed oils tend to be strong flavored and are best when added judiciously to dishes at the last minute for added spice, or when combined with olive oil in a vinaigrette. All oils should be stored in a cool place.

Almond Oil: Pressed from sweet almonds, this delicate, fragrant oil is used in baking and is good mixed with other oils in a salad. It can turn rancid quickly and should be refrigerated after opening.

Avocado Oil: A light, colorless oil made from the pits and flesh of avocados.

Canola Oil: Pressed from rapeseed, this tasteless oil is the lowest in saturated fat of any oil. With a high smoking temperature, it's suitable for frying.

Corn Oil: Thick, buttery, and heavy, corn oil is high in polyunsaturated fats and a good all-purpose oil for baking and sautéing.

Ghee: Popular in India, this oil is made from clarified butter.

Grapeseed Oil: Made from grape seeds, this light, delicate oil is high in polyunsaturated fats. With a high smoking point, it is suitable for frying. It's also good for marinades and mayonnaise.

Hazelnut Oil: A versatile nut oil with a deep, nutty aroma and flavor. Delicious in a salad dressing or marinade, it can also be added at the last minute to sautéed or braised vegetables or other dishes. Keep refrigerated after opening.

Olive Oil: See pages 70-71.

Peanut Oil: This all-around oil has a high smoking temperature, and is good for sautéing and frying.

Poppyseed Oil: When left unrefined, this is a light, aromatic oil that benefits salads and crudités. It is called huile blanche in France.

Pumpkin Seed Oil: An ebony-colored oil reminiscent of toasted pumpkin seeds. Delicious sprinkled on steamed vegetables or salads.

Safflower Oil: A versatile, unrefined oil high in polyunsaturated fats. With a high smoking temperature, it's suitable for frying or stir-fries.

Sesame Oil: Used in ancient Egypt, sesame oil is available light or dark. Light sesame oil is pressed from raw sesame seeds and has a mild sesame flavor, whereas dark sesame oil is fragrant and rich, made from roasted sesame seeds. With a high smoking temperature, it's suitable for frying and is also delicious as a seasoning. Keep refrigerated after opening.

Soybean Oil: Also known as soyabean oil, this light, all-purpose oil pressed from soybeans is rich in polyunsaturated fats. Good in salad dressings and other seasonings.

Sunflower Oil: A light, neutral, inexpensive, all-purpose oil, high in polyunsaturated fat. Due to its lower smoking point, it is best in cold sauces or low-temperature frying.

Vegetable Oil: Made by blending various oils (which means that it can be high in saturated fats), this is an all-purpose cooking oil.

Walnut Oil: A delicate, nutty oil, delicious as a seasoning in salad dressings and other dishes. Also known as huile de noix in France. Keep refrigerated after opening.

SPECIALTY OILS

Appendices

Essential Ingredients

Allspice: Although allspice sounds like a spice blend, it is actually a brown dried berry from Jamaica (also known as Jamaican pepper), with an aroma of nutmeg, cinnamon, and cloves combined. Used in both sweet and savory dishes, allspice is a key ingredient in jerk seasonings. If you can find whole berries, grind them yourself.

Amaranth: A tiny grain the size of a sesame seed, with a nutty, earthy flavor.

Ancho Chile: These dried poblano chiles are slightly sweet, with an earthy, rustic flavor and the aromas of tobacco and berries. Anchos (which means "wide" in Spanish) can be mild or medium hot, depending on the source.

Angostura bitters: A cocktail flavoring from Trinidad made with various herbs.

Annatto: A natural food coloring that imparts a bright red-orange color to soups, sauces, cheeses, and other foods. Rich in vitamin C, annatto is good with rice, grains, and legumes, and in stews, soups, curries, and egg dishes. Also known as achiote, bija, and roucou, it is an integral part of Mexican Yucatán cooking.

Arbol chiles: See page 37.

Arborio rice: A plump, short-grain rice used for the Italian dish risotto. Do not rinse arborio before cooking; rinsing removes the starch that is released during cooking and gives the rice its creamy texture.

Baby bananas: Similar to bananas, but the size of fingers. They are ready to eat when flecked with brown sugar-colored spots.

Basmati rice: An Indian rice with long slender grains, a distinctive perfume, and an almost nutty flavor. The rice is named after a tropical flower, the Basmatic, and hails from the foothills of the Himalayas in northern India. Texans and Californians grow their own varieties, which they modestly call Texmati and Calmati.

Black-eyed pea: Also known as the cow pea, this small, creamy-colored bean has a black dot on the skin.

Borlotti: Perhaps the most popular dried bean in Italy, this legume is also known as *rose coco* and is a tan-colored bean with red flecks. Kidney beans may be substituted.

Buckwheat: A mild, nutty grain. When toasted, it becomes stronger flavored and chewier and is known as kasha.

Buckwheat noodles: Flat grayish brown noodles made from buckwheat, with a somewhat nutty flavor. Rich in protein, they are called soba noodles in Japan and can be found in Asian markets or health food stores.

Bulgur: A light, mild grain with a wheaty flavor. Sometimes called cracked wheat, it is the key ingredient in the Middle Eastern salad tabbouleh.

Cactus pear: A tart fruit with a taste reminiscent of cherries and a thick green outer membrane. Look for cactus pear that's been dethorned.

Cannellini: A large, white, starchy, flavorful kidney bean. Navy beans may be substituted.

Cardamom: An exquisite spice created by grinding the tiny aromatic seeds found in the husk of cardamom pods. With a sweet warm flavor, cardamom is often used in curry pastes and to flavor cakes and pastries.

Cascabel chile: About the size of a walnut, with the distinct sound of a rattle when shaken, these medium-hot chiles are woody and nutty.

Cayenne chile: Long, bright red, and slender, the cayenne provides a quick-burning fire. It's available fresh (seed packets that simply say "hot peppers" often feature cayenne chiles) and when dried is ground into cayenne pepper.

Channa dal: Hulled split peas. The whole peas are called chick-peas.

Chayote: Also known as *christophine* in the West Indies, *chouchoute* in Polynesia, and *mirleton* in Florida, this tropical squash has a light green skin and resembles a pear in shape. The skin is edible, though chayote should be cored. With a high water content, it's mild tasting, with a crisp white flesh that is good raw in salads or grilled in thin slices.

Chipotle chile: A versatile dried chile that is made by smoking red jalapeño peppers (see page 37 for more information). Chipotles have an intense woody smell and flavor, with midlevel heat. If you can't find dried whole chipotles, substitute approximately 1 teaspoon canned chipotle chiles in adobo sauce for 1 dried chile.

Chipotle chiles in adobo sauce (also called chipotles en adobo): A canned mixture of chipotle chiles packed in vinegar and spices, often found in Mexican markets and the international section of grocery stores.

Coconut milk: Coconut milk is made from the liquid found in fresh coconuts, with some water added. If you can't find it in stores, Indian cooking authority Madhur Jaffrey recommends combining 2 cups unsweetened dried coconut with 2 1/2 cups water. Bring the mixture to a boil, remove from heat, and allow to cool, then mix in a blender for 2 minutes and strain through a tea towel. Makes 2 cups.

Coriander: An aromatic plant cultivated for its musky seeds, which can be purchased whole or ground, or its delicate spicy leaves, which are called cilantro. In some markets, coriander and cilantro are used interchangeably.

Cotijo: A Mexican cow's milk cheese.

Couscous: A pasta made with semolina (and sometimes barley or green wheat) that has been moistened and rolled into tiny pellets. When cooked, couscous is drier and fluffier than other pasta. Cook couscous like rice in a small enough amount of water to be absorbed by the grain.

Cumin: A member of the parsley family, the cumin plant has small seeds, which are cultivated whole or ground into a nutty, fragrant spice. A strong spice popular in North African, Mexican, and Indian cuisines, it should be used sparingly. Toasting the seeds before grinding yields a warmer flavor.

Fenugreek: With almost a chalky taste, fenugreek is a key spice in Indian curries (and in some Caribbean hot sauces). The seeds should be lightly dry-roasted before grinding, otherwise they can be bitter (overroasting will also make them bitter). Quite pungent, a little bit of fenugreek goes a long way.

Fish sauce: Used as a salty seasoning in Southeast Asian cooking (much like soy sauce), fish sauce is made by fermenting fish in salt. It is used to enliven stir-fries and other dishes. Substitute 1/4 teaspoon salt dissolved in 1/2 cup water for every 1/2 cup of fish sauce.

Five-spice powder: Popular in Chinese dishes, five-spice powder is a mixture of fennel seeds, Chinese cinnamon, star anise, Szechwan peppercorns, and cloves. To make your own, see page 310.

Focaccia: An Italian flatbread, focaccia is similar to pizza. The main difference is the flavor is found mostly in the focaccia dough rather than in the topping.

Ginger: A pungent, rather hot, slightly sweet root that can be peeled, then grated, minced, or sliced into many dishes.

Gorgonzola cheese: A sharp, blue-veined, crumbly Italian cheese traditionally made from cow's milk. Good crumbled on salads, canapés, and gratins.

Grits: Traditionally, corn that is coarsely ground and served as a popular porridge-like dish in the South. Soy grits, barley grits, and buckwheat grits (packaged as a cream of buckwheat cereal) are also available on the market.

Guajillo chile: A mahogany-colored dried chile, about 4 to 5 inches long, that has an earthy heat and almost raisinlike flavor.

Habanero chile: Shaped like a walnut, this pepper is 50 to 100 times hotter than a jalapeño. It is grown throughout Mexico and the Caribbean, where it is also known as the goat pepper, datil pepper, and Bahama Mama. It is similar to the Scotch bonnet pepper, although slightly more elongated and less crinkly. Blisteringly hot, the habanero is also quite fruity, and used sparingly, can add a delectable zip to many meals. It's particularly good in fruit salsas and is the main ingredient of many Caribbean hot sauces.

Hibiscus: Throughout Mexico and the Caribbean, Jamaica hibiscus flowers are used to make refreshing drinks. In the markets, they are called Jamaica flowers, hibiscus flowers, and sometimes sorrel (not to be confused with the green-leafed garden sorrel).

Hoisin sauce: A Chinese soy-based sauce made from fermented soybeans and spiked with chiles and peppercorns.

Hungarian wax chile: A crisp, pale-yellow mild to medium-hot chile measuring about 6 inches.

Jicama: A Mexican tuber vegetable. Remove the skin, and you'll find crisp, white flesh with a sweet, subtle taste and high water content (almost like an apple). It's delicious served raw as a snack, sliced thin for crudités, or cut into matchsticks for a salad.

Kaffir lime: Larger than common limes, with skin that is more pitted. Kaffir lime leaves are small and glossy. Found in Asian markets, they are delicious slivered and added to soups and other dishes.

Kosher salt: The only salt that's at least 99 percent pure and contains no additives. Kosher salt is milder and has a cleaner flavor than regular table salt.

Lemongrass: A dry grass with a bulbous root that is prized in Asian cooking for its lemony flavor and fragrance. Strip away the outer leaves, slice off the bulb, and use the inner stalk. It is found in Asian markets and can be frozen. If lemongrass is unavailable, substitute the zest of 1/2 a lemon for 1 stalk of lemongrass.

Lentil: This small, disk-shaped bean cooks quickly and is delicious in soups, sauces, and burgers.

Macho chile: Well-named, with a scorching heat, similar to the pequin chile.

Manchego: A firm, cream-colored Spanish cheese made from ewe's milk.

Masa harina: A finely ground cornmeal made from posole and used to make tamales and tortillas.

Millet: A small, yellow, versatile grain that goes well in burgers, stuffings, and pilafs. When cooked, its fluffiness makes it an attractive substitute for rice.

Miso: Fermented soybean paste. Miso is found in Asian markets or in the refrigerated section of some supermarkets.

Mung bean: This bean plant, originally from Asia, is cultivated for its shoots, popularly known as bean sprouts.

Mustard greens: Spicy and pungent, these greens are as long as lettuce, with green leaves and frilly edges.

Mustard seed: The name "mustard" comes from the Latin *mustum ardens* ("burning must"), an ancient reference to the fact that the seeds were crushed with unfermented grape juice, or *must*. There are three varieties of mustard seed: white, black, and brown. White mustard seeds (also called yellow mustard seeds) are actually wheat-colored and are the most commonly found in the United States, used in prepared mustards and dry mustard powder. Black mustard seeds (which can actually be quite reddish) are prized by Indian cooks and have a strong, pungent flavor. Brown seeds, also popular in Asian cooking, can be hot and aromatic. They should be crushed to bring out the heat or toasted to bring out a nutty, earthy sweetness.

Navy bean: A mild, dense, white bean, also known as the small white bean or pea bean.

New Mexico chile: Arguably the definitive chile pepper of the Southwest, New Mexico chiles are available red or green and have a mild to medium heat. With a strong vegetable flavor and fresh quality, they are often served roasted or stuffed (chiles rellenos). In the fall, you'll find New Mexican shops and houses decorated with long strings (ristras) of dried New Mexico chiles. Californians have dubbed a similar chile grown on California soil the Anaheim chile.

Orzo: A small pasta that looks like rice and is commonly served in cold pasta salads or stuffings.

Pasilla chile: The pasilla chile (which means "little raisin," due to its raisinlike aroma) is a mild, dark brown dried chile with a mellow flavor. Also sold as chile negro.

Passion fruit: The size of a plum, this fruit has a dark reddish purple skin. Counterintuitively, the wrinklier the skin, the riper the fruit.

Pequin chile: A tiny, pearl-shaped chile, with a quick-burning heat and citric aftertaste.

Plantain: A type of banana from South America and the Caribbean. Always served cooked, they should be bought green and allowed to ripen, when they'll be their sweetest. (You'll know they are ripe when they turn completely black.) Difficult to peel, they can be sliced with a knife to easily remove the skin.

Poblano chile: A mild, dark purply green chile pepper shaped like a gardener's spade with an undulated surface. Popular in Mexican cuisines, they are delicious roasted or stuffed. Dried poblanos are called anchos.

Polenta: Italian in origin—and perhaps comparable in popularity to American-style mashed potatoes or hominy grits—polenta is a creamy cornmeal dish that is good by itself (especially served with a dab of butter and freshly grated cheese) or in lieu of pasta with tomato sauce.

Plum tomato: Pear-shaped, also known as a Roma tomato. Plum tomatoes are often used in Southwestern cooking and sometimes preferred because they have a lower juice content than the standard garden tomato varieties.

Pumpkin seeds: Raw, hulled pumpkin seeds are used in Mexican cooking to thicken sauces. They are available at health food stores.

Queso fresco: A popular multipurpose Mexican cheese used for toppings and stuffings.

Quinoa: From the Andes, a small grain (pronounced keen-wah) about the size of mustard seed, with a mild flavor and fluffy texture when cooked. A good substitute for bulgur in tabbouleh or other salads. Do not overcook, or it will get mushy. Perhaps most startling about quinoa is that, when cooked, each grain will have a small white spiraling thread dangling from it. It is very nutritious, with more iron than any grains and high amounts of folic acid, magnesium, phosphorus, and potassium.

Rice noodles: Dry rice noodles are available at Thai markets. They come packaged as semitranslucent, thin flat noodles about 1/8 inch wide and 8 to 10 inches long. The noodles double in weight when soaked in cold water. They are rather tasteless, but soak up the flavors of the other ingredients.

Scotch bonnet pepper: See habanero.

Serrano chile: Shaped like a bullet and the size of a pinkie finger, serrano chiles have a fresh, vegetable flavor and piercing heat.

Sesame seeds: Cultivated from the ancient sesame plant, sesame seeds are used extensively in Indian and Middle Eastern cooking. Seeds vary in color from white to brown to black, with the black seeds containing the least oil.

Sorrel: *See* hibiscus.

Split peas: A quick-cooking legume.

Squash blossom: A pretty yellow flower attached to a squash plant. I've never found them in supermarkets—I go to a local farm stand and ask the farmer if I might pick a few blossoms in the field out back.

Szechwan peppercorns: A small, dried berry that is similar (but unrelated) to black pepper, from a small Chinese ash tree. Highly aromatic, with a tingly, mildly hot taste.

Tabasco chile: A thin-skinned chile with short-lived heat, used in McIlhenny's famous sauce. Similar in flavor to cayenne chiles. Not widely available on the market.

Tamari soy sauce: Standard soy sauce is made with fermented soybeans and wheat, whereas tamari is a soy sauce brewed without wheat. In Western markets, "tamari" is often used as a generic term to describe Japanese-style soy sauces.

Tamarind: A sour-sweet fruit of a tree that grows in Africa, the Caribbean, India, and Southeast Asia. Tamarind is used in chutneys, jams, soups, drinks, and condiments. See page 293 for more information.

Thai chiles: Long, thin, and pointy, Thai chiles have a lingering heat and are often found in Asian dishes.

Tomatillo: Also known as *tomate verde* (green tomato) in Mexico (where tomatillos are an integral part of the cuisine), tomatillos are not actually tomatoes, but rather a fruit that hails from the *Physalis* family (a relative of the Cape gooseberry). Light green with a tart freshness, tomatillos are a good substitute for tomatoes in the winter and widely available in U.S. markets. They can range in size from a shallot to a lemon and have a papery husk that should be removed before cooking.

Wasabi: A spicy root, similar to horseradish.

White peppercorns: Removing the outer husk of a peppercorn with a saltwater solution creates white peppercorns, which are more subtly spicy than black peppercorns.

Wild rice: With long dark grains, this dense, nutty rice is cultivated from grasses grown in the Great Lakes region of North America and Canada. Wild pecan rice is a buttery-tasting hybrid from Louisiana.

Stovetop Cooking Instructions

Beans

Bean Type	Dry amount	Water	Cooking Time	Yield
Adzuki	1/2 cup	2 cups	45 to 60 minutes	1 1/2 cups
Anasazi	1/2 cup	1 1/2 cups	90 minutes	1 cup
Black (turtle)	1/2 cup	1 1/2 cups	1 to 1 1/2 hours	1 cup
Black-eyed peas	1/2 cup	2 cups	45 to 60 minutes	1 1/2 cups
Cannellini	1/2 cup	1 1/2 cups	90 minutes	1 1/2 cups
Fava	1/2 cup	2 cups	45 to 60 minutes	1 cup
Garbanzo	1/2 cup	1 1/2 cups	1 1/2 to 2 hours	1 1/4 cups
Great Northern	1/2 cup	1 1/2 cups	1 to 3 hours	1 cup
Kidney	1/2 cup	1 1/2 cups	1 to 2 hours	1 1/2 cups
Lentils*	1/2 cup	1 1/2 cups	20 to 30 minutes	1 1/2 cups
Lima	1/2 cup	2 2/3 cups	45 minutes	1 1/3 cups
Mung	1/2 cup	2 cups	40 to 60 minutes	2 cups
Navy	1/2 cup	2 cups	1 to 1 1/2 hours	1 1/2 cups
Pinto	1/2 cup	2 cups	1 to 1 1/2 hours	1 1/2 cups
Split peas*	1/2 cup	2 cups	35 minutes	1 cup

*Doesn't require soaking

Freshly cooked beans are far superior to canned beans and, with a little planning, are easy to prepare. First, pick over the dried beans, then rinse thoroughly. Put the beans in a large bowl with 4 times more water than beans, and leave to soak for 8 hours or overnight to tenderize them.

Drain off soaking water and put beans in a heavy saucepan with the specified amount of water. Bring the beans to a boil, lower the heat, cover, and simmer until tender. As a rule, salt should not be added, as it will toughen the skins of the beans, with the exception of beans with soft skins—such as limas and black soybeans—which depend on the salt to keep the beans intact. The cooking time will depend on how old the beans are; those harvested in the last 6 months will cook faster and taste better. Begin checking the beans for doneness about 30 minutes before the allotted time is up; beans are cooked when they yield easily when squeezed between your thumb and finger.

Rice

Rice Type	Dry Amount	Water	Cooking Time	Yield
Arborio	1/2 cup	3/4 cup	15 minutes	1 1/2 cups
Basmati	1/2 cup	1 cup	15 minutes	1 cup
Brown	1/2 cup	1 cup	30 to 40 minutes	1 1/2 cups
Sticky	1/2 cup	1/2 cup	25 minutes	1 cup
White	1/2 cup	1 cup	20 minutes	1 1/2 cups
Wild	1/2 cup	2 cups	50 to 55 minutes	2 cups
Wild pecan	1/2 cup	1 cup	20 minutes	1 1/2 cups

Rinse rice well. Bring specified amount of water to a boil in a saucepan, add rice, and stir. Bring rice to a boil again, lower heat and cover, and simmer for required time. Remove from heat and stir to fluff before serving.

Grains

Grain	Dry Amount	Liquid	Cooking Time	Yield
Amaranth	1/2 cup	1 1/4 cups	20 minutes	1 cup
Barley (hulled)	1/2 cup	1 1/2 cups	90 minutes	2 cups
Barley (pearl)	1/2 cup	1 1/2 cups	60 minutes	1 3/4 cups
Barley (flakes)	1/2 cup	1 1/2 cups	30 minutes	1 cup
Buckwheat	1/2 cup	1 cup	10 minutes	1 cup
Bulgur	1/2 cup	1 cup	20 minutes	1 1/2 cups
Couscous	1/2 cup	1 cup	1 minute plus 10 minutes standing	1 1/2 cups
Job's Tears	1/2 cup	1 1/4 cups	60 minutes	1 1/2 cups
Millet	1/2 cup	1 1/2 cups	30 minutes	1 1/2 cups
Oats	1/2 cup	1 cup	60 minutes	1 cup
Quinoa	1/2 cup	1 cup	15 minutes	2 cups
Teff	1/2 cup	1 1/2 cups	15 minutes	1 cup
Whole barley	1/2 cup	1 1/2 cups	60 minutes	1 cup

Rinse grain well under cold water. In a saucepan, cook in specified amount of liquid for time indicated.

Recommended Daily Allowances for Adults

Below is a general recommended allowance of vitamins and minerals that are needed for adults to maintain good health. Individual needs will vary according to weight, age, sex, stress, pregnancy, and other circumstances. These guidelines were developed by the Food and Nutrition Board of the National Research Council. For more nutritional information, I highly recommend *The Wellness Encyclopedia of Food and Nutrition* by Sheldon Merge, M.D., and the editors of the *University of California at Berkeley Wellness Letter*, from which much of this material was drawn. Vitamin D, vitamin K, iodine, and selenium are not included in this chart.

Vitamin A   **RDA: 800 (female) to 1000 (male) mcg RE***

1 cup raw broccoli	1,542 IU (39% female RDA, 31% male RDA)
1 cup raw snap beans	668 IU
1 cup raw brussel sprouts	883 IU
1 1/3 cups raw carrots	28, 129 IU
2 cups shredded romaine lettuce	2,600 IU
2 raw red hot chiles	10,750 IU

* Retinol equivalents. One retinol equivalent=1mcg retinol or 6 mcg beta carotene. Calculate the IU value for vegetables and fruits by multiplying the RE value by ten.

Vitamin E   **RDA 8 (female) to 10 (male) mg x-TE**

12 prunes	3 mg (38% female RDA, 30% male RDA)
1/2 mango	1 mg
2/3 cup dry rye	1 mg
3/4 cup dry-roasted whole almonds	21 mg
3/4 cup dry-roasted sunflower seeds	20 mg

* X-tocopherol equivalents. One mg d-x tocopherol = x-TE

Vitamin C   **RDA: 50 to 60 (male, female) mg**

1 cup raw brussel sprouts	85 mg (142% RDA)
1 cup chopped fennel	93 mg
1 1/2 cups chopped kale	120 mg
2 cups raw arugula	91 mg
1 large kiwifruit	98 mg
2 raw red hot chiles	243 mg

Thiamine — RDA: 1–1.1 (female), 1.2–1.5 (male) mg

3/4 cup cooked garbanzo beans — 0.1 mg (11% female RDA, 8% male RDA)

Riboflavin — RDA: 1.2–1.3 (female), 1.4–1.7 (male) mg

5 raw button mushrooms — .4 (31% female RDA, 24% male RDA)
3/4 cup sliced raw water chestnuts — .2 mg
1/2 cup dry amaranth — .2 mg
3/4 cup cooked fresh pasta — .2 mg

Niacin — RDA: 13–15 (female), 15–20 (male) mg NE*

1/2 baked potato — 2 mg (13% RDA)
2/3 avocado — 2 mg
12 dates — 2 mg
3/4 cup cooked enriched spaghetti — 2 mg

* One NE (niacin equivalent) equals 1 mg of niacin

Vitamin B6 — RDA: 1.4–1.6 (female), 1.7–2.0 (male) mg

2 cups chopped spinach — 28 mg (12% female RDA, 10% male RDA)
1 banana — .6 mg
1/2 cup cooked pinto beans — .2 mg
12 prunes — .3 mg
3/4 cup sliced raw water chestnuts — .3 mg

Folic Acid (Folate; folacin) — RDA: 150–180 (female), 150–200 (male) mcg

3/4 cup raw sliced beets — 93 mcg (52% female RDA, 47% male RDA)
1 cup raw chopped broccoli — 71 mcg
2 1/2 stalks celery — 28 mcg
1/3 cup corn kernels — 46 mcg
2 cups shredded romaine lettuce — 136 mcg
3/4 cups cooked garbanzo beans — 172 mcg

Vitamin B12 — RDA: 2 mcg

2/3 cup 1% milk — .8 mcg (40% female RDA)
3 1/2 ounces Cheddar cheese — .8 mcg
2 large eggs — 1 mcg

Calcium

RDA: 800–1,200 mg

1 cup fennel	109 mg (155% female RDA)
2 1/2 cups raw beet greens	119 mg
2 1/2 cups dandelion greens	187 mg
2 cups raw arugula	309 mg
2 cups raw watercress	120 mg

Phosphorus

RDA: 800–1,200 mg

1/2 cup dry amaranth	455 mg (57% RDA)
1/2 cup dry quinoa	410 mg
3/4 cup fresh cooked pasta	63 mg
3/4 cup dry-roasted sunflower seeds	1,155 mg

Magnesium

RDA: 280–300 (female), 270–400 (male) mg

1 cup sliced raw okra	57 mg (20% female RDA, 16% male RDA)
2 cups chopped spinach	79 mg
2/3 avocado	34 mg
1 banana	29 mg
1/2 cup cooked pearl barley	133 mg
3/4 cup dry-roasted whole almonds	304 mg

Iron

RDA: 10–15 (female), 10–12 (male) mg

1 cup chopped fennel	3 mg (20% female RDA, 30% male RDA)
2 1/2 cups beet greens	3 mg
2 raw red hot chiles	1 mg
1/2 cup cooked pearl barley	4 mg

Zinc

RDA: 12 (female) to 15 (male) mg

1/2 cup dry amaranth	3 mg (25% female RDA)
1/2 cup cooked pearl barley	3 mg
1/2 cup dry quinoa	3 mg
2/3 cup dry rye	4 mg
3 1/2 ounces Cheddar cheese	3 mg

Recipes for All Occasions

Perfect for a Crowd

My Favorites

For Picnics

Dishes That Make a Meal with Bread or Salad

For Sunday Brunch

Gifts for the Holidays and Housewarmings

Hot As Hell

Mail-Order Sources

Chiles, Herbs, and Spices

Colorado Spice Company, 5030 Nome St., Unit A, Denver, CO 80239, 800-677-7423

Dean & DeLuca, 560 Broadway, New York, NY 10012, 800-221-7714

Don Alfonso Foods, Box 201988, Austin, TX 78720, 800-456-6100 (Mexican chiles, canned chipotle chiles in adobo sauce)

Frontier Cooperative Herbs, Box 299, Norway, IA 52318, 800-669-3275

Pacific Spice Company, 722 Stanford Ave., Los Angeles, CA 90021, 213-626-2302

Shepherd's Garden Seeds, 30 Irene St., Torrington, CT 06790, 203-482-3638 (seeds for flowers, vegetables, and chiles)

The Pepper Gal, P.O. Box 23006, Fort Lauderdale, FL 33307, 305-537-5540 (hundreds of chile seeds)

Rafal Spice Company, 2521 Russell St., Detroit, MI 48207, 800-228-4276

San Francisco Herb Company, 250 Fourteenth St., San Francisco, CA 94103, 800-227-4530

Stonewall Chili Pepper Company, Box 241, Highway 290 East, Stonewall, TX 78671, 800-232-2995

Tierra Vegetables, B684 Chalk Hill Rd., Healdsburg, CA, 707-433-5666 (chipotle chiles and morita chiles smoked over fruitwood and grapevine cuttings)

Asian Ingredients

Katagari & Company, Inc., 224 East 59th Street, New York, NY 10022, 212-755-3566

Nancy's Specialty Market, P.O. Box 327, Wye Mills, MD 21679, 800-462-6291

Nature's Key Products, P.O. Box 1146, New Hyde Park, NY 11040, 516-775-5279

Star Market, 3349 North Clark Street, Chicago, IL 60657, 312-472-0599

Indian Ingredients

House of Spices, 76-17 Broadway, Jackson Heights, NY 11373, 718-476-1577

Southwestern Ingredients

Chile Hill Emporium, Box 9100, Bernalillo, New Mexico 87004, 505-867-3294 (unsprayed ristras, pure chile powders, books)

Coyote Cafe General Store, 132 West Water St., Santa Fe, NM 87501, 505-982-2454 (beans, chiles, posole, salsas, sauces, books)

Monterrey Foods, 3939 Brooklyn, Los Angeles, CA 90063, 213-263-2143

Louisiana Ingredients

Sambet's Cajun Store, 8650 Spicewood Springs Rd., Ste. 111, Austin, TX 78759, 512-258-6410

Tabasco Country Store, McIlhenny Company, Avery Island, LA 70513, 800-634-9599

Heirloom Beans

Adobe Milling Company, P.O. Box 596, Dove Creek, CO 81324, 800-542-3623 (for Anasazi beans)

Dean & DeLuca, 560 Broadway, New York, NY 10012, 800-221-7714

Elizabeth Berry, Gallina Canyon Ranch, P.O. Box 706, Abiquiu, NM 87510, 505-685-4888 (a wonderful source for heirloom beans)

Oils

Dean & DeLuca, 560 Broadway, New York, NY 10012, 800-221-7714

Lila Jaeger, Rutherford Hill Winery, Box 410, St. Helena, CA 94574, 707-963-1871

Organic Products

Gold Mine Natural Food Company, 3419 Hancock St., San Diego, CA 92102, 800-475-FOOD

Hardwood Charcoal and Grilling Supplies

People's Smoke 'n Grill, 55 Mill St., Cumberland, RI 02864, 401-725-2700

Tropical Fruit

Frieda's, Box 58488, Los Angeles, CA 90058, 800-241-1771 (tropical fruit and vegetables, as well as fresh and dried chiles)

Hot Sauces, Salsas, Chutneys, and Other Condiments

Calido Chile Traders, Oak Park Mall, Oak Park, KS 66214, 800-LOTT-HOT

Chile Today Hot Tamale Hot Sauce of the Month Club, 919 Hwy. 33, #47, Freehold, NJ 07728, 800-468-7377

Flamingo Flats, Box 441, St. Michael's, MD 21663, 800-468-8841

Hot, Hot, Hot, 56 South Delacey Ave., Pasadena, CA 91105, 800-959-7742

Hot Stuff, P.O. Box 2210, Stuyvesant Station, New York, NY 10009, 800-WANTHOT

International Hot Stuff, 905 North California St., Chicago, IL 60622, 800-555-9798

Isla Vieques Condiment Company, P.O. Box 1496, Vieques, PR 00765, 809-741-0848

Le Saucier, Quincy Market, North Canopy, Boston, MA 02109, 617-868-9139

Mo Hotta, Mo Betta, Box 4136, San Luis Obispo, CA 93403, 800-462-3220

Old Santa Fe Pottery, 2485 South Santa Fe Dr., Denver, CO 80223, 303-871-9434

Peppers Gift Shop, 2009 Hwy. 1, Dewey Beach, DE 19971 800-998-FIRE

Salsas, Etc., 126 Great Mall Way, Milpitas, CA 95035, 800-40-SALSA

Some Like It Hot, 3208 Scott St., San Francisco, CA 94123, 415-441-7468

Supernatural Food, 142 Walton St., Syracuse, NY 13202, 315-424-2545

Tropical Syrups and Teas

Caribbean Spice Company, 2 South Church St., Fairhope, AL 36532, 800-990-6088

Island Bound, P.O. Box 1268, St. Thomas, U.S. Virgin Islands 00804, 800-424-8055

Sunny Caribbee Spice Company, Box 3237 VDA, St. Thomas, U.S. Virgin Islands 00803, 809-494-2178

Jump Up and Kiss Me Products

JT² Productions, 560 North Hoosac Rd., Williamstown, MA 01267, 413-458-2882

Bibliography and Sources for Quotes

I am grateful to those who have paved the way with intelligent books about food and cooking, which have helped me in my research. They include:

Andrews, Jean. *Peppers: The Domesticated Capsicums*. Austin, TX: University of Texas Press, 1984.

Arora, David. *Mushrooms Demystified*. rev. ed. Berkeley, CA: Ten Speed Press, 1990.

Atlas, Nava. *Vegetariana: A Rich Harvest of Wit, Lore & Recipes*. Boston: Little, Brown and Company, 1993.

Clayton, Bernard, Jr. *The Complete Book of Breads*. New York: Simon and Schuster, 1973.

Dolamore, Anne. *The Essential Olive Oil Companion*. New York: Interlink Books, 1994.

Elliot, Rose. *The Complete Vegetarian Cuisine*. New York: Pantheon Books, 1988.

Green, Jonathon, ed. *Consuming Passions*. New York: Fawcett Columbine, 1985.

Kennedy, Diana. *The Cuisines of Mexico*. New York: Harper & Row, 1986.

Lang, Jennifer Harvey, ed. *Larousse Gastronomique: The American Edition of the World's Greastest Encyclopedia*. New York: Crown, 1988.

Margen, Sheldon. *The Wellness Encyclopedia of Food and Nutrition*. New York: Rebus, 1992

McMahan, Jacqueline Higuera. *The Chipotle Chile Cookbook: Fire with Flavor*. Lake Hughes, CA: Olive Press, 1994.

Miller, Mark. *Coyote Cafe*. Berkeley, CA: Ten Speed Press, 1989.

Miller, Mark. *The Great Chile Book*. Berkeley, CA: Ten Speed Press, 1991.

Ortiz, Elisabeth Lambert. *The Complete Book of Caribbean Cooking*. New York: Ballantine Books, 1986.

Ortiz, Elisabeth Lambert. *The Encyclopedia of Herbs, Spices, & Flavorings*. New York: Dorling Kindersley, 1992.

Robbins, Maria Polushkin, ed. *The Cook's Quotation Book*. Wainscott, NY: Pushcart Press, 1983.

Sahni, Julie. *Classic Indian Vegetarian & Grain Cooking*. New York: William Morrow and Company, 1985.

Saltzman, Joanne. *Amazing Grains: Creating Vegetarian Main Dishes with Whole Grains*. Tiburon, CA: HJ Kramer Inc., 1990.

Sass, Lorna. *Complete Vegetarian Kitchen*. New York: Hearst Books, 1992.

Tannahill, Reay. *Food in History*. New York: Stein and Day, 1973.

Also by Jennifer Trainer Thompson

BOOKS

The Great Hot Sauce Book

A comprehensive guide to the best hot sauces on the market.
$14.95 (paperback), 192 pages.

Trail of Flame

An irreverent guide to spicy restaurants and the culture of hot food.
$11.95 (paperback), 160 pages.

POSTERS

Hot Sauces I & Hot Sauces II

A beautiful set of posters highlighting 249 hot sauces in screaming color.
$20 each or both for $30.

Olive Oils

A beautiful color poster featuring the finest oils from around the world, surrounded by an olive branch border. Elegant and airy, suffused with soft gold light, this poster will brighten any kitchen.

American Microbrewery Beers

A handsome color poster featuring 126 premier microbrews. Sleek printing on fine paper, black background, with a varnished finish. $20.

Classic Beer Guide

An informative color poster illustrating the major beer syles with world-class examples. Includes taste profiles, serving suggestions, glass styles, and a description of the beer-making process. Beer lovers go nuts for this poster, exquisitely printed with a soft gold background. $20.

All items are available from Ten Speed Press/Celestial Arts, Box 7123, Berkeley, CA 94707, (800) 841-BOOK. Please include $3.50 for shipping and handling for the first item and 50 cents for each additional item. California residents include sales tax. Write for a free catalog of more than 500 books, posters, and tapes.

 For more about hot sauces, syrups, and other Jump Up and Kiss Me foodstuffs by Jennifer Trainer Thompson, contact her at JT² Productions, 560 North Hoosac Road, Williamstown, MA 01267 or e-mail her at 75050.1417@compuserve.com.

Index